MASTER
CHEFS
OF
EUROPE

ACADÉMIE INTERNATIONALE
DE LA GASTRONOMIE

MICHEL GÉNIN, PRESIDENT

MASTER
CHEFS
OF
EUROPE

PHOTOGRAPHS BY MICHAEL BOYS

EDITED BY PEPITA ARIS

MACDONALD
ORBIS

A Macdonald Orbis Book

Text © The International Academy of Gastronomy 1988
Photography and design of this volume © Macdonald & Co 1988

First published in Great Britain in 1988
by Macdonald & Co (Publishers) Ltd
London and Sydney

A member of Maxwell Pergamon Publishing Corporation plc

British Library Cataloguing in Publication Data

Ronay, Egon
   Master Chefs of Europe
   1. Food: European dishes – recipes
   I. Title
   641.594
   ISBN 0-356-15630-3

Editorial Direction: Coralie Dorman
Art Direction: Bobbie Colgate-Stone
Designer: Miranda Kennedy
Translation: Lesley Bernstein
Indexer: Marcus Bell

Filmset by Bookworm Typesetting, Manchester
Printed in Italy by New Interlitho SPA

Macdonald & Co (Publishers) Ltd
Greater London House
Hampstead Road
London NW1 7QX

Contents

Introduction by
RAYMOND BLANC

In the last fifteen years cuisine has moved drastically away from classicism, whose codified rules had been stifling creativity and made cuisine rigid and static.

The immediate effect of this change of direction, however, was rather unfortunate. The promotion of the new resulted in a complete discarding of the old and a denial of tradition. What ensued was an unruly, 'fashionable', reactionary and confused movement. The prime ingredients of a recipe became merely cosmetic, there was 'novelty at any cost' and all too often these daring experimental dishes lacked the most important ingredient: honesty.

If the root of a tree is cut, it will not grow new branches or bear fruit. Rather than discard the old, a renovation or polishing and refining process should take place, so that we keep the roots of the tree 'cuisine' alive and so that healthy branches can bear wonderful fruit. We are now beginning to reach the heart and purity of the cookery revolution, and do away with its superficial affectations. Hence today's cuisine can become tomorrow's tradition. 'Nouvelle cuisine' (or today's cuisine, if you like) has never been as healthy and triumphant as it is now, enjoying its newly found freedom. It uses all repertoires, regional, family, bourgeoise and haute cuisine, to create a cuisine sans frontière, incorporating influences from the Far East, the Tropics and all continents, resulting in a most exciting combination of ideas, flavours and ingredients.

You will find the generals, field marshals and captains of the movement in this book. They are all part of this great change, always fuelled on by their tremendous strength and belief, their constant striving for excellence, in the knowledge that they are creating unique and magical events in their guests' memories.

Each chef contributor has his own views and philosophy. Cooking is the language of chefs; it is through dishes that we communicate our thoughts on what creates harmony. This book offers an insight into what the very best think about cuisine's direction at the present time. The recipes are inspired and inspiring, for chef, amateur cook or general reader.

Preface by

MICHEL GÉNIN

The purpose of the Académie Internationale de la Gastronomie is to 'promote and develop a better knowledge of gastronomy both universally and amongst individual consumers'. It was in this spirit that, as Chairman, I decided to publish a book of menus and recipes, collected from some of the finest chefs in Europe. I wanted the book to be both a guide which would arouse the traveller's curiosity and prompt him or her to try out the restaurants in the book, and also to provide a collection of recipes which can be cooked at home, giving everyone the opportunity to discover the best of foreign cuisine.

Without a doubt, the most difficult part of our task was actually choosing who was to be included in the book. There are many chefs in Europe who are of an equally high standard, and selecting the very top fifty of them seemed an insurmountable problem. Finally, we managed to make an objective choice, thanks to the serious hard work of the various national academies, whose members are lovers of fine food and are enlightened, independent and unbiased in their opinions.

The criteria used were strict ones. In keeping with the principles of the Académie Internationale, the selection was made by considering the authenticity of the chef's cooking. By this, we mean the use of high quality ingredients whose flavour is brought out by the way in which they are cooked, the regional or national nature of the cooking, and the chef's own interpretations of his country's culinary traditions. This means that the book portrays not only the truly famous chefs, but also a number of chefs who are less well-known but whose cooking is of an extremely high quality and who show great promise.

Mention must be made of the warm welcome received from the chefs featured in this book. They carried out their work in producing the book with seriousness and good grace and they showed an intuitive grasp of what the book was striving to achieve.

I would also like to express my gratitude to all my friends in the various countries for their valued cooperation, in particular Egon Ronay, President of the British Gastronomic Academy, without whose constant help the book could not have been completed. My thanks therefore, to Eckart Witzigmann from Germany, Klaus Lukas in Austria, Count Louis de Meeus d'Argenteuil for the Benelux countries, Don Rafael Anson from Spain, Jean Ferniot and Maurice Letulle in France, Count Giovanni Nuvoletti from Italy, Charles Florman in Sweden and Pierre Sciclounoff for Switzerland. Our thanks must also go to General Henri Broussaud and Francine Toy-Riont, who undertook the massive task of collecting all the information from each country involved.

· 8 ·

EGON RONAY

The tide of uniformity in restaurant food all over Europe is upon us. Rationalisation, efficiency, the priority of profit over quality, mass tourism and catering chains with their unquenchable thirst for takeovers add up to a dangerous threat. The individual restaurateur finds it increasingly difficult to compete financially, to use his imagination, do his own thing and practise his traditional skills at the highest level. Worse still: the majority of the public is, alas, inclined to conform and we, the minority, are under pressure by a climate increasingly intolerant of elitism, in the name of democracy; ignoring that elitism is a sine qua non *in gastronomy. The threat of uniform mediocrity to individual excellence has never been greater.*

This is why we, in the International Academy of Gastronomy, advocate with such conviction the preservation of individuality, whether national, regional or personal. It is our raison d'être. *Bouillabaisse, pasta faggioli, bread and butter pudding, Apfel Strudel, gravadlachs, waterzoi or every one of the thousands of farm cheeses may sound irrelevant in a broader international context, but it is precisely such manifestations in everyday life that reflect national characteristics. Obliterate them and who could deny that the marvellous difference between one nation and another will diminish? More specifically, the erosion of regional gastronomy within each country often has social and economic consequences beyond culinary considerations. Regional produce and dishes are just as much part of their respective countries' heritage as their history or art.*

All these considerations have brought about this unique book. Unique because our International Academy, through its national member Academies, has carefully chosen and invited the most respected and widely recognised 51 chefs of Europe to demonstrate the differences we are fighting to preserve. Nearly all the chefs are owners of the establishments in which they function – an important circumstance: as well as proving their professional worth in their career, they have staked all on their own skills. This is a more idealistic act of faith than it may seem, for most of the highest-rated restaurants today maintain standards so elevated that, contrary to belief, they do not leave room for a commensurate level of profit. And we ourselves, the International Academy, do not operate for gain.

We are grateful to the 51 eminent chefs for demonstrating the importance of being different and individual, and we trust that readers and users of this exceptional collection will find pleasure in stepping into the shoes of Europe's greatest masters.

France

Everything ends this way in France — everything.
Weddings, christenings, duels, burials, swindlings, diplomatic affairs —
everything is a pretext for a good dinner.

Michel Guérard

LES PRÉS D'EUGÉNIE
40320 Eugénie-les-Bains telephone: 58 51 19 01

Culinary innovator, chef, pastry-cook and expert on wine, Michel Guérard is certainly one of the most talented chefs of his generation. The son of a butcher at Vétheuil, north of Paris in Claude Monet country, he served an apprenticeship in the most exacting of kitchen skills, as a pastry cook. The apprentice won his first prize. Following military service and further training in a number of celebrated Paris restaurants, he became pastry cook at the Crillon, where he won the Meilleur Ouvrier de France in 1958.

In 1965 he decided to open his own restaurant and bought modest premises at Asnières in the Paris suburbs. At Le Pot au Feu he started to put his own ideas into practice, rebelling against the constrictions, but not the well-proved virtues, of the French classical tradition. It won him his first Michelin rosette.

A change in locality and culinary direction came as a result of marriage, in 1972, to Christine Barthélemy, whose father owned several spas and hydros. Together they opened Les Prés d'Eugénie et Les Sources d'Eugénie in south-west France. In 1977 he was awarded three Michelin rosettes for the perfection of his cooking. His style at the time was cuisine gourmande *and not the one for which the hotel is now famous. But a connection between health and high class cooking had been made, and he went on to develop* grande cuisine minceur, *a new health-conscious cuisine, combining lightness, flavour and appeal, which caused a revolution in the world of cooking.*

MENU

SALADE DE HOMARD AUX TOMATES CONFITES
Lobster salad with tomato confit

FEUILLANTINE D'AILES DE CAILLES TRUFFEES DE CEPES
Pastry puffs of quail wings truffled with ceps

SOUFFLE LEGER A LA PECHE DE CARAMAN
Light peach soufflé

SALADE DE HOMARD AUX TOMATES CONFITES

Lobster salad with tomato confit

Serves 2

2 live lobsters, each about 500-550g/1lb 4oz-1lb 6oz,
preferably female
2L/3½pt court bouillon (see below)
¼ garlic clove, very finely chopped
1 sprig of thyme, leaves rubbed
fresh basil leaves
200g/7oz green beans, cooked in salted water
a few sprigs of chervil

For the tomato confit

4 very ripe tomatoes, about 100g/3½oz each
100ml/3½fl oz groundnut oil
salt and ground white pepper
1 teaspoon sugar
1 sprig of thyme, leaves rubbed
1 unpeeled garlic clove, crushed

For the pink mayonnaise

1 egg yolk
½ teaspoon strong mustard
85ml/3fl oz olive oil
1 teaspoon lemon juice
1 tablespoon tomato ketchup
1 teaspoon Armagnac
1 heaped tablespoon chopped tarragon and chervil

Make the tomato confit

Blanch the tomatoes in boiling water, peel them, cut them in half and seed them. Use a brush to grease a small oven dish with part of the oil. Put in the tomatoes cut side down and baste them with the rest of the oil, mixed with salt, pepper and sugar (which takes the edge off the tomatoes' acidity). Sprinkle thyme leaves and garlic juice over them.
Place in an oven at 120°C/245°F/gas ½ for 1½ hours, then leave to cool.

Cook and prepare the lobsters

Bring the court bouillon to a rapid boil, then plunge in the lobsters, head first. Cook for 10 minutes then remove, drain and let them cool, lying on their backs.
If the lobsters are female, remove the coral, which is held between the tail fins and the back

legs, and save it for garnishing the dish.
Use large scissors to cut open the lobsters on the underside, the length of the tail. Then remove the tailmeat in one piece. Slice the meat from each lobster into 6 medallions. Crack 2 claws (the others are not used in this dish), but do not remove the shell. Reserve the lobster heads for garnishing.

Make the pink mayonnaise

Put the egg yolk and mustard in a bowl and whisk in the oil, a little at a time, to make a mayonnaise. Finish the sauce by gradually whisking in the lemon juice, ketchup, Armagnac and the chopped herbs.

Presentation

Arrange the tomato confit attractively in the middle of two plates and sprinkle with garlic and thyme. Arrange fresh basil leaves on top and stand a claw in the middle. Arrange the lobster medallions all round. With a spoon spread a fine coat of pink mayonnaise on each medallion and then add a sprig or so of chervil. If you have coral, sprinkle the eggs over the sauce. Surround it all with a delicate green bean frieze. Place a lobster head on the edge of each plate as a garnish.

My wine suggestion: Clos Uroulat Jurançon 1986. Charles Hours at Monein (P.A.)

Chef's note: Though this is for cooking shellfish, I use a.court bouillon entirely of vegetables. Double it – or cook the lobsters in sequence. Chop the following vegetables into 2mm/⅛in slices to permit swift cooking: 2 carrots, the white of one leek, 30g/1oz celery stalk, 60g/2oz onion, 2 shallots and cover with 1.25L/2pt water. Add 30g/1oz coarse salt, 5 strips of lemon zest, 2 unpeeled garlic cloves, 25 green peppercorns, a clove, 6 parsley stalks, ½ bay leaf, a little sprig of fresh fennel and a thyme sprig. Simmer very slowly, uncovered, for 30 minutes. Add 250ml/9fl oz dry white wine and just bring back to the boil. Strain.

Salade de homard aux tomates confites

Feuillantine d'ailes de cailles truffées de cèpes

Les Prés d'Eugénie

FEUILLANTINE D'AILES DE CAILLES TRUFFEES DE CEPES

Pastry puffs of quail wings truffled with ceps

Serves 4

2 quail
350g/12oz made weight puff pastry
85g/3oz foie gras
1 egg beaten with salt, to glaze
500g/1lb small potatoes, all the same size
100g/3½oz butter
your choice of garnish, such as lambs' lettuce, cooked
asparagus spears and carrot slices and fresh herbs

For the marinade

100ml/3½fl oz red wine
60ml/2fl oz cognac
1 tablespoon olive oil
1 carrot, chopped
1 shallot, chopped
1 garlic clove, chopped
1 juniper berry, crushed
1 small bouquet garni

For the cep stuffing

120g/4oz chicken livers, trimmed
40g/1½oz lard
85g/3oz shallots, finely sliced
120g/4oz ceps, finely chopped
150g/5oz mushrooms, finely chopped
few drops of lemon juice
150ml/¼pt cognac
salt and freshly ground black pepper
200ml/7fl oz double cream

For the red wine sauce

85g/3oz onions, roughly chopped
85g/3oz carrots, roughly chopped
200g/7oz butter
10g/⅓oz black peppercorns
1 bouquet garni
100ml/3½fl oz red wine vinegar
60ml/2fl oz cognac
100ml/3½fl oz red Tursan wine

Marinate the quails

Remove the legs and each quail breast complete with wing. Bone out the wings, leaving the flesh attached to the breasts. Combine the marinade ingredients and marinate the breasts and un-boned legs for 12 hours.

Prepare the cep stuffing

Fry the chicken livers, cut in small pieces, in lard with the shallots in a frying pan over a low heat. Add the ceps and mushrooms and moisten with a few drops of lemon juice. When nicely browned, deglaze the pan with the cognac, season and mix in the cream. Cool.

Make the pastry puffs

Roll out the puff pastry and cut 4 circles, each 12cm/4½in diameter and 3mm/¹⁄₁₀in thick. Put a tablespoon of stuffing in the centre then a quail breast with an unboned leg – this will stick out of the pastry slightly. Add 20g/⅔oz foie gras and a little more stuffing. Dampen the pastry edges and fold over one half (like a turnover) pinching the edges tightly together.

Roll out the trimmings and cut leaves. Stick them onto the puffs with beaten egg, then brush the parcels with egg glaze.

Make the red wine sauce

Brown the onions and carrots in a little butter. Add the peppercorns and bouquet garni. After 5 minutes add the vinegar and cognac, stirring to deglaze the pan; boil and reduce until the mixture is almost dry. Add the red wine and reduce by a third.

Strain the sauce into a small pan and then enrich it by whisking in 100g/3½oz butter, a few pieces at a time, adding more just before they melt, so that the sauce retains its texture. Season to taste and add a few drops of vinegar.

Cook the pastry puffs and potatoes

Cut the unpeeled potatoes into discs about 5mm/¹⁄₅in thick. Heat 100g/3½oz butter until it begins to colour and fry the slices for 2 minutes on each side.

Meanwhile bake the pastry puffs in an oven at 190-200°C/375-400°F/gas 5-6, for 8-10 minutes, depending on the size of the quail.

Presentation

Pour red wine sauce on to one side of 4 plates, place a pastry in the centre and the potatoes at one side, garnishing them as you wish.

My wine suggestion: Vieux Château Saint-André 1983, Montagne Saint Emilion, Proprietor Jean Cl. Berrouet at Lussac.

SOUFFLE LEGER A LA PECHE DE CARAMAN

Light peach soufflé

Caraman is a village near Les Sources d'Eugénie, where they grow the most delicious peaches.

Serves 6

5 beautifully ripe peaches, weighing about 120g/4oz each, or 500g/18oz peaches preserved in syrup
½ lemon
60g/2oz caster sugar
1½ tablespoons peach liqueur
5 egg yolks
12 egg whites
a pinch of salt
2 tablespoons icing sugar

For the peach syrup
1L/1¾pt water
100g/3½oz caster sugar
1 vanilla pod, slit lengthways

For the soufflé dishes
20g/⅔oz softened butter
30g/1oz caster sugar from a shaker

Make the peach purée
Put the water, sugar and vanilla pod for the syrup into a pan and bring to the boil. Peel and quarter the peaches, removing the stones and rubbing them with the half lemon to preserve the colour. Cook them in the syrup for 15 minutes then drain in a colander.
Purée the drained peaches carefully in a blender with 60g/2oz caster sugar, the peach liqueur and the 5 egg yolks. Transfer the mixture to a large bowl.

Prepare the dishes and make the soufflés
Brush the inside of four 150ml/¼pt soufflé dishes lightly but thoroughly with the softened butter. Sprinkle the buttered dishes with sugar from a shaker, then turn them upside down and tap the bases to dislodge any surplus sugar.
Put the egg whites and a pinch of salt in a copper or another large bowl, and whisk to a soft snow with a hand or electric whisk, without making them too firm. Towards the end of the operation, incorporate the icing sugar, whisking all the time.
Stir one-quarter of the whites into the peach mixture with a spoon to soften it. Then gradually fold in the remaining egg whites, using a wooden spatula and lifting the mixture lightly to keep it airy.

Bake and present the dish
Heat the oven to 220°C/425°F/gas 7. Fill the soufflé dishes to the top and level the surface with the side of a palette knife. Using your thumb, push the mixture away from the edges of each dish, to enable the soufflés to rise more easily.
Cook for 10 minutes and serve the moment they are removed from the oven.

My wine suggestion: champagne rosé, because it is both good and pretty to look at – try the new Bollinger.

Tea by the pool at les Prés d'Eugénie

Soufflé léger à la pêche de Caraman at les Prés d'Eugénie

ALAIN CHAPEL

Mionnay, 01390 St-André de Corcy telephone: 7 891 82 02

Born in Lyons, a city famous for its fine food, and the son of a restaurateur, Alain Chapel moved with his parents to La Mère Charles twenty kilometres from the city. He became his father's apprentice, already showing something of the great commitment and steadfastness of purpose which was to mark him later. Another apprenticeship followed with Jean Vignard, a close friend and highly talented colleague of Fernand Point, the father of nouvelle cuisine. He went on to learn at La Pyramide itself, under Point's successor. At the age of thirty he became head chef at La Mère Charles, working for his father who was restaurant manager. Within a year he had gained a second Michelin rosette for the restaurant. In 1970, on his father's death, he brought a new style to the restaurant, becoming the chef-owner of what is now one of the best restaurants in France. A third Michelin rosette was awarded in 1973 when he was thirty-four.

Alain Chapel is mad about cooking. Twinned with his nouvelle cuisine *training is a wish to promote the traditions of the Bresse-Lyons region; for example, simple local vegetables accompany his creations. Despite the fame of the restaurant now bearing his name, he is concerned to cater for his locality. He feels it is part of the restaurant's character to be a provincial* auberge. *Unusually for a restaurant of such eminence, the dining room is stone-flagged and rough-plastered and looks into the kitchen. His wife Suzanne adds a touch of comfort and refinement to surroundings that might otherwise be a trifle severe.*

MENU

BOUILLON DE CHAMPIGNONS DE
PRINTEMPS COMME UN CAPUCCINO
Bouillon of spring mushrooms like a 'capuccino'

ROGNONS DE VEAU ROTIS DANS LEUR
GRAISSE EN COCOTTE
Calf's kidneys roasted in their own suet

POIRES WILLIAMS A LA FIGUE ET GLACE
AU LAIT CARAMELISE
William pears with figs and caramelised milk ice cream

BOUILLON DE CHAMPIGNONS DE PRINTEMPS COMME UN CAPUCCINO

Bouillon of spring mushrooms like a 'capuccino'

A frothy head tops each bowl of creamy mushroom soup, and hides the crayfish and chervil beneath.

Serves 4

250g/9oz button mushrooms
40g/1½oz butter
1.2L/2pt water
salt
milled white pepper or cayenne
375ml/13fl oz double cream

For the garnish
12 crayfish tails
about 750ml/1¼pt fish stock (page 161)
120g/4oz wild mushrooms
20g/⅔oz butter
salt
8-12 sprigs chervil

Make the mushroom soup

Peel and wash the button mushrooms and cook gently in the butter without allowing them to brown. Add the water, season with a little salt and leave to cook over the lowest possible heat until the liquid has reduced to 750ml/1¼pt. Strain it back into a pan and add the cream. Cook for 10 minutes, then taste and season.

Poach the crayfish tails in hot fish stock for about 3 minutes, then peel and remove the vein. Wash the wild mushrooms and sauté them in a pan in the butter. Season with salt. Add the crayfish tails, then the chervil and sauté briefly.

Presentation

Transfer the mushroom and crayfish tail mixture to 4 warmed soup bowls.

Froth the boiling mushroom bouillon in a blender (a little at a time and taking care); this gives the creamy soup a capuccino-like head. Pour into the bowls and serve.

My wine suggestion: Chablis 'les Butteaux' 1984 Jean-Marie Raveneau, which has a suave fresh bouquet with an aroma of mushrooms.

ROGNONS DE VEAU ROTIS DANS LEUR GRAISSE EN COCOTTE

Calf's kidneys roasted in their own suet

Serves 4

2 calf's kidneys, as clean as possible, in their own suet,
which should be white and crumbly
salt and freshly ground black pepper
150g/5oz butter
20 shallots, peeled whole
4 tablespoons Madeira
175ml/6fl oz meat stock (page 133)
flat-leaved parsley
juice of 2 crushed garlic cloves

Cook the kidneys

Trim excess suet from the kidneys and season them with salt. Use a small cast-iron casserole and 30g/1oz butter to brown the kidneys whole in their suet in an oven at 230°C/450°F/gas 8. Cook for 15 minutes, turning frequently.

Pour out all the fat and replace with 60g/2oz fresh butter, then add the shallots. As they begin to cook, they will become soft. Crush to a purée using a fork. The sugar they contain will bind the kidney juice and caramelise slightly. When the kidneys have lost their blood and feel firm to the touch, remove and leave them to rest separately in a dish, keeping them hot.

Make the shallot and Madeira sauce

Stir the Madeira into the juices in the casserole and then add the stock, a little at a time. Boil to reduce to a syrupy liquid, then strain. Pour the juice that has run from the kidneys into the reduced sauce and whisk in 30g/1oz butter, in pieces, to thicken it.

Presentation

Carve the kidneys with the suet into thick slices. Arrange on a dish and sprinkle with a few drops of melted butter to give a marbled effect.

Blanch the parsley in boiling salted water then dry on a cloth. Melt 15g/½oz butter with the garlic juice and add the parsley, stirring continuously until just crisp. Garnish with parsley.

My wine suggestion: Hermitage 1978 Gérard Chave; it has all the body of a great red wine, but is fine, smooth and full, with a distinctive but not overpowering bouquet.

POIRES WILLIAMS A LA FIGUE ET GLACE AU LAIT CARAMELISE

William pears with figs and caramelised milk ice cream

Serves 4

4 small red William pears
8 small green figs
40g/1½oz butter
4 ripe purple figs

For the caramelised milk
200g/7oz sugar
1 teaspoon liquid glucose
200ml/7fl oz milk
pinch of bicarbonate of soda

For the custard
300ml/½pt milk
6 eggs
30g/1oz sugar
85ml/3fl oz crème fraîche

For the poaching syrup
175g/6oz sugar
300ml/½pt water

Caramelise the milk

Cook the sugar with the glucose until it is lightly coloured. Meanwhile bring the milk to the boil with the bicarbonate of soda. Off the heat slowly pour the milk on to the caramel. Be careful because the mixture will froth up a lot. Reheat very gently and leave to reduce by half. Skim the froth from the surface from time to time. Save 3-4 tablespoons caramelised milk for making the purple fig purée.

Make the custard and freeze it

Put the caramelised milk and the milk for the custard together. Beat the eggs and sugar in a bowl until light, then pour on the hot milk. Return to the saucepan and cook, over very gentle heat, until thickened, stirring continuously. The custard is ready when a finger drawn across the back of a spatula leaves a clean mark. Leave until cold, stirring occasionally, then add the crème fraîche.

Turn into an ice cream maker, or freeze in a freezer, beating several times before it's stiff.

Prepare the fruit

Cut across the base of the pears so that they will stand up, but leave them whole and unpeeled.

Make the poaching syrup by bringing the sugar and water to the boil slowly.

Melt a little butter in a sauté pan and add the pears, turning to cook them on all sides. Add the syrup gradually and cover the pan. Cook gently for about 8 minutes, until almost cooked, spooning the syrup over the pears continually. Add the green figs to the pan, standing them upright in the gaps, as they are extremely fragile. Continue with the basting. When cooked, remove the pears and figs. Let the syrup cool until somewhat stiffened, then use to glaze the cooked fruit.

Scrape out the inside of the purple figs and mash to a smooth pulp with a fork, working in a little caramelised milk to make a sauce.

Presentation

Use large plates for the dessert and spoon a little purple fig purée on to each one at the top left. Place a pear upright at the bottom of the plate, with a green fig on either side. Spoon over a little cooking syrup, diluted if necessary, to moisten. Spoon a small quenelle (oval shape) of caramelised milk ice cream on to the purple fig sauce.

My wine suggestion: Banyuls 'Solera Hors d'Age' from Dr. André Parcé. Extremely suave, with an Eastern flavour, it has a complex blend of aromas among which can be discerned a hint of fresh fig.

Claude Peyrot

LE VIVAROIS

192 Avenue Victor Hugo, 75116 Paris telephone: 45 04 04 31

Born in the rugged but hospitable region of the Ardèche, at the village of Saint-Félicien, Claude Peyrot began his cooking career there, at the family inn. From this modest beginning, he went on to become one of those chefs so respected and established that they are listed by name, next to that of the restaurant, in the Michelin red guide and to become the holder of two Michelin rosettes.

After studying at the Ecole Hôtelière in Grenoble, he took a succession of jobs to build up his expertise, working in the kitchens of restaurants whose names are known throughout the world, with Fernand Point at La Pyramide in Vienne, wih Raymond Thuilier at L'Oustau de Baumanière in Provence and at the Lucas Carton and Ritz in Paris.

In 1966, when he was forty-one, he opened his own restaurant Le Vivarois in Paris, where his dazzling style of cooking quickly won a Michelin rosette. The restaurant also became a place where young chefs wished to train.

His wife Jacqueline presides in the restaurant over a decor of sombre grey marble. The kitchen houses an artist who is completely serious about his work but does not take himself too seriously. He is, he says 'a provincial at heart, who loves the mountains'; he is also a keen jogger. His cuisine is subtly seductive — traditional cooking updated but without gimmickry. It is characterized by an innate culinary sense of perfectionism.

MENU

HUITRES GRATINEES AU CURRY
Curried oyster gratin

FOIE GRAS D'OIE EN POULARDE
Galantine of chicken with foie gras

TRANCHES D'ANANAS POELEES SUR
GLACE VANILLE
Fried pineapple slices with vanilla ice cream

HUITRES GRATINEES AU CURRY

Curried oyster gratin

Serves 6

36 oysters
1 garlic clove
30g/1oz butter
600g/1¼lb spinach, washed and stalks removed
paprika

For the curry hollandaise sauce
6 egg yolks
salt
juice of 1 lemon
1 tablespoon water
200g/7oz clarified butter, tepid (see right)
cayenne
3 teaspoons curry powder

Open the oysters and prepare the shells
Choose nice fat oysters, open them with a knife through the hinge and remove from the shells, saving the juices. Carefully clean the shells and keep for presentation.

Cook the spinach
Rub the inside of a saucepan with the cut side of the garlic clove, add the butter and then the washed trimmed spinach. Cook gently, turning the top to the bottom once or twice, then season.

Arrange the spinach in the oyster shells.

Make and flavour the hollandaise sauce
Put the yolks into a bowl which will fit over simmering water and add salt, the lemon juice and water. Place over gentle heat and whisk until the yolks start to thicken. Whisk in the tepid, liquid butter, starting with a small stream, as you would for mayonnaise and whisking well to the bottom of the pan. Add more as the butter is incorporated, taking care that the sauce never gets really hot and using almost all the butter. Taste and adjust the seasoning, using cayenne instead of black pepper.

In a small pan warm the remaining butter and stir in the curry powder. Make sure this mixture is not too hot when added to the hollandaise.

Poach and serve the oysters
Poach the oysters in their own liquid for 30 seconds. Arrange them in the shells on the spinach leaves and top with curry hollandaise. Sprinkle with paprika and brown quickly under a hot grill.

My wine suggestion: Condrieu 1986 of Georges Vernay, which has greenish-gold reflections and a flowery flavour.

CLARIFIED BUTTER

400g/14oz unsalted butter

Melt the butter in a medium-sized pan. Chefs usually do this in the course of the recipe, skimming the froth and pouring off the oily liquid underneath as needed. However amateurs may find it easier to let the foam subside and the casein in the milk drop to the bottom of the pan, where it forms a milky residue. The butter can be poured off it easily.

It is important that the butter is tepid when used, at the same temperature as the egg yolks, neither cold nor too hot, if a smooth emulsion is to be obtained.

FOIE GRAS D'OIE EN POULARDE

Galantine of chicken with foie gras

Serves 6

2.5kg/5½lb chicken
600g/1¾lb foie gras, cleaned (page 85)
toasted pain de campagne or brown bread to serve

For the poultry stuffing

150g/5oz chicken flesh from the drumsticks
1 tablespoon double cream
½ egg white
salt and milled white pepper

For the jellied glaze

60ml/2fl oz red port
500ml/18fl oz well-reduced chicken stock (page 250)
85g/3oz shin of beef, finely chopped
60g/2oz chicken flesh, chopped
1 tablespoon chopped white of leek
1 tablespoon chopped onion
1 tablespoon chopped carrot
2 cloves
1 egg white, lightly whisked with a fork

For the garnish

your seasonal choice from:
Agen prunes, braised in brown stock (page 178)
green olives, stuffed with foie gras purée
asparagus tips, steamed
quartered orange slices, glazed with jelly

Bone out the chicken through the neck

Ask your butcher to bone out the chicken through the neck. Cut off the wings at first joint, the drumsticks and neck (keeping some neck skin attached). Clean the bird and remove all the bones through this aperture. This will give you a hollow tube of chicken flesh, open at both ends, enclosed by skin. The action of boning out from inside will pull the flesh of both thighs and wings inside the chicken, neatening the exterior shape. Remove the fat from inside the vent end and move the small, loose fillet inside each breast to pad the skin on the backbone side.

Make the poultry stuffing

Mince the chicken flesh finely in a food processor beating in the cream and the egg white. Season to taste and press through a sieve; the stuffing must be extremely light, as it is there solely to provide a coating for the inside of the chicken, to help the foie gras adhere.

Stuff and roast the chicken

Smear the stuffing over the inside of the chicken then fold the two lobes of the foie gras together and insert into the bird. Close the neck and the vent, patting the flesh close to the liver and cutting off excess neck skin. Tie a string round the galantine lengthways and across in several places to hold it in place. Salt and pepper the skin.

Roast the chicken in an ungreased roasting tin at 160-180°C/325-350°F/gas 3-4 for 1¾ hours, basting it regularly with the juices that run from inside, but without adding any butter or fat, which would spoil the unique fat that comes from the foie gras itself. Remove the galantine from the pan and leave to cool.

Make the jelly for the glaze and clarify it

Set the tin over low heat and deglaze, stirring port into the juices; reduce by three-quarters. Add the chicken jelly. Pour the juices into a jug and leave until cold, then remove all trace of fat. Return the jelly to a saucepan and clarify it. Add the chopped beef and chicken flesh, vegetables, cloves and egg white, and bring the liquid slowly to the boil. The additions will cohere and rise to form a crust; simmer for 20 minutes. Push the crust gently aside in one place and ladle the liquid from underneath pouring it over the crust, which will act as a strainer. When the liquid is clear, pass through a muslin-lined sieve and leave to cool.

Prepare the cooked garnishes and cool

Prepare for presentation

The following day melt the jelly and lightly coat the base of a serving platter; chill to set. Slice the galantine and arrange the slices on the jelly. Using jelly chilled to the point of setting, coat each slice till it shines. Coat the chosen fruit or vegetable garnish and chill on a rack to set, then arrange round the galantine on the platter.

Serve with toasted pain de campagne.

My wine suggestion: L'Oeil de Perdrix, Domaine de Dujac 1986; a light black Pinot which is almost rosé with a hint of strawberry.

TRANCHES D'ANANAS POELEES
SUR GLACE VANILLE

Fried pineapple slices with vanilla ice cream

Serves 6

1 large pineapple
120g/4oz butter
100g/3½oz sugar

For the vanilla ice cream
500ml/18fl oz milk
½ vanilla pod, split lengthways
6 egg yolks
100g/3½oz sugar
250ml/9fl oz single cream

Make the vanilla ice cream
Bring the milk to the boil with the split vanilla pod. In a bowl whisk the egg yolks with the sugar and then strain in the boiling milk, whisking all the time. Return to a pan and set over simmering water. Cook, stirring constantly, until the custard coats the back of a spatula. Leave until cold, stirring occasionally.
Stir in the cream and turn into an ice cream maker, or freeze in the freezer, beating several times before the ice cream is firm.

Caramelise the pineapple
Cut off the top and bottom of the pineapple and then all the sides. Slice neatly into 6. Heat the butter in a large frying pan and stir in the sugar and cook until it caramelises. Put in the pineapple slices and cook on both sides, turning, until coated.

Presentation
To serve, arrange the hot caramelised pineapple slices on plates and top each one with a ball of ice cream.

My wine suggestion: Muscat de Rivesaltes 'Taïchac', a light wine with a scent of fresh almonds and a taste of honey.

Marc Meneau

L'Espérance

Saint-Père-sous-Vézelay, 89450 Vézelay telephone: 86 33 20 45

The owner of one of France's great restaurants, Marc Meneau was born in Vézelay where he still lives, an old Burgundy village where his father was the harness-maker and his mother ran a café-bar-cum-grocery business. His first thought was to take a white collar job and he went to hotel school in Strasbourg — to learn to be a manager. This was abandoned when he married a pretty girl, Françoise, who was a highly enthusiastic cook and the daughter of local restaurateurs. This induced him to exchange his white collar for the cook's white overalls and in 1970 the café-grocery was turned into a restaurant. Two years later it gained a Michelin rosette. Having no cookery training, all his information and inspiration came from books but he combined this with the tough professional apprenticeship — running a renowned restaurant. Another link with the past was a friendship with Alex Humbert, head chef at Maxim's during the Grand Epoque.

In 1975 L'Espérance moved to its present home, under the hill in Vézelay, and gained its second Michelin rosette. A charming nineteenth century house set against big trees, it has a small river — with quacking ducks — running through the grounds. The third Michelin rosette was awarded in 1984, when he was thirty-nine.

His enthusiasm for the local produce is as much for the humble things as for the more spectacular. There is a continuity about using the local food and the local approach to it which he values. In each dish he is looking for an essential correctness of taste, and the success of his dishes may be characterised by saying they are full of natural grace.

MENU

HUITRES A LA GELEE D'EAU DE MER
Oysters jellied in their own sea juices

CANARD SAUCE AU SANG A LA PRESSE AVEC GALETTE AUX DEUX POMMES
Duck in its own juices served with potato and apple pancakes

POIRE CARAMELISEE GLACE A LA REGLISSE
Caramelised pears with liquorice ice

Huîtres à la gelée d'eau de mer

HUITRES A LA GELEE D'EAU DE MER

Oysters jellied in their own sea juices

Serves 4

30 special oysters, no 3
½ bunch of watercress, 250-300g/8-10oz

For the oyster cream
30-40g/1-1½oz chopped shallots
60g/2oz butter
150ml/¼pt single cream
juice of ¼ lemon
salt and freshly ground black pepper

For the jelly
juices from the oysters
½ leaf gelatine
freshly ground black pepper

Open the oysters, saving their sea juices. Remove them from their shells and lay them on a cloth.

Make the jelly
Warm the oyster liquid to 40°C/105°F. Break up the gelatine leaf and soften it in 1 tablespoon cold water. Dissolve, stirring over hot water then let it cool again. Add it to the sea juices, stirring very gently so as not to disturb the juice too much. Add a grinding of pepper and chill in the refrigerator until half set.

Make the oyster cream
Chop 6 oysters with a knife. Sweat the shallots in melted butter until soft then leave to cool. Blend the chopped oysters, shallots, cream, lemon juice and seasoning.

Completion and presentation
Wash, scrub and dry all the shells. Into each one scoop a teaspoonful of oyster cream and place an oyster on top. Grind a dash of pepper over them and cover with washed and picked watercress leaves.
Take out the jelly, which should be a sticky consistency (if necessary stand in a bowl of ice-and-water to help thicken it). Fill the shells with jelly and leave in a cool place until set. Serve on a bed of crushed ice.

My wine suggestion: Chablis Montmains.

CANARD SAUCE AU SANG A LA PRESSE AVEC GALETTE AUX DEUX POMMES

Duck in its own juices served with potato and apple pancakes

Serves 4

2 Challans ducks (strangled duck), each 1.5kg/3½lb
salt and freshly ground black pepper
60g/2oz butter
2 shallots, chopped
300ml/½pt red wine

Prepare and roast the ducks
Draw the ducks, if necessary, and prepare them for roasting seasoning inside and out with salt and pepper. Using 20g/⅔oz butter for each bird, rub it over the breasts and thighs with the palms of your hands.
Roast the ducks in an oven at 190°C/375°F/gas 5, basting frequently, for 15 minutes or better still, cook them on a spit if your cooker has one. At the end of this time, wrap the ducks in aluminium foil and leave them for 6 or 7 minutes until the heat has got through to the inside. Then take off the breasts and thighs.

Press the carcasses and make the sauce
Chop the carcasses with a cleaver and wring them in a cloth, squeezing it hard down on them, to extract the blood. Collect this with great care. In the restaurant we use a duck press and the operation is done before the guests, to enhance their pleasure in the food.
Meanwhile sweat the shallots in the rest of the butter, then add the red wine to the pan in three lots, each time reducing the sauce to syrup before adding the next glass.

Add the blood to the sauce
When your guests are ready to eat the duck, gently rewarm the breasts and thighs. Slice the breasts into 5 or 6 pieces.
Replace the pan of reduced wine on the heat, pour in the blood and cook very gently – only to 66°C/140°F – to cook the sauce without coagulating it too much. Finishing at this point requires great care if you are not to have a grainy liquid. Correct the seasonings and add any juices from carving.

Presentation

Pour sauce onto one side of the plate and arrange the breast on top. Centre a thigh on each plate and arrange the apple and potato galettes opposite each breast. Serve at once.

My wine suggestion: Irancy Palotte.

Editor's note: Challans ducks are among the finest in France. Reared in the Vendée, on the Bay of Biscay below the mouth of the Loire, they are often known as Nantes ducks – the railway station from which they travel.

The reason for strangling them is that this method sheds no blood; preserved within the meat, it makes it very red and moist. Rouen ducks are smothered for the same reason. All other ducks in France and elsewhere are bled after killing, which enables them to be refrigerated safely for a period. Strangled ducks must be cooked almost immediately.

GALETTE AUX DEUX POMMES

Potato and apple pancakes

Serves 4

85g/3oz potatoes, preferably Binch
20g/²/₃oz flour, sifted
2 whole eggs
250ml/9fl oz skimmed milk
salt and freshly ground black pepper
freshly grated nutmeg
2 Granny Smiths or crisp dessert apples
40g/1½oz butter, plus extra for frying the pancakes

Wash and boil the potatoes. Purée them and add the flour, eggs, milk, salt, pepper and nutmeg. Mix well and leave to stand in a cool place.
Meanwhile cut the apples into slices 1cm/½in thick and fry until golden in the butter.
A few minutes before serving take a frying pan 10cm/4in diameter, melt some butter and put in 1½ tablespoons potato batter. Top with 4-5 slices of apple and cover with about the same amount of potato mixture. Cook on both sides, then keep them warm while you cook three more pancakes. Serve with the duck.

POIRE CARAMELISEE GLACE A LA REGLISSE

Caramelised pears with liquorice ice

Serves 4

4 ripe pears
30g/1oz butter
60g/2oz sugar
150ml/¼pt water

For the liquorice ice
40g/1½oz liquorice root
750ml/1¼pt milk
12 egg yolks
150g/5oz sugar

Make the liquorice ice
Chop the liquorice root finely. Add to the milk in a pan over high heat and bring to the boil.
Put the egg yolks and sugar in a bowl and whisk vigorously. When the milk boils, pour it onto the egg and sugar mixture, continuing to whisk all the time. Pour it back into the saucepan and return to a very gentle heat; it must not exceed 93°C/200°F. Cook it, stirring all the time with a spatula until it is thick enough to coat the back. Test by running a finger across the spatula – it should leave a clean line. When the custard is fully cooked, pass it through a sieve and leave until cold.
Freeze the custard in an ice cream maker or in a freezer, beating several times before it becomes firm.

Caramelise the pears
Peel and core the pears and slice them lengthways. In a frying pan melt the butter and fry the slices until a good golden colour. Add the sugar and the water and cook gently for 15 minutes, making sure the sugar does not burn.

Presentation
Fan out the hot pear slices on one side of 4 pretty dessert plates and set 2 balls of liquorice ice next to them.

My wine suggestion: Marc de Bourgogne.

Canard sauce au sang à la presse avec galette aux deux pommes

L'Espérance

Poire caramelisée glace à la réglisse

Firmin Arrambide

LES PYRÉNÉES

Place du Général de Gaulle, 64220 Saint-Jean-Pied-de-Port telephone: 59 37 01 01

Born in the French Basque country, in Saint-Jean-Pied-de-Port in south-west France, Firmin Arrambide grew up among people who knew about good food. 'My grandmother was a cook and my father was a cook and from the earliest age I could never imagine entering another métier than that of cook.' He served his apprenticeship with his father in the kitchen of the inn that the family has owned since 1939.

An old coaching inn at the foot of the Roncevalles pass, on the main route to Spain and the pilgrim shrine of Santiago de Compostella, Les Pyrénées will stay in the family for yet another generation, as his son Philippe is training to join him. In sight of the mountains, but surrounded by the green Basque country, the hotel is in the middle of one of the prettiest local villages, huddling round a Vauban fortress, and it looks out on the ramparts. The young Firmin Arrambide made his own 'grand tour' of France's best restaurants then, in 1970, returned to take charge of the kitchen and to marry Anne-Marie. Aware of the new phenomenon of the French kitchen, 'I refashioned and updated the cooking, while respecting the classical tradition of my father'. His links with Basques south of the border are strong and he has been influential in taking modern French cooking to Spain.

His style of cooking is 'a synthesis between the cooking of the Basque country, with the maximum use of the products of the region — and the traditions of the region — and a more modern style of cooking'. His aim is to combine the precision of classical cooking with a totally modern emphasis on presentation and on using seasonal ingredients. A Maître Cuisinier de France, his success has been acknowledged by his first Michelin rosette in 1975 and a second in 1985.

MENU

POIVRONS FARCIS A LA MORUE
Peppers stuffed with salt cod

LAPIN FARCI AUX PETITS LEGUMES
Rabbit stuffed with little vegetables

TERRINE DE FRUITS FRAIS
A LA MOUSSE D'AMANDES
Terrine of fresh fruit with almond mousse

POIVRONS FARCIS A LA MORUE

Peppers stuffed with salt cod

Serves 4

250g/9oz salt cod
8 red peppers
150ml/¼pt olive oil
salt and freshly ground black pepper
100g/3½oz onions, sliced
3 garlic cloves, chopped
60g/2oz breadcrumbs
150ml/¼pt whipping cream
a pinch of caster sugar
1 egg
flour
3 sprigs parsley, chopped

Soak the salt cod ahead

Soak the salt cod in cold water for 36 to 48 hours, changing the water three or four times, to remove the salt.

Prepare and stuff the peppers

Pierce each pepper with the prongs of a fork and hold over a gas flame (or put under a hot grill) turning continuously, until its skin begins to blister and blacken. Rinse in cold water and peel. Remove the stalks and de-seed the peppers through the hole, using a teaspoon.

Place them side by side on a platter, sprinkle with 60ml/2fl oz olive oil, salt them all over and cook in an oven at 200°C/400°F/gas 6 for 15 minutes. Remove and let them cool.

Meanwhile put the onions and garlic into a saucepan with a tablespoon of oil and cook over gentle heat, stirring frequently. Drain the cod, strip off all the skin, and bone and flake it. Add the flaked fish to the softened onion, stir for no more than 1 minute and remove from the heat. Add the breadcrumbs and adjust the seasoning. Drain the peppers and cut off a slice from the open end, about 2cm/¾in wide, leaving a neat cup. Chop the trimmings and cook with the cream over gentle heat. Simmer for 15 minutes, then purée in a blender and pass through a conical strainer. Add salt and the sugar to this sauce.

Fry the peppers

Beat the egg yolk and white together in a shallow dish. Put a little flour in another dish. Stuff each pepper with the salt cod mixture. Heat the rest of the oil in a frying pan over moderate heat. Roll each pepper in flour, shaking off the excess, then in the beaten egg. Fry them, turning, until golden on all sides.

Presentation

To serve, coat the bottom of a warmed serving dish with some of the creamy pepper sauce. Arrange the peppers on top, sprinkling them with chopped parsley. Pass the remaining sauce in a sauce boat.

My wine suggestion: Jurançon sec, Domaine de Cauhapé from M. Ramonteu at Monein, a young dry and fruity white – or a Chablis.

LAPIN FARCI AUX PETITS LEGUMES

Rabbit stuffed with little vegetables

Serves 4

1.2kg/3lb farmed rabbit
4 small artichokes, trimmed to the base
280g/10oz can baby carrots
100g/3½oz fresh spinach, trimmed
1 pork caul (page 165)
¼ teaspoon ruby port
1 teaspoon sherry vinegar
salt and freshly ground black pepper
chervil to garnish

For the stuffing
100g/3½oz meat taken from the neck and shoulders of the rabbit
60g/2oz pork back fat, chopped
20g/⅔oz breadcrumbs
100ml/3½fl oz milk
1 egg
1 sprig of basil

For the vegetable base
2 tablespoons olive oil
3 carrots, finely sliced
2 shallots, finely sliced
1 onion, finely sliced
250ml/9fl oz dry white wine, preferably Jurançon
3 tomatoes, blanched, skinned, seeded and flesh chopped
1 garlic clove, crushed
1 bouquet garni
1 sprig of basil
1 sprig of rosemary
1L/1¾pt brown chicken stock (page 250)

Bone the rabbit and make the stuffing
Your butcher will do this. Remove the head and feet and bone it out completely, saving the liver and kidneys and the bones. Lay the boned rabbit out flat and cut away 100g/3½oz meat from the neck area for the stuffing. Put this meat and pork fat into the food processor, add the breadcrumbs (soaked in milk then squeezed out), the egg, basil, salt and pepper. Mix to a fine mass then chill.

Prepare the vegetables
Cook the artichoke hearts in salted boiling water for 18 minutes. Cook the carrots for 3-4

minutes. Refresh the artichokes and remove the chokes. Steam the spinach for 30 seconds, refresh and spread out on a cloth.

Make a vegetable base for braising
Brown the chopped rabbit bones in a casserole in the olive oil. Then sweat the vegetables for 10 minutes, stirring occasionally. Moisten with the white wine, boil until dry, then add the tomato flesh, garlic, bouquet garni, sprigs of basil and rosemary, chicken stock and some seasoning. Simmer gently.

Stuff and cook the rabbit
Soak the caul for ½ hour then pat dry and spread it out on a large sheet of greaseproof paper. Lay out the boned rabbit. Cut the thick part of the fillets and thighs into slices to open them out and trim to a uniform thickness. Season with salt, pepper and a few drops of port and sherry vinegar. Trim the liver, removing the gall (and any dark parts that have been in contact with it) and cut into four. Season these and the kidneys. Spread the rabbit with a thin even layer of stuffing. Put 2 layers of spinach leaves on top. Cover with a second layer of stuffing. Arrange the quarters of liver and kidney in the centre, then 4 rows of little carrots and the halved artichoke hearts, staggered. Cover with more stuffing.

Fold the rabbit in half with the help of the greaseproof paper and wrap in caul, trimming away the surplus. Wrap the rabbit in paper, folding the ends together like a large parcel. Tie up like a roast. Set the rabbit on the vegetable base and cook in an oven at 170°C/325°F/gas 3 for 1½ hours, basting frequently and turning over halfway through cooking.

Serve the rabbit
Take the rabbit from the casserole and remove the paper. Brown the caul under the grill. Sieve the braising vegetables, adding ½ teaspoon sherry vinegar and seasoning to taste. Slice the rabbit, arrange on plates and coat with the sauce. Garnish with chervil.

My wine suggestion: Château Haut-Marbuzet from M. Duboscq at St-Estèphe, a fruity wine of substance and lots of charm, or a Madiran wine, Château Montus from M. Brumont of Maumusson.

TERRINE DE FRUITS FRAIS A LA MOUSSE D'AMANDES

Terrine of fresh fruit with almond mousse

Serves 4

200ml/7fl oz whipping cream
175g/6oz butter
150g/5oz icing sugar
100g/3½oz ground almonds
2 tablespoons Grand Marnier
500g/1lb strawberries
4 kiwi fruit
400g/14oz can yellow peach halves in syrup
(or slices of fresh mango)
60g/2oz caster sugar
½ lemon
20 sponge fingers

The night before (or at the latest 2 hours before you start preparing the rest of the dish) place the whipping cream and a mixing bowl in the refrigerator, and take out the butter to warm to room temperature.

Make the almond mousse
Into the mixer put the butter, sifted icing sugar, ground almonds and Grand Marnier. Beat until the mixture is white and smooth. Put the chilled cream into the cold bowl and whip until thickened. With the help of a spatula, carefully cut the whipped cream into the almond mixture. Refrigerate immediately.

Prepare the fruit
Wash the strawberries then remove the stalks (never in the reverse order as they would otherwise soak up some of the washing water). From the total weight sort out 250g/9oz attractive, sound fruit, reserving the rest for the sauce. Cut the selected berries into cork shapes, by trimming off both ends, adding the trimmings to the berries for sauce. Peel the kiwi fruit and cut lengthways into quarters. Drain the peaches in a colander over a bowl. Pat them dry with absorbent paper and cut them into quarters.

Make the strawberry purée
Put the sauce berries and trimmings into a blender with the caster sugar and juice of ½ lemon. The lemon juice, whilst giving the strawberries a slightly acidic flavour, will help them to retain their attractive colour. Blend to a purée and then place in the refrigerator.

Make the fruit terrine
Assemble all the fruit for the terrine with the sponge fingers and almond mousse. Line a 850ml/1½pt terrine with a sheet of aluminium foil large enough to hang over the edge. Soak the sponge fingers lightly in peach syrup, then line the base and sides of the terrine with them. Put a little mousse in the bottom, then a layer of fruit and fill the terrine in alternate layers in such a way that the fruit will make a decorative pattern when it is cut. Cover with a final layer of fingers and chill overnight.

Presentation
Just before serving, carefully turn out the terrine. Spoon a little strawberry purée on to each plate. Slice the terrine with a sharp knife and arrange one slice on each plate on the purée with the help of a gateau slice.

My wine suggestion: a mellow Jurançon blanc, a Clos Cancaïllou from B. Barrère of Lahourcade, with a flavour of mature fruit and vanilla, or a good Sauternes.

Bernard Pacaud

L'AMBROISIE
9 Place des Vosges, 75004 Paris telephone: 1 42 78 51 45

Bernard Pacaud spent his youth in Lyons, sometimes described as 'the stomach of France'. Perhaps this explains his interest in food, for among his Breton parents and family, no one was a cook. He began his apprenticeship at the Col de la Luère, a place of great tradition for it had been the restaurant of Mère Brazier, who thirty years before was one of France's very few women chefs to gain Michelin's highest rating.

He rose through the ranks in the kitchen to become assistant then deputy chef in a number of different establishments, all of them Michelin starred. The Mère Brazier was followed by the Tante Alice in Lyons, then ten years in Paris, starting at La Coquille. In 1976 he went to work for Claude Peyrot at Le Vivarois. Here he found his true inspiration and he regards the chef as his mentor.

Five years at Le Vivarois gave him the confidence to open his own restaurant, L'Ambroisie, which was then on the Quais de la Tournelle. It was awarded one Michelin rosette in 1982, then two in 1983, when he was thirty-five.

In 1986 the restaurant moved to a former private mansion in the Place des Vosges, one of the most beautiful squares in Paris. Here in surroundings he describes as 'elegant but discreet' – marble floors and doors, tapestries and seventeenth century pictures – he serves food of equal quality. How does he characterise his own style? He has never been a follower of nouvelle cuisine; in essence 'it is a cuisine based on its produce – treated with great sensibility.' Michelin agreed and the third rosette was awarded in 1988.

MENU

SUPREME DE BAR A L'EMULSION D'HUILE
D'OLIVE, PUREE DE FENOUIL
*Fillet of perch with an emulsion of olive oil and fennel
purée*

QUEUE DE BOEUF BRAISEE EN CREPINE
Oxtail braised in caul

SAVARIN A L'ANCIENNE
Babas the classic way

SUPREME DE BAR A L'EMULSION D'HUILE D'OLIVE, PUREE DE FENOUIL

Fillet of perch with an emulsion of olive oil and fennel purée

Serves 4

1.5kg/3½lb perch
250g/9oz fennel bulb
1 carrot
2 teaspoons chopped coriander leaves
250ml/9fl oz olive oil
1 tomato
1 lime
dill leaves
flat-leaved parsley to garnish
salt and freshly ground black pepper

Make the accompaniments

To make the fennel purée, peel and chop the fennel and carrot. Steam them with the chopped coriander for 20 minutes, until tender, then pass through a sieve. Stir 2 teaspoons of oil into the purée and keep warm.

To make the olive oil emulsion, blanch, peel and deseed the tomato and chop the flesh. Blend to a purée with the juice of the lime and dill to taste. Season with salt and pepper, then stir in 150ml/¼pt olive oil.

Prepare and cook the perch

Fillet the perch, cutting each fillet in half. Season with salt and pepper, then fry, skin side down in 2 teaspoons hot olive oil until cooked through.

Presentation

To serve, pour a pool of olive oil emulsion on to warmed dinner plates. Place the perch fillets on top, skin side up, to one side and centre a quenelle of fennel purée opposite. Garnish with sprays of flat-leaved parsley.

My wine suggestion: Meursault 'Les Narvaux' from B. Michelot – a white Burgundy with an attractive greenish-gold colour, well balanced, with a freshness, subtlety and elegance.

QUEUE DE BOEUF BRAISEE EN CREPINE

Oxtail braised in caul

Serves 4

2 oxtails, chopped in pieces
salt and freshly ground black pepper
2 onions
2 carrots
2 shallots
1 garlic clove
1 tablespoon olive oil
2 70cl bottles of Cornas red wine
1 bouquet garni
200g/7oz caul (page 165)
freshly cooked carrots to serve

Casserole the oxtail ahead

The day before you wish to serve the dish, season the oxtails with salt and pepper. Finely chop the vegetables and garlic to make a mirepoix. Heat the oil in a heavy pan and brown the oxtails on all sides. Remove and transfer to a casserole then brown the mirepoix in the pan and transfer. Pour in the wine and bring to the boil. Skim, add the bouquet garni and cook in an oven heated to 150°C/300°F/gas 2 for 8 hours. Leave to cool then chill.

Cook the oxtail in caul parcels

Place the caul in a colander and leave under gently running cold water for 15 minutes then drain. Spread it out and cut pieces of a size to enclose each piece of oxtail.

Remove the layer of fat from the casserole, then spoon out the pieces of oxtail, scraping any vegetables adhering to them back into the sauce. Wrap the pieces individually in the caul and tuck them back into the casserole.

Cook over a moderate to high heat, basting the tops of the parcels often, until they are lightly golden and heated through, and the sauce is well reduced – about 30 minutes.

Serve simply on hot dinner plates with the sauce, accompanied by freshly cooked carrots.

My wine suggestion: Cornas 1984 from Barjac, a very typical red Côtes du Rhône, robust, with an earthy flavour for a rustic dish. Use it for cooking and to drink.

Suprême de bar à l'émulsion d'huile d'olive,
purée de fenouil

Queue de boeuf braisée en crépine

L'Ambroisie

Savarin à l'ancienne

SAVARIN A L'ANCIENNE

Babas the classic way

Since the days when the Polish king Stanislaus Leczinski was exiled to France, where his daughter was Louis XIV's queen, babas have been adopted by the French. Stanislaus poured a glass of rum over his favourite cake, and set it alight. Enchanted by the result, he called it Ali Baba, after the hero of his favourite story. A century later a pair of Paris pastry cooks turned the cake into a ring and poured rum syrup over it, naming it after the gastronome Brillat-Savarin. These babas are a classic and enduring feature of the dessert trolley.

Serves 4

100g/3½oz plain flour
a pinch of salt
1 teaspoon sugar
1 egg, lightly beaten
5g/⅕oz fresh yeast
20g/⅔oz butter, melted
500g/1lb fresh raspberries
fresh mint leaves to garnish (optional)

For the kirsch syrup
120g/4oz sugar
300ml/½pt water
2 teaspoons kirsch

For the sabayon sauce
2 egg yolks
60g/2oz sugar
2 teaspoons kirsch

Make the babas
Place the flour, salt, sugar and egg in a mixing bowl. Dissolve the yeast in a little warm water, leaving it in a warm place until frothy. Then add it to the bowl (don't use a food processor for this). Work the paste thoroughly until the consistency resembles a thick pancake batter; it is ready when it starts to come away cleanly from the beaters.
Cover with a cloth and leave in a warm place until doubled in volume – about 30 minutes.
Add the melted butter and knead again.
Divide the dough and place it in four individual ring baba moulds.
Bake in the oven at 220°C/425°F/gas 7 for 10 minutes. Then reduce the heat to 150°C/300°F/gas 2 and bake for a further 10 minutes until risen and golden. Remove from the oven and leave to cool slightly in the tins, then unmould the babas.

Soak the babas in kirsch syrup
Dissolve the sugar in the water slowly then boil for 2 minutes and add the kirsch. Immerse the babas in the syrup, then drain on a wire rack.

Make the sabayon sauce
Whisk the egg yolks with the sugar in a bowl suitable for standing on a saucepan. Set it over simmering water and whisk hard until the sauce is fluffy and thick, then stir in the kirsch.

Presentation
Coat four dessert plates with sabayon sauce. Place a baba on each one and pile the centre high with raspberries, and garnish with fresh mint if you wish.

My wine suggestion: dry champagne.

Paul and Marc Haeberlin

AUBERGE DE L'ILL
Illhaeusern, 68150 Ribeauvillé telephone: 89 71 83 23

Tradition played its part in the establishment of one of the world's most celebrated restaurants, at Illhaeusern. For more than a century the Haeberlin family has owned a restaurant there; it was called *L'Arbre Vert* when the brothers Paul and Jean-Pierre were born. Paul, the elder of the two, wanted to cook from the age of four and was apprenticed to Edouard Weber, formerly chef to the Czar and half the crowned heads of Europe, at Ribeauvillé. In this small restaurant, where the cuisine was traditional yet creative, he was quietly able to develop his own style – projections of traditional Alsatian dishes, but taking them in directions that had not been previously explored.

After a spell at the Rôtisserie Périgourdine and the Poccardi in Paris to broaden his experience, he returned to Illhaeusern in 1950, to cook in the family restaurant. Michelin rosettes confirmed his success: one in 1952, a second five years on. His perfectionism and sense of style means the restaurant has held all three since 1967.

The war had not been kind to the Haeberlin brothers. They ended up (through no fault of their own) in opposing armies, and the family restaurant was also destroyed. Here the talents of Jean-Pierre came into play. The gabled restaurant was rebuilt under his architect's eye and his flair was also applied to the job of restaurant manager.

In 1976 the family team was joined by Paul's son Marc. In preparation he studied at Strasbourg and then with those French masters, Paul Bocuse and the Troisgros brothers, as well as a stint at the Erbprinz in Germany.

MENU

TERRINE DE FOIE GRAS TRUFFE
Terrine of foie gras with truffle

SELLE DE CHEVREUIL AUX CHAMPIGNONS SAUVAGES
Saddle of venison with wild mushrooms

PECHES HAEBERLIN
Peaches Haeberlin

TERRINE DE FOIE GRAS TRUFFE

Terrine of foie gras with truffle

Serves 8

1 foie gras of 800g/1¾lb
15g/½oz spiced salt
20ml/⅔fl oz cognac
20ml/⅔fl oz red port
1 truffle of 40g/1½oz, chopped
100g/3½oz goose fat
chopped jellied chicken stock (page 250) to garnish

Using a small paring knife, cut the liver in two horizontally. Scrape away the bile and remove any blood vessels. Season the two pieces of liver inside and out with the spiced salt. Place in a dish, pour on the cognac and port and leave to marinate for 24 hours.

Make and cook the terrine
Place the liver in a terrine into which it fits well, preferably one of earthenware or porcelain and press in well. Using your finger make an opening down the centre of the liver and insert the chopped truffle. Pull the foie gras together again and cover the terrine.

Cook in a bain-marie surrounded by boiling water, in an oven at 150°C/300°F/gas 2 for 40 minutes. Remove the terrine lid and cover the surface with melted goose fat. Chilled, this terrine will keep for two weeks.

Presentation
Use a spoon dipped in hot water to scoop out portions of foie gras. Accompany the terrine with chopped, jellied chicken stock and pass freshly-made toast.

My wine suggestion: Tokay-Pinot Gris 1983 from Jos Meyer of Wintzenheim; an expressive wine with a good bouquet, full of body and perfectly balanced.

SELLE DE CHEVREUIL AUX CHAMPIGNONS SAUVAGES

Saddle of venison with wild mushrooms

Serves 4

1 saddle of venison, 2kg/4½lb
150g/5oz butter
2 tablespoons tomato purée
1 bouquet garni
salt and freshly ground black pepper
60ml/2fl oz cognac
150ml/¼pt crème fraîche
1 tablespoon redcurrant jelly

For the marinade
75cl bottle red wine
1 onion, diced
1 small carrot, diced
1 parsley stalk
1 sprig of thyme
½ bay leaf
1 clove
1 pinch of rosemary
6 juniper berries, crushed

For the garnish
4 dessert apples, halved and cored
500ml/18fl oz white wine
100g/3½oz preserved bilberries or cranberries
250g/9oz chanterelles
30g/1oz butter

Marinate the venison
Bone out the venison and trim neatly. Soak the fillets in a marinade of red wine with the onion, carrot, parsley, thyme, bay leaf, clove, rosemary and juniper berries. Leave to marinate overnight.

Make game stock
Fry the off-cuts from the venison in a little butter, then add the diced onion and carrot from the marinade. Brown well and then pour in the marinade. Add the tomato purée and bouquet garni and simmer for 1 hour in an open pan, skimming off any scum from time to time. Strain the stock.

Cook the fillets and make the sauce
Cut the venison into 8 thick slices and season with salt and pepper. Fry in some of the butter until the meat is still slightly pink, 3 minutes on each side.

Stir the cognac into the juices in the pan and then add the game stock. Stir in the crème fraîche, then whisk in the remaining butter quickly. Add the redcurrant jelly and season to taste.

Presentation

Poach the apple halves in white wine for 10 minutes and heat the bilberries or cranberries. Sauté the chanterelles lightly in butter.
Arrange the venison on hot plates and cover with the sauce. Arrange an apple half on one side and top with the red berry preserve.
Arrange the chanterelles on the other side.

My wine suggestion: Wasserstriwela.

PECHES HAEBERLIN

Peaches Haeberlin

Serves 8

8 peaches
375g/13oz sugar
600ml/1pt water
1 vanilla pod
200ml/7fl oz whipping cream to decorate

For the pistachio ice cream

500ml/18fl oz milk
500ml/18fl oz double cream
1 vanilla pod
250g/9oz sugar
10 egg yolks
150g/5oz pistachios, freshly ground
2 drops bitter almond essence

For the champagne sabayon

8 egg yolks
150g/5oz sugar
½ bottle champagne

Poach the peaches

Make a vanilla syrup by dissolving 350g/12oz sugar in the water with the vanilla pod. Bring to the boil, then boil 1 minute. Cool then remove the pod. Lower the peaches into boiling water for 10 seconds then peel. Poach for 4 minutes in vanilla syrup, remove and cool.

Make the pistachio ice cream

Bring the milk and cream to the boil with the vanilla pod and half the sugar.
In a basin whisk the egg yolks with the remaining sugar, then pour on the boiling milk. Pour back into the pan and cook over very low heat, or on the top of a double boiler, over simmering water, stirring all the time until the mixture coats the back of a spoon.
Remove from the heat and add the freshly ground pistachios and a few drops of bitter almond essence; let it cool. When cold freeze in an ice cream maker, or in a freezer, beating several times before firm.

Make the champagne sabayon

In a saucepan whisk the egg yolks with the sugar until pale in colour. Add the bottle of champagne. Place on a double boiler over simmering water and whisk until the mixture thickens. Remove from the heat and whisk until cold.

Presentation

Place each peach in a shallow dish with two large balls of pistachio ice cream. Pour on the champagne sabayon. Whisk the cream with 30g/1oz sugar and decorate each one with a little cream chantilly.

My wine suggestion: Gewürztraminer Sélection des Grains Nobles 1983 Lorentz Bergheim wine, which has a Sauternes-like liqueury taste but typical Alsatian bouquet.

Jöel Robuchon

JAMIN

32 Rue de Longchamp, 75116 Paris telephone: 1 47 27 12 27

One of France's most highly respected chefs, Jöel Robuchon has a reputation far beyond her borders, and at home holds three Michelin rosettes and four toques from Gault Millau, one of only eleven restaurants in the world to do so. He first became interested in cooking while helping the Sisters at a small seminary in Poitiers, a town where his father was a stone-mason. He became an apprentice at the Relais de Poitiers in Chasseneuil du Poitou. While still an unknown provincial chef, he set out to make a name for himself by entering every competition possible. His success was outstanding: the Prosper Montagné prize in 1969, the Pierre Taittinger prize the following year. He was Meilleur Ouvrier de France in 1976 and is now the holder of nineteen medals. After working in a number of restaurants, including four years as chef at the Concorde Lafayette, he became director at the Hôtel Nikko. Here he was discovered by Gault Millau, who immediately awarded him two toques; Michelin followed later with two rosettes. In 1982 he set up on his own at Jamin.

'What follows nouvelle cuisine?' Robuchon's answer has been called la cuisine de grand'mere. The man who put an exquisite purée of potatoes back on to the fashionable menu believes the way forward is to return to the values of provincial cooking. But it should be educated and reformed by the lessons of the new wave – freshness of produce, attention to quality, perfect timing and a strictness about the matching of flavours. A simple message must triumph. From this common French heritage he has created a style that is supremely personal.

MENU

TARTE FRIANDE AUX TOMATES ET BASILIC
Tomato and basil tartlets

VEAU CUIT A L'ETOUFFEE AUX OIGNONS ET CHAMPIGNONS
Braised veal with onions and mushrooms

POIRE CARAMELISEE AU GLACE DE MIEL
Caramelised pears with honey ice cream

TARTE FRIANDE AUX TOMATES ET BASILIC

Tomato and basil tartlets

Serves 4

3kg/6½lb large tomatoes
3 green peppers with thick flesh
1 large onion
150g/5oz butter
100ml/3½fl oz olive oil
salt and freshly ground black pepper
4 garlic cloves, peeled
1 bouquet garni
2 tablespoons tomato purée
20g/²⁄₃oz caster sugar
4 sheets filo pastry
2 tablespoons fresh chopped basil
4 sprigs of green thyme, rubbed

Prepare the vegetables

Drop the tomatoes in turn into a pan of boiling water for 10 seconds. Transfer to iced water then peel and quarter them and remove the seeds.

Using a 2.5cm/1in cutter, cut the tomato flesh into rounds. Crush and reserve the remaining flesh.

Remove the stalks, seeds and pith from the peppers and slice lengthways into 3. Using the same cutter, cut rounds from the peppers. Blanch them in boiling water for 10 seconds, transfer to iced water then drain.

Make a tomato sauce

Finely chop the onion and place in a pan with 30g/1oz butter and 60ml/2fl oz olive oil over moderate heat. Salt lightly and stir continuously for 3-4 minutes, without allowing the onion to brown.

Add the garlic, bouquet garni, crushed leftover tomato and the tomato purée. Season with salt, pepper and sugar to taste. Cook, uncovered, over a moderate heat until all the liquid has evaporated, then remove the garlic cloves and the bouquet garni.

Make the filo tartlets

Cut 4 rounds of greaseproof paper about 13cm /5in diameter. Cut 20 rounds the same size from the filo pastry sheets. Place one filo round on a baking sheet, brush a thin film of softened butter over it and top with a second round. Continue until you have 5 layers, leaving the top unbuttered. Make 4 such piles and refrigerate the tray.

Melt the remaining butter and give a generous coating to the rounds of tomato and pepper. Arrange the tomato and pepper rounds (skin side up) on the 4 greaseproof paper circles, overlapping them to form a circle and alternating 2 pieces of tomato with 1 of pepper. Chill until the butter layer sticks the vegetables on to the paper.

Baking and presentation

Bake the filo 'tarts' in an oven heated to 200°C/400°F/gas 6 for 10 minutes until golden.

Gently reheat the tomato sauce, check the seasonings and add the chopped basil. Spread the pastry rounds with the tomato sauce, smoothing it evenly with the back of a spoon or spatula. Take the paper circles with the tomato and pepper rounds sticking firmly to them and turn them, face down, on top of the pastry. Bake (with the paper on top) for 8 minutes. When cooked, remove the paper. Season with salt and pepper, rubbed thyme and a sprinkling of olive oil. Serve on warm plates.

My wine suggetion: Châteauneuf du Pape Blanc 1985 Propriétaire Paul Avril – Clos des Papes; a full-bodied, rounded wine, suitably aromatic and well-matched.

Tarte friande aux tomates et basilic

Veau cuit à l'étouffée aux oignons et champignons

VEAU CUIT A L'ETOUFFEE AUX OIGNONS ET CHAMPIGNONS

Braised veal with onions and mushroooms

Serves 6

2.5kg/5½lb breast of veal
250g/9oz carrots
2 large onions
250g/9oz fat bacon, cut into matchstick strips
salt and freshly ground black pepper
2 calf's feet
60ml/2fl oz groundnut oil
300g/11oz butter
1 bouquet garni
500ml/18fl oz brown bone stock (page 178) or water

For the garnishing vegetables
40 tiny pickling onions
1 teaspoon sugar
salt and freshly ground black pepper
1 shallot, finely chopped
120g/4oz butter
400g/14oz chanterelles
1 tablespoon chopped flat-leaved parsley

Make all the preparations

Bone out the breast of veal, trim off the fat and neaten the shape, keeping the trimmings. Dice the carrots and onions coarsely into cubes about 1cm/½in. Season the bacon strips with salt and pepper then use a larding needle to prick the veal and insert them at regular intervals; this will keep the veal moist during cooking.

Bone the calf's feet (your butcher will do this, but ask for the bones). Blanch the feet in boiling water for 30 seconds, transfer to iced water then drain. Break up the bones and reserve with the veal bones and trimmings.

Braise the veal

Choose a casserole which fits the veal with a close-fitting lid and heat the oil with 15g/½oz butter in it. Add the bones and veal trimmings with the diced carrots and onions. Cook, stirring occasionally, until nicely browned. Remove from the pan and reserve.

Add 85g/3oz butter to the pan and the well-seasoned breast of veal. Brown gently on both sides, taking care the butter does not burn. When nicely brown, remove the veal and return the bone and vegetables mixture to the bottom of the pan, putting in the feet, bouquet garni and then the breast of veal.

Seal hermetically. Cook in an oven at 150°C/300°F/gas 2 for 5-6 hours, basting frequently with the cooking juices and resealing; cooking must be very slow. Once cooked, remove the breast of veal and calf's feet; keep warm.

Attend to the sauce

Finely chop the meat from the feet and return to the casserole. Add the brown bone stock, stirring to deglaze the pan and simmer very gently to reduce by half, to give a thick, golden, slightly syrupy sauce.

Cook the garnishing vegetables

Put the tiny onions in a saucepan with a teaspoon of sugar and a pinch of salt. Cover them with a round of greaseproof paper, pricked with small holes, and cook over high heat at first for 1 minute. Then stir and reduce the heat to very low. Cover the pan and cook for 20 minutes until the onions are golden and gleaming.

Fry the shallot in a small saucepan in 20g/⅔oz butter with a pinch of salt. Cook over very moderate heat without letting it brown then remove.

Heat the remaining butter in a frying pan; when it is nicely frothy, toss in the chanterelles. Cook over high heat for 2 minutes, stirring continuously, then season with salt and pepper. Add the shallot and cook for another 30 seconds, add the onions and stir well.

Add the finishing touches

Strain the veal gravy into a pan and add the chopped meat from the feet back to it. Bring to the boil.

Carve the veal breast into thin slices. Arrange the slices, slightly overlapping, on a serving dish. Pour on the hot gravy. Place some of the chanterelles and onions in the centre of the platter and the remainder round the edge. Sprinkle with chopped parsley.

My wine suggestion: Margaux Château Labégorce-Zédé 1982 – a cru bourgeois; an excellent Margaux but full-bodied and delicate, extremely smooth on the palate despite its youth.

POIRE CARAMELISEE AU GLACE DE MIEL

Caramelised pears with honey ice cream

Serves 4

2 large dessert pears
200g/7oz caster sugar
200ml/7fl oz water
1 lemon
½ vanilla pod
200g/7oz granulated sugar
8 mint leaves

For the honey ice cream
250g/9oz honey
4 egg yolks
250ml/9fl oz milk
150ml/¼pt single cream

For the chocolate sauce
100g/3½oz chocolate
100ml/3½fl oz water
20g/⅔oz butter, flaked

Cook the pears

Make a syrup by dissolving the sugar in the water, then boil for 1 minute. Peel the pears and core from the end opposite the stalk, using an apple corer. Coat generously with lemon juice. Split the ½ vanilla pod and add to the syrup with the pears. Cook over a low heat until done but still firm. Remove from the pan, cut in half, drain and leave till cold.

Make the honey ice cream

Measure the honey – warm it slightly if necessary and then let cool. Beat it with the yolks until the mixture is thick and pale. Bring the milk to the boil and pour on to the yolks, stirring. Pour back into the pan and thicken over a very low heat, stirring continuously. The custard is ready when a finger drawn across the back of the spatula leaves a clean mark. Cool then add the cream.

Freeze in an ice cream maker or in a freezer, beating it several times before it is firm.

Prepare the chocolate sauce

Grate the chocolate coarsely and add to the boiling water in a pan. Whisk until melted then bring back to the boil, stirring continuously.

Remove from the heat. At the last moment before serving, whisk in the flaked butter, to give the sauce a gloss.

Presentation

Slice the four half pears across thinly (to make them easier to eat) then reform them. Cover with granulated sugar and caramelise this by holding a red-hot iron (a salamander, see page 237) over them.

Pour chocolate sauce in the centre of 4 warmed plates to make a long oval shape. Lay a half pear in the middle and arrange the mint leaf in the natural place. Use a spoon to make 2 long scoops of honey ice cream for each person, letting them roll up. Place one roll on either side of each pear at the base.

My wine suggestion: Muscat de Beaumes de Venise 1985 Proprietor Castaud-Morin, Domaine des Bernadins. This wine is made from small Muscat grapes, naturally sweet and rich – drink it well chilled.

Poire caramelisée au glace de miel

The cheese board at Jamin

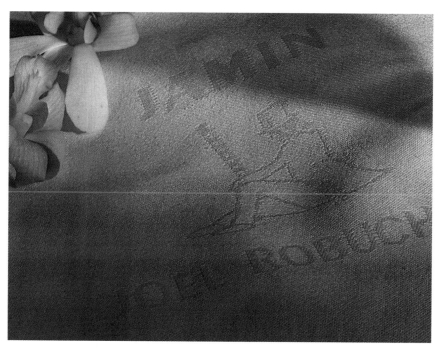

Napkins at Jamin

Georges Blanc

GEORGES BLANC
01540 Vonnas telephone: 74 50 00 10

To be born grandson of La Mère Blanc, one of France's best-known women chefs, celebrated by Curnonsky as 'the best cook in the world,' was a good start for Georges Blanc. But it was his own talent as a chef that has earned the family restaurant, now bearing his name, three Michelin rosettes and 19.5 out of 20 in the Gault Millau guide. Born in Bourg-en-Bresse, home of the world's most famous poultry, the restaurant was founded as an inn for marketing farmers. A tradition of local produce used to the best advantage and hearty, butter-based cooking made Elisa Blanc's inn famous to an ever-widening circle. This tradition was passed on to the wife of her eldest son and subsequently to Georges, who joined the family business in 1965 and took over in 1968. His choice of career was never in doubt and he went via the hotel school and military service (where he cooked for the Admiral on the Foch and Clémenceau) to work with his mother. The restaurant had become increasingly fashionable after the war and, as chef, Georges Blanc took it to new fame, becoming a Maître Cuisinier de France in 1975. His attachment to tradition is such that some of the famous old recipes are still served − three of them are given here − but he has succeeded in developing and adapting it with new ideas, acknowledged by the third Michelin rosette in 1981. He has also been the instigator of many drives to promote French cuisine abroad. His books include Mes Recettes (1981, 1982) and Ma Cuisine des Saisons (1984).

MENU

CUISSES DE GRENOUILLES SAUTÉES COMME EN DOMBES
Sautéed frogs' legs, the Dombes way

FRICASSÉE DE POULET DE BRESSE A LA CRÈME GRAND-MÈRE BLANC AVEC CRÊPES VONNASSIENNES
Grandma Blanc's fricassee of Bresse chicken in cream served with Vonnas pancakes

TARTE AU CHOCOLAT AMER
Bitter chocolate cake

CUISSES DE GRENOUILLES SAUTEES COMME EN DOMBES

Sautéed frogs' legs, the Dombes way

Serves 4

*800g/1¾lb fresh frogs' legs, preferably not too large
(about 7-10 legs per person)
flour for coating
400g/14oz butter
salt and freshly ground black pepper
2 tablespoons finely chopped parsley
1 garlic clove, finely chopped*

Wash the skinned frogs' legs, in plenty of cold water. Bend the legs at the knee to cross each other in pairs. At the last minute before cooking coat them lightly in flour – as you would if preparing fish for frying *à la meunière.*
Melt 85g/3oz butter per portion in one or two large, thin-bottomed frying pans over a very fierce heat. Add the frogs' legs immediately, filling the pans well. Season with salt and pepper. As soon as they begin to brown slightly, turn them over one by one, using a large carving fork. Turn down the heat and continue cooking until they are gently golden all over. Keep a close watch on them, as cooking frogs in butter is a delicate operation, and it is important not to let them dry out. Add a little extra butter if the butter in which they are cooking starts to brown.

Presentation

Arrange in a very hot enamel fish dish. Melt the remaining butter and pour over them, to give plenty of froth. Mix parsley and garlic and sprinkle on top. Serve immediately.

My wine suggestion: Mâcon Quintaine by Thévenet; one of the best Chardonnay wines from the exceptional Quintaine soil, it is dry and fruity with a lingering flavour.

FRICASSEE DE POULET DE BRESSE A LA CREME GRAND-MERE BLANC AVEC CREPES VONNASSIENNES

Grandma Blanc's fricassee of Bresse chicken in cream served with Vonnas pancakes

This plain, traditional recipe from Bresse is particularly straightforward. If the poultry is of really good quality – as they are in Bresse where the birds are *appellation contrôlée* – there is no need to use stock as a cooking liquid. The cut chicken and the juices obtained by browning successfully will impart their delicious flavour to the sauce.

Serves 4

*1 plump Bresse chicken, about 1.8kg/4lb
150g/5oz butter
salt and freshly ground black pepper
2-3 tablespoons flour
500ml/18fl oz double cream
3 egg yolks
½ lemon*

For an aromatic garnish
*1 whole onion, spiked with a garlic clove
1 garlic clove, peeled
1 small sprig of thyme
½ bay leaf*

Cut up the chicken

Draw and singe the chicken if your butcher has not done so. Cut it into pieces with the help of a heavy knife. First remove the legs, separating them into the drumsticks and thighs. Take off the two wings and remove the tips. Split the carcass in two lengthways and from it cut the breasts, which should then be halved. Chop up the carcass, neck and wing tips and reserve.

Make the fricassee

Put a generous amount of butter into a large frying pan over fierce heat. Add the chicken pieces, seasoning them well with salt and pepper. Let them brown slightly, before turning them and continue frying until they are golden all over. Add the aromatic garnish and the chicken trimmings to the pan. Add a little more butter and work the flour into it, allowing the flour to brown and cook for a while. Then stir in enough water to just cover the chicken pieces. Let this come to the boil, shaking the pan as the liquid starts thickening to combine them. Cover and reduce the heat, letting the chicken simmer for about 30 minutes, depending on the size of the pieces. At the end of cooking time use a carving fork to shift the chicken pieces into a frying pan, ready to complete the sauce.

Complete the sauce

Strain the cooking sauce over the chicken pieces and put the pan over gentle heat. Mix the cream and yolks and add, stirring them in gently. Warm through until thickened, but don't let the mixture come to the boil again after adding this cream liaison. If the consistency of the sauce needs correcting a little, add a little water or cream. Taste and adjust the seasonings and balance the flavour with a dash of lemon juice. Serve immediately in a large dish, either alone or with a garnish of Creole rice or Vonnas pancakes.

My wine suggestion: Morgon, Château de Bellevue from the Domaine Princesse Lieven; a grand cru beaujolais and a typical example of the appellation. 'Il morgonne,' as it is called, goes very well with this traditional regional dish.

CREPES VONNASSIENNES
Vonnas pancakes

The pancakes of the celebrated Mère Blanc are still served in the restaurant of her grandson. They can be eaten salted as an accompaniment to chicken or meat (as here) or served as a sweet course, sprinkled with brown sugar.

Serves 6

500g/1lb potatoes
400g/14oz butter
salt
3 tablespoons flour
3 whole eggs
4 egg whites
60ml/2fl oz milk
3 tablespoons double cream

Clarify the butter

Heat the cubed butter in a saucepan to drive off the water and to obtain a perfectly clear oil. Skim off the scum as it rises. When fully melted, pour off through a strainer lined with muslin to remove any butter dregs that have settled on the base of the pan. (These are excellent in strong cheese, but it is this casein that burns at high cooking temperatures.) You will have about 300g/11oz clarified butter. The melted butter can then be poured into earthenware pots ready for use or storing.

Make the pancake batter

Cook the peeled potatoes in salted water and then purée them, adding a little water if needed. Leave to cool in the bowl ready for making batter. Work in the flour with a wooden spatula, then add the whole eggs, one at a time, and then the egg whites, without whipping them in any way. Cream the mix together gradually and stir in the milk and cream without overworking the batter, until its consistency is that of relatively thick cream (it can be thinned after testing). The batter, or just the purée, can be made a day ahead.

Fry the pancakes

Take a large frying pan with a good flat bottom and put in the amount of melted butter that you would use for an omelette. Heat over fierce heat until very hot, and pour in about ¾ tablespoon batter at a time; it will form rounds almost as if in a deep-fat fryer. In a average-sized frying pan you will be able to cook 6-7 pancakes at a time – they cook very quickly. Flip them over with a palette knife with a flexible blade. Transfer to a serving dish and serve very hot.

TARTE AU CHOCOLAT AMER
Bitter chocolate cake

Serves 4
120g/4½oz cooking chocolate
100g/3½oz fine unsalted butter
60g/2oz flour
150g/5oz caster sugar
4 eggs

For the dark glaze
100g/3½oz dark dessert chocolate, or cooking chocolate
20g/⅔oz butter
85ml/3fl oz whipping cream, hot
cocoa powder (unsweetened)

Make the chocolate sponge
Gently melt the chocolate and butter together over simmering water. In a large bowl mix together the flour and sugar then the eggs with a wooden spatula. Beat in the chocolate and work them together for 10 minutes. The consistency should be beautifully smooth and thick, and leave a ribbon on top when the spatula is lifted. Pour into a greased *moule à manqué* tin (a cake tin with sloping sides, 3cm/1¼in deep) or a sponge tin of 20cm/8in diameter. Bake in an oven at 200°C/400°F/gas 6 for 30 minutes. Check that the cake is cooked by piercing with a needle or small knife – it should come out clean. Turn out on to a cake rack and leave until cold.

Prepare the glaze
Melt the chocolate and butter over simmering water. Add the boiling cream and stir vigorously to a smooth paste. Using a metal palette knife, coat the top and sides of the cold cake with chocolate cream. Allow to set slightly then mark out portions on the surface of the cake using the back of a long knife. Sprinkle with cocoa powder. The cake may also be served more simply, without the chocolate glaze, just sprinkled with icing sugar.

My wine suggestion: Madeira 1971.

Pierre Gagnaire

PIERRE GAGNAIRE
3 Rue Georges-Teissier, 62000 St-Etienne telephone: 77 37 57 93

During the St-Etienne's book fair in 1987, eleven chefs with thirty Michelin rosettes between them gathered in Paul Gagnaire's restaurant. It was a proud moment for the host, who was cooking for those European Masterchefs who were also authors.

Pierre Gagnaire was born in a Loire village into a family of restaurateurs – his grandmother managed one in the country on her own for years. His parents moved to St Priest-en-Jarez and, as he was the eldest son, it was obvious he should join the business. He went to work, but with no special enthusiasm, until he was apprenticed in Lyons to Jean Vignard, who was one of Alain Chapel's teachers. 'Going to Alain Chapel's I had my first big cooking thrill. Suddenly I realised that was what I wanted to do – how I felt about it.'

After working briefly at the Mère Lyonnaise and Tante Alice in Charbonnière, with a longer stay at the Casino, he did his military service in the navy (as a cook aboard a flagship). Paris at the Intercontinental and the Lucas Carton followed, then Maxim's at Orly, before becoming chef in 1975 of La Bastide of Tourtour, a famous inn on the Côte d'Azur. In 1976 he took over the family business and then moved it to St Etienne in 1981, when he was thirty. The restaurant is in a small street in the centre of the town and decorated by his wife Gabrielle; it is modern and bright with flowers and contemporary paintings that 'go well with my cooking'. Michelin rosettes, one in 1983, the second in 1986, mark out the quality of his talent.

MENU

ASSIETTE D'HUITRES ET SAUMON FRAIS A LA BETTERAVE ROUGE
Deep dish of oysters, fresh salmon and red beetroot

SUPREME DE PINTADE AUX HUIT EPICES, SALADE DE FRUIT SECS
Guinea fowl breasts in eight spices with dried fruit salad

SOUPE SOUFFLEE AU CHOCOLAT NOIR, GANACHE TIEDE
Dark chocolate soufflé with a warm chocolate cream

ASSIETTE D'HUITRES ET SAUMON FRAIS A LA BETTERAVE ROUGE

Deep dish of oysters, fresh salmon and red beetroot

Serves 4

24 oysters, size 0
120g/4oz fresh salmon
salt and freshly ground black pepper
120g/4oz cooked beetroot, diced
1 chicory head
2-3 tablespoons olive oil
100g/3½oz butter
3 shallots, finely chopped
5 tablespoons dry white wine
½ teaspoon chopped chives
juice of 1 lemon

Open the oysters, carefully saving their juices, and remove from the shells. Cut the salmon into domino-sized pieces and season lightly. Put them in 4 deep-bowled plates and dot with the diced beetroot.

Pull all the leaves from the chicory, pile in wads one on top of the other, then cut across to make matchstick strips. Season these lightly with olive oil, salt and pepper.

Make the dressing

Melt 15g/½oz butter in a small, heavy-bottomed pan. Add the chopped shallots and cook for a little while until beginning to soften. Add the reserved oyster liquid and white wine. Bring to the boil. Whisk in the remaining butter, a few pieces at a time. Add the chives and lemon juice and boil for 40 seconds, then remove from the heat. Pour into a cold jug.

Presentation

Pour the sauce – it should be warm, not hot or cold – on to 4 plates and scatter with the strips of chicory. Serve with the deep dishes of seafood and eat together.

My wine suggestion: a Condrieu, a local wine from the northern Rhône.

SUPREME DE PINTADE AUX HUIT EPICES, SALADE DE FRUITS SECS

Guinea fowl breasts in eight spices with dried fruit salad

Serves 4

2 guinea fowl, each 800g/1¾lb
salt and freshly ground black pepper
1 tablespoon groundnut oil
15g/½oz butter
100ml/3½fl oz double cream

For the marinade

1 pinch of cinnamon
2 pinches of curry powder
1 pinch of cumin
2 pinches of paprika
10 coriander seeds, crushed
4 cardamom seeds, out of the pod
2 cloves
120ml/4fl oz yoghurt

For the stock

1 tablespoon groundnut oil
3 shallots, grated
1 small onion, finely chopped
1 carrot, chopped
a sprig of thyme
¼ chicken stock cube
20ml/⅔fl oz red port

For the fruit salad

15g/½oz green walnuts
20g/⅔oz dried apricots, cut into strips
20g/⅔oz dried figs, cut into strips
15g/½oz almonds, toasted
15g/½oz cashew nuts, toasted and crushed
85ml/3fl oz yoghurt
2 tablespoons whipped cream
juice of 1 lemon

Macerate the breasts in spices

Ask the butcher to cut the breasts from the two birds and to bone out the thighs.

Crush all the spices to powder, add the yoghurt, salt and pepper and daub the guinea fowl breasts with the mixture. Leave in a cool place overnight.

Make the stock

Bruise the carcass and the drumsticks and sauté them in a thick frying pan in the groundnut oil. When the bones are well browned, add the shallots, onion, carrot, thyme sprig and chicken cube. Pour in the port and enough water to cover. Simmer gently for 50 minutes then strain.

Cook the guinea fowl breasts

Mix all the fruits and nuts with the yoghurt, the whipped cream and the lemon juice. Keep cool.
Fry the guinea fowl breasts in the oil and butter rapidly to colour, then add just sufficient stock to cover them and the cream. Cook for a further 10 minutes. If there is too much liquid, remove the breasts and boil to reduce to a good flavour. Taste and correct the seasonings.
At the same time the flesh of the thighs can be grilled and later served with the cheese.

Presentation

Serve the breasts with the fruit salad on the side. Coat the breasts with a little cream sauce and pass the rest in a sauce boat.

My wine suggestion: St-Joseph Luis Cheze; light ruby in colour and smelling of blackcurrants, it is less tannic, less pronounced than the Hermitage wines.

Chef's note: The guinea fowl thighs can be used to make an amusing little salad with two attractive cheeses. Boil a potato (not too big) in salted water, peel it and cut into 4 neat slices (discarding the ends). Cut 4 cleaned Paris mushrooms into little cubes. Put these into a bowl with the cut cress from 1 box. Dress with 3 tablespoons of hazelnut oil with truffle juice from the smallest size can and season very lightly. Arrange on 4 plates. Cut a thin slice of *Fourme de Montbrison* into fingers and then crumble it round the salads.
In a very hot pan sauté 2 *Rigottes de Condrieu* in a little olive oil. Slice them in 2 and arrange on the salad, cut side down. Grill the guinea fowl thighs well and arrange on top of the salads. Serve with slices of milk loaf.

SOUPE SOUFFLEE AU CHOCOLAT NOIR, GANACHE TIEDE

Dark chocolate soufflé with a warm chocolate cream

Serves 4

85g/3oz bitter chocolate, melted
8 eggs, separated
4 tablespoons granulated sugar
2 tablespoons cognac
melted butter and sugar for the bowls

For the sauce
60g/2oz bitter chocolate
85ml/3fl oz whipping cream, hot

Make the chocolate soufflé

Prepare 4 dessert bowls by painting them with melted butter, sugaring them and tipping out the excess.
Melt the chocolate over hot water. Warm a mixing bowl thoroughly then in it whisk the egg yolks, sugar and cognac. Stir in the melted chocolate.
Whisk the egg whites to soft peaks then whisk in the chocolate mixture – no great care is necessary.
Fill the bowls and cook in the oven at 220°C/425°F/gas 7 for 6-7 minutes, when the middle should be soft, almost runny.

Make the ganache sauce

Melt the chocolate and stir into the boiling cream. Keep hot until the soufflé is ready.

Presentation

Powder the surface in each bowl with icing sugar. Pour a spoonful of the sauce into the centre of each soufflé and serve at once. The soufflé could also be served with fresh strawberries, lightly creamed together.

My wine suggestion: Gewürztraminer Grains Nobles, Clos des Capucins from the Domaine Weinbach de Madame Faller – *'c'est absolument extraordinaire!'*

Antoine Westermann

BUEREHIESEL
4 Parc de l'Orangerie, 67000 Strasbourg telephone: 88 61 62 24

The Buffet de la Gare restaurant in Strasbourg was where the fourteen-year-old Antoine Westermann started cooking. Born in Wissembourg, right on the French-German border, he had wanted to be a cook since he was a child, although there were no chefs in the family, only good cooks and an aunt who was a priest's housekeeper. Meanwhile he studied at the local hotel school and after a year, had his first opportunity to perform as a chef. He then spent two years building up his knowledge in several restaurants, including Feyel of Strasbourg, a specialist in foie gras. His military service passed pleasantly as a cook for the Military Governor General of Strasbourg, in one of France's greatest gourmand cities, and he gained further experience in Germany and Paris, at the same time mastering the three languages (English is the third) he now speaks.

In 1970, with his wife Viviane, he bought the Buerehiesel – 'the peasant's cottage' – a typically Alsatian house, timber-framed and gabled with magnificently carved beams and situated in the very pretty garden of the Orangerie park. Here his talent was rewarded in 1975 by his first Michelin rosette; the second came nine years later.

Like many of the new generation of cooks with impeccable classical training, he now prefers to be more inventive and imaginative. But he looks to the traditional recipes of Alsace to inspire him and is determined to maintain the Buerehiesel as a gastronomic high point.

MENU

TERRINE DE CHEVREUIL AU FOIE GRAS DE CANARD, AU CELERI ET AU JUS DE TRUFFES
Terrine of venison with duck foie gras, celery and truffle juice

LE BAEKEOFFE D'AGNEAU AUX LEGUMES CONFITS
Alsatian lamb stew with steeped vegetables

PETITES CREPES CROUSTILLANTES AUX COINGS, GLACE A LA VANILLE
Crispy pancakes with quince and vanilla ice cream

TERRINE DE CHEVREUIL AU FOIE GRAS DE CANARD, AU CELERI ET AU JUS DE TRUFFES

Terrine of venison with duck foie gras, celery and truffle juice

Serves 6

250g/9oz raw duck foie gras
salt and freshly ground black pepper
250g/9oz venison fillet, cut in strips 1cm/½in thick
1 small dense head of celery (400g/14oz)
200ml/7fl oz Pinot Noir d'Alsace
about 1 tablespoon groundnut oil
½ lemon
a few sprigs of chervil
2 tablespoons truffle juice
wholemeal toast to serve

For the game stock
200g/7oz venison bones
½ calf's foot, cut up
60g/2oz carrots, chopped
60g/2oz onions
½ bay leaf
1 sprig thyme
2 juniper berries, crushed
2 tablespoons groundnut oil
200ml/7fl oz Pinot Noir d'Alsace
500ml/18fl oz water

Salt then cook the foie gras

Slit open the foie gras to remove the veins and season with salt and pepper. Leave it in a cool place for 12 hours then blot with absorbent paper. Cook the foie gras in a small pan into which it fits neatly, standing in a bain-marie of boiling water, in the oven at 60°C/140°F/gas low, for 30 minutes.
Allow to cool, press it lightly and chill.

Prepare the venison and make stock

Next day, season the venison then fry the strips for 20 seconds each side in a little fat skimmed from the duck foie gras after cooking. Drain them on absorbent paper and leave to cool.
Fry the venison bones, calf's foot, vegetables and herbs in groundnut oil until well coloured. Moisten with the Pinot Noir and water, season and cook slowly for 3 hours, skimming occasionally. The liquid should remain clear and reduce by half the original quantity.
Season then strain through a muslin-lined sieve and chill until jellied then remove any surface fat.

Assemble the terrine

Use a mandolin to cut 20 paper-thin slices from the celery heart. Put the Pinot Noir in a pan, season and blanch the celery for 30 seconds. Dry the slices immediately on absorbent paper.
Cut the foie gras into strips the same size as the venison. Line an 850ml/1½pt terrine with a large enough piece of greaseproof paper to hang about 2cm/¾in over the sides. Arrange some celery slices across the bottom and round the sides, reserving the rest.
Arrange the venison and foie gras strips alternately so they will cut to chequerboard squares. Melt the jelly and pour in 2 tablespoons after each layer.
Fold the paper inwards and press with a board. Pour the remaining stock into a shallow dish. Chill for at least 12 hours. Turn it out on to greaseproof paper and chop it into small dice with a long knife.

Presentation

At the last moment, cut the reserved celery into matchsticks and season with salt, pepper, a drop of lemon juice and oil. Chop the jelly with a long knife. Turn out the terrine carefully, using the paper.
Using a fine-bladed knife dipped in hot water, cut 2 thin slices of terrine for each person and lay them in the middle of the plate. Round them alternate chopped jelly dice, celery strips and sprigs of chervil. Sprinkle truffle juice and a few drops of oil over the terrine slices. Serve at once with wholemeal toast.

My wine suggestion: Riesling Moenchberg grand cru 1983 Andlau, a fine distinctive wine with a fruity bouquet and a taste of lime and iris.

LE BAEKEOFFE D'AGNEAU AUX LEGUMES CONFITS

Alsatian lamb stew with steeped vegetables

A classic Alsatian dish of layered meats and vegetables marinated in wine.

Serves 6

*2kg/4½lb shoulder of lamb, boned out
400g/14oz carrots
400g/14oz small turnips
1kg/2lb small potatoes, preferably Rosenwald
500g/1lb leeks
24 garlic cloves
24 shallots
salt and freshly ground black pepper
20g/⅔oz coriander seeds, crushed
1 pig's trotter, in 6 pieces
70cl bottle Riesling
2 sprigs of thyme
2 cloves
1 bay leaf
60g/2oz parsley, bruised
green salad to serve*

Steep the casserole in wine ahead
Cut the lamb into 4cm/1½in chunks and season. Skin the carrots and turnips and cut them into large sticks 3 x 1cm/1¼ x ½in. Peel the potatoes and cut them through lengthways. Cut the leek white into 3cm/1¼in pieces. Skin the garlic cloves and shallots. Season all the vegetables and sprinkle them with coriander.
Take a terracotta terrine and lay in the pieces of pig's trotter, then alternate layers of meat and vegetables. Cover with Riesling and add all the thyme, cloves, bay leaf and parsley. Cover the terrine with foil and replace the lid. Leave to marinate for 12 hours.

Cook and serve the casserole
Cook the casserole in the oven at 200°C/400°F/gas 6 for about 4 hours. The white wine should be reduced by half. Present the casserole in its terrine, accompanied by a green salad.

My wine suggestion: Tokay Pinot Gris, Saint Landelin 1985 Rouffach, a full-flavoured and fine wine with a beautiful golden colour and aromas of peach and candied fruit.

PETITES CREPES CROUSTILLANTES AUX COINGS, GLACE A LA VANILLE

Crispy pancakes with quince and vanilla ice cream

Serves 6

*1.5kg/3½lb quinces
60g/2oz butter
85g/3oz sugar
1 lemon
vanilla ice cream (page 201)*

For the pancakes
*150g/5oz flour
3 eggs
500ml/18fl oz milk
60g/2oz sugar
60g/2oz butter
60g/2oz icing sugar*

Make and dry the tiny pancakes
Put the flour into a bowl and beat in the eggs, stirring in the milk and sugar to make a smooth batter. Heat the butter until lightly browned and work in. Stand for an hour, then strain.
Make some very thin pancakes. Use a 4cm/1½in biscuit cutter to cut 36 discs from them. Spread these out on a baking sheet and dry them in an oven at 70°C/160°F/gas low for 2 hours.

Prepare the quinces
Peel the fruit and dice three-quarters of them. Cook in a small covered pan with the butter, 60g/2oz sugar and the juice of ½ lemon, shaking the pan occasionally, until done.
Chop and stew the remaining fruit with the remaining sugar and juice, purée and reserve.

Cook the pancakes and serve
Sprinkle the small pancakes with icing sugar and glaze them under the grill on both sides, turning and resugaring them. Put 3 on each plate, with a spoonful of warm quince purée in the middle. Top with another pancake each. Pour warmed stewed quince round them and centre a scoop of vanilla ice cream.

My wine suggestion: Gewürztraminer late vintage 1983 Husseren Les Châteaux; a full-bodied mature wine, very fruity, with aromas of cinnamon, clove and pepper.

Italy

No two Italians cook alike – and all of them are competing with their mothers!

In a country with few common national culinary traditions,

every chef seeks inspiration in the dishes of his own locality.

Pierantonio Ambrosi

VECCHIA LUGANA

Via Vecchia Lugana, 25019 Colombare di Sirmione telephone: 30 919012

In a quiet corner on the shores of Lake Garda, Pierantonio Ambrosi's parents own a hostelry with a 1300-year-old history. Sheltered by three centuries-old trees, it has been in the family, with all fishing rights, for nearly eighty years. Perhaps because children of restaurateurs see the chores of the life without understanding the pleasures, Pierantonio chose to become a lawyer. But in the late 1960s he took a wine course, purely out of interest, which entirely changed his view. He found himself 'reading fewer and fewer books on criminal and Roman law and more and more by Escoffier, Carnacina and Vergese'. He returned to run the family restaurant. An expert sommelier, he plans all the menus with his chef, Carmine Gazineo. These are seasonal menus, based on the highest quality ingredients, with daily dishes chosen to suit what he finds in the market.

The Vecchia Lugana has always been a traditional stopping place on the road from north to south, and so a good place to observe the changing traditions of the Italian kitchen. Pierantonio Ambrosi's main interest has been to protect and foster typical Italian cooking, 'dishes that are rooted in tradition, but not simply reproduced in exactly the same way they were all those years ago'. He wants to 'bring them up to date and change them so they are new and fresh, creating a mixture of tradition and modernity'. He is a founder-member of the Linea in Cucina, *based at the magazine* Cucina Italia, *which collects and preserves regional recipes, and of a group meeting to improve Italian cooking:* Le Soste. *He is also a member of the* Club della mela d'oro, *safeguarding Italian cookery abroad.*

MENU

TERRINA DI PESCE GARDESANO ALLE VERDURE PRIMAVERILI
Terrine of Lake Garda fish with spring vegetables

PETTO DI ANITRA SELVATICA CON SALSA AGLI AGRUMI
Mallard breasts with citrus sauce

TORTA DI FRAGOLINE
Wild strawberry tart

TERRINA DI PESCE GARDESANO ALLE VERDURE PRIMAVERILI

Terrine of Lake Garda fish with spring vegetables

Serves 6

150g/5oz tench
150g/5oz trout
150g/5oz freshwater whitefish (see note)
150g/5oz sardines
60g/2oz carrots
60g/2oz courgettes
60g/2oz spinach
60g/2oz potatoes
salt and freshly ground black pepper
fresh bay leaves to garnish
toast and butter to serve

For the fish fumet
the heads and bones of the fish, without the skin
60g/2oz onion, sliced
1 carrot, sliced
1 celery stalk, sliced
20g/²/₃oz parsley
2 sprigs of thyme
1L/1¾pt water
salt

For the herb mayonnaise
100ml/3½fl oz mayonnaise
1 tablespoon cognac
2 tablespoons double cream
1 sprig of rosemary
1 sage leaf
1 chive
1 sprig of parsley
1 sprig of fennel
2 tablespoons Tanit or Moscato di Pantelleria
(or another sweet muscat wine)

Make the fish fumet

Clean and bone all the fish. Put the bones (but no skin) in a large stockpot with the sliced vegetables, herbs and water. Salt only lightly and simmer for 1 hour, uncovered, then strain. Taste and adjust the salt. The stock will be well reduced and jellied.

Make the fish terrine

Peel and slice the vegetables lengthways. Blanch in salted boiling water, drain then refresh under cold running water. Drain again and pat dry.

Cover the base of a terrine 30 x 11cm/12 x 4¼in and 6cm/2¼in deep with foil. Put a thin layer of tench over the bottom and up the sides, saving enough tench to cover the top. Continue putting in layers of fish, then vegetables, seasoning very lightly between the layers and moistening each one with 2 tablespoons of fish fumet. Cover with foil and cook in a bain marie, with boiling water half way up the sides, in an oven at 180°C/350°F/gas 4 for about 1 hour.

Put a board on top of the foil that fits inside the terrine rim and weight it down to force out spare liquid. Leave to cool then chill for 24 hours.

Presentation

Finely chop all the herbs and mix together all the mayonnaise ingredients. Turn the terrine out on to a platter, using the foil, and cut into slices. Arrange these on plates, garnishing them with fresh bay leaves and serve with herb mayonnaise. Pass toast and butter with the dish.

My wine suggestion: Lugana D.O.C., a fresh, dry and gentle wine from the Trebbiano grape, best drunk in the year it is made.

Editor's note: The fish used here is *coregone*, or a *laveret* in French. The English is houting – not easily found. The nearest related British whitefish are vendace, pollan and powan.

Terrina di pesce gardesano alle verdure primaverili

PETTO DI ANITRA SELVATICA CON SALSA AGLI AGRUMI

Mallard breasts with citrus sauce

Duck shooting over the lakes is an Italian passion. The *cacciatori* wait for migrating birds, flying south across Italy in November and December. They are less good on the spring return, after their long northward flight.

Serves 4

*the breasts of 2 mallards
orange and grapefruit slices to garnish
glazed brussels sprouts to serve*

For the citrus sauce
*1 tablespoon sugar
60ml/2fl oz orange juice
60ml/2fl oz grapefruit juice
85g/3oz butter
salt and freshly ground pepper*

For the duck stock
*duck carcasses
2 carrots, chopped
2 onions, chopped
2 garlic cloves, chopped
2 tablespoons sunflower oil
fresh bouquet garni, made from 20g/²/₃oz parsley,
2 sprigs of thyme, 1 bay leaf and ½ celery stalk
750ml/1¼pt meat stock (see right)
60ml/2fl oz red wine*

Start by making the duck stock
Brown the chopped vegetables in the oil in a large saucepan with the broken duck carcasses (reserving the legs for another dish). Add the fresh bouquet garni, meat stock and wine. Cover and leave to simmer for at least 2 hours, skimming off the fat from time to time. Check occasionally that the liquid covers the carcasses and add more meat stock if necessary. Strain through a sieve. Let the stock stand then again skim off all fat.

Make the garnish and start the sauce
Peel the zest thinly from the orange and slice into julienne strips. Blanch in boiling water for 2 minutes, then refresh in cold water. Squeeze the fruit for their juice.

Put the sugar in a small pan and heat until it caramelises. Add the duck stock – be careful initially, it will boil up – and the citrus juices. Boil until reduced to 200ml/7fl oz.

Cook the breasts and finish the sauce
Meanwhile season the duck breasts and roast them on a greased tray in an oven at 180°C /350°F/gas 4 for 10 minutes.

With the heat very low, whisk the butter, a few dice at a time, into the citrus fruit sauce, adding more butter just before the last lot melts, so the texture is creamy. Season to taste.

Presentation
Slice each breast into 3 or 4 and arrange, overlapping, on warm plates. Arrange the citrus julienne on top and pour on the sauce. Quarter the orange and grapefruit slices and arrange a trio on the side of the plate. Glaze the brussel sprouts and add to the plate.

My wine suggestion: Foianeghe rosso from the Trento; ruby red with orange tints, this is a wine of breeding including both cabernet grapes.

BRODO DI CARNE

Meat stock

*5 veal bones
1 carrot
1 celery stalk
½ onion
1 sprig of parsley
5L/8pt water
2 egg whites
500g/18oz minced beef
salt*

Wash the veal bones under running water. Slice the vegetables and put them with the bones in a stockpot and add the water. Work the egg whites into the minced beef to make a paste and add this to the liquid with the salt. Bring to simmering then turn down the heat and leave to simmer slowly for 2 hours, skimming from time to time. Strain the liquid and taste and adjust the salt.

TORTA DI FRAGOLINE
Wild strawberry tart

In season we make this tart with local wild strawberries. It is, of course, delicious with cultivated ones too – you can glaze these (see note), but it is not absolutely necessary.

Serves 6-8
600g/1¼lb wild or alpine strawberries
200g/7oz caster sugar
75ml/2½fl oz dark rum
1-2 tablespoons dried breadcrumbs
cream or kiwi fruit purée to serve

For the sweet shortcrust
300g/11oz flour
150g/5oz caster sugar
pinch of salt
grated zest of 1 lemon
150g/5oz unsalted butter, at room temperature
3 egg yolks

For the Marsala custard
500ml/18fl oz milk
1 vanilla pod, split lengthways
150g/5oz caster sugar
3 egg yolks
60g/2oz flour
60ml/2fl oz dry Marsala
200ml/7fl oz double cream

Start by making the pastry
Put the flour, caster sugar, a pinch of salt and the grated lemon zest on to a pastry board and mix them together. Make a well in the centre, dice the butter and put it in the well with 3 egg yolks. Pull the dry ingredients into the yolks with your fingers, working to break up the butter, until you have a smooth dough. Make a ball, wrap in oiled paper and chill for around 2 hours.

Macerate the strawberries
Mix the sugar and rum and pour over the strawberries in a bowl. Stand in a cool place for 10 minutes.

Make the Marsala custard
Bring the milk to the boil with the vanilla pod and sugar. Put the egg yolks and flour into a bowl and use a wooden spoon to mix them well. A little at a time, work in the Marsala, taking care that the mixture doesn't go lumpy. Then, still stirring, strain in the boiling milk. Return the mixture to the pan and put over very gentle heat, stirring continuously until the mixture comes to the boil. Pour into a bowl; leave to cool.

Make the tart case
Butter a flan tin about 28cm/11in diameter, sprinkle with a few breadcrumbs and shake out the excess. Roll out the pastry sufficiently larger than the tin. Move it, rolled round the pin, and line the base and sides of the tin. Turn down the edges so they are the same height all round then pinch the edge.
Prick the base all over with a fork, cover with a piece of oiled paper, put dried beans on top and bake in an oven at 190°C/375°F/gas 5 for about 40 minutes.
At the end of cooking time, remove the beans and paper. Cool then remove the pastry case from the tin and put on a serving dish.

Assemble the tart
Whip the cream and fold it into the cold marsala custard. Pour this into the tart and smooth the top. Drain the strawberries well and arrange on top of the tart.

My wine suggestion: Vin de la Fabreseria de San Rocco – sweet, soft and warm.

Editor's note: To glaze the strawberry tart, purée 175g/6oz strawberries in a blender, then rub through a sieve into a small pan. Mix 1½ teaspoons cornflour to a paste with 2 tablespoons water and add to the pan with 3 tablespoons sugar. Stir over gentle heat until thickened, then stir in 1 teaspoon lemon juice. Brush over the berries.

The dessert table at Vecchia Lugana

Petto di anitra selvatica con salsa agli agrumi

Torta di fragoline

Andrea da Merano

VILLA MOZART

Via San Marco 26, 39012 Merano telephone: 473 30630

'Become a chef, you will see the world — and you will always be able to eat', said his mother. This advice made a lasting impression on the young Andrea Hellrigl, born during the period of uncertainty and poverty after the war, in Alto Adige, near the Swiss-Austrian border. Preliminary training in Switzerland then an apprenticeship followed, in Münich at the Vier Jahreszeiten, presided over by the legendary Alfred Walterspiel.

He returned to Italy to work at the Quirinal Hotel in Rome and the Grand in Venice and then arrived in Merano, the resort in the north of Italy whose name he was to adopt. He cooked in the principal hotels and opened his first restaurant, the Andrea, there. For twelve years he ran the Kursaal, organizing memorable banquets like the wedding of the world ski champion Gustav Thoeni and a national convention of the Cordon Bleu de France.

The Villa Mozart, a hotel with mighty cedars of Lebanon in the grounds and a view of the Alto Adige mountains, was established in 1979. It is furnished and decorated — everything from seats to clocks and cutlery — in the elegant form of art nouveau made famous by the Viennese Secessionists School. The restaurant was awarded a Michelin rosette in 1985. When the thirteen leaders of the Common Market met in June 1985, Andrea da Merano was chosen as chef. They agreed rather more readily about his food than they did about policy. He was chef again for the Economic Summit in Venice in 1987. In 1986 he became co-owner of the Palio, at the Equitable Center in New York. An early Italian award for regional cooking was followed by the title of the Chef of Europe in 1985; three years later he was Chef of the Year in America, for his promotion of Italian food.

MENU

SCAMPI CON PORRI CROCCANTI
Dublin Bay prawns with crispy leeks

ANITRA IN PORCHETTA
Duck in the style of a sucking pig

TORTA CAPRESE
Chocolate almond cake from Capri

SCAMPI CON PORRI CROCCANTI

Dublin Bay prawns with crispy leeks

Scampi are served as a starter in this menu, but the dish also makes an attractive main course.

Serves 4

24 Dublin Bay prawn tails, 30g/1oz each
unshelled
250ml/9fl oz white wine
2 tablespoons lemon juice
2 tablespoons cognac or brandy
6 saffron strands
2 garlic cloves, finely chopped
175ml/6fl oz extra virgin oil
salt and freshly ground black pepper
2 tablespoons chopped parsley

For the vegetable garnish
8 leeks, white only
olive oil for deep frying

Put the white wine, lemon juice, cognac or brandy, saffron strands and garlic in a saucepan and boil until reduced to 75ml/2½fl oz. Peel the scampi tails, removing the black gut down the back.

Pour the reduced wine into a shallow pan and add the olive oil. When hot and bubbling add the scampi tails. Place the pan under a hot grill for 4 minutes until bubbling.

Meanwhile wash the leeks, pat dry and cut the white part into julienne strips 2.5cm/1in long. Deep fry quickly in hot oil until golden brown and crisp, then drain on absorbent paper and salt lightly.

Use a slotted spoon to transfer the scampi to 4 warmed plates. Simmer the sauce for a couple more minutes, season and add the parsley. Pour over the scampi. Spoon crisp leeks on to the side of each plate.

My wine suggestion: Pigato di Albenga, a lively white wine – buy the most recent vintage.

Chef's note: The scampi can be heated in 150ml/¼pt olive oil for 4 minutes and then drained and served in the sauce, made with 60ml/2fl oz oil only.

ANITRA IN PORCHETTA

Duck in the style of a sucking pig

Serves 4

2.5kg/5½lb duckling, liver reserved
85g/3oz pork sausagemeat
30g/1oz prosciutto
pinch of freshly grated nutmeg
pinch of ground coriander
1 clove, ground
1 garlic clove, finely chopped
250ml/9fl oz red wine
250ml/9fl oz meat stock (page 68)
60g/2oz fresh foie gras
30g/1oz butter
30g/1oz small dice of 1-day old bread
1 egg yolk
120ml/4fl oz milk
salt and freshly ground black pepper

For cooking the duck
2 tablespoons olive oil
mirepoix consisting of 60g/2oz each diced onion, carrots
and celery
2 bay leaves
1 garlic clove, bruised
pinch each of rosemary, thyme and sage, finely chopped
200ml/7fl oz white wine

For the sauce
500ml/18fl oz red wine
500ml/18fl oz meat stock (page 68)

Bone out the duck and make forcemeat
Your butcher will do this for you, starting by cutting down the backbone. Leave all the skin intact, but remove the leg meat from the bird. Save all the bones. Leave the breast meat in place attached to the skin, but slice into it then bat it flat so that it is equally distributed.

Mince the leg meat with the liver, sausagemeat and prosciutto. Add the spices and chopped garlic. Boil the red wine and meat stock together until reduced to 120ml/4fl oz and work in.

Cut the foie gras into small pieces and sauté them quickly in a dry hot pan. In a frying pan melt the butter and toss the bread cubes until crisp. Stir the foie gras, croûtons, yolk and milk into the forcemeat and season well.

Stuff and cook the duck

Place the forcemeat on top of the duck, patting it into a log shape. Roll up the duck round it, slightly overlapping the skin on the backbone side, folding skin round the ends and trimming off spare neck skin. Tie all down its length and round the ends with string. Season the outside.

Heat the olive oil in a roasting tin. Place the duck roll in the tin with the bones, mirepoix, bay leaves, garlic, rosemary, sage and thyme round it. Add the white wine and put in the oven heated to maximum for 15 minutes. Reduce the heat to 180°C/350°F/gas 4 and roast for a further 15 minutes. Remove the duck from the tin and let it rest on a platter for 10 minutes.

Make the sauce and serve the duck hot

Skim off all fat from the roasting tin. Pour the red wine over the bones and mirepoix and boil to reduce by a third. Add the meat stock and reduce again to 500ml/18fl oz then strain. Check the consistency, boiling to reduce a little more, if necessary, now the vegetables are removed. Pour the sauce into a blender and add enough duck fat to give it a rich unctuousness.

Serve the duck hot, sliced across, accompanied by the hot duck gravy.

My wine suggestion: Taurasi, with its deep ruby red, authoritarian and very personalised flavour, complements game well.

TORTA CAPRESE

Chocolate almond cake from Capri

Makes 12 slices

250g/9oz butter
250g/9oz almond flour (see note)
250g/9oz caster sugar
5 egg yolks
120g/4oz semi-sweet dark chocolate, grated
5 egg whites

For the creamy vanilla sauce
500ml/18fl oz double cream
1 vanilla pod, split lengthways
6 egg yolks
120g/4oz sugar
450ml/¾pt whipping cream

Make and bake the almond cake

In a food processor or electric mixer beat the butter, almond flour, 100g/3½oz sugar and the 5 yolks until light and white. Grate the chocolate and mix it with 85g/3oz of the sugar. Fold this into the cake batter.

Butter a 23cm/9in cake tin, about 7cm/2½in deep, and line the base with non-stick baking paper. Butter this again. Whisk the egg whites until soft peaks form. Sift the remaining sugar over the top and fold in. Fold this into the cake batter and turn into the lined cake tin. Bake in an oven at 150°C/300°F/gas 2 for 50-60 minutes, until a skewer inserted into the centre comes out clean. Remove from the oven, let it stand in the tin for 5 minutes, then turn it out on to a cake rack and leave until cold.

Make the creamy vanilla sauce

Bring the double cream to the boil with the vanilla pod. Put the egg yolks and sugar in a bowl and whisk until light and white. Pour in half the hot cream, whisking all the time. Remove the vanilla pod and pour in the remaining cream, then return the mixture to the pan. Over a very low heat, or simmering water, cook the custard, stirring with a wooden spoon, until it will coat the back of the spoon. Leave until cold then chill.

Before serving whisk the chilled whipping cream and stir it in.

Presentation

Serve the cake on a platter, accompanied by the chilled vanilla sauce.

My wine suggestion: Moscato rosa del Trentino Alto Adige 1985, recommended for its graceful flavour and bouquet and its colour – from rose to pale ruby – which draws you, as Luigi Veronelli says in his book on Italian wine, 'to a state of meditation'.

Editor's note: Not ground almonds, but flour, made from almonds which have been dried out, then ground to powder. This may be difficult to find outside Italy, so try drying out 350g/12oz almonds at the lowest possible heat for 24 hours, then grinding them.

Pina Bellini

LA SCALETTA

Piazzale Stazione Genova, 20144 Milan telephone: 2 835 0290

'I never expected to be so successful' says Pina Bellini. 'In the 1940s it was virtually impossible for a woman to get a job in a major kitchen. Then I was terrified by those stars and the points system of the gastronomic guides – but they spurred me to keep going and adapt to change and new demands.' Pina Bellini started work aged sixteen, in Milan and her skill at pasta – she was born in Bologna – gained her a place in the kitchens of some great chefs, such as Polonelli and Talamona, where she learned a broader cuisine.

Married at nineteen then widowed, in 1970 she and her son Aldo opened a little restaurant, Il Riservino, up in the Brianza hills near Milan. A Michelin rosette marked its success. Six years later she moved back to Milan, opening La Scaletta – seating thirty at the most – as a wine bar. Designed by the architect Gianfranco Frattini, it is very strict, very simple, while her collection of Murano glass gives it the atmosphere of a private house.

Within six months the wine bar became a restaurant.

Only the second woman in Italy, after Cantarelli, to gain two Michelin rosettes, Pina Bellini attributes part of her success to continuing curiosity. 'I've always tried to cook as an Italian should cook, and tried to get away from the labels which are so prevalent in today's cooking. Italian cuisine still has whole fields left to be explored.'

MENU

INSALATA DI BACCALA MARINATO IN
OLIO, LIMONE E ERBA CIPOLLINA
Salt cod marinated in oil, lemon and chives

FARFALLE, BROCCOLETTI E VONGOLE
Pasta bows with broccoli and mussel sauce

ROGNONE DI VITELLO CON FUNGHI
PORCINI E CRESCIONE
Calf's kidneys with fresh ceps and watercress

MOUSSE DI MELONE CON SALSA DI KIWI,
FRAGOLE E ANANAS
Melon cream with kiwi, strawberry and pineapple sauce

INSALATA DI BACCALA MARINATO IN OLIO, LIMONE E ERBA CIPOLLINA

Salt cod marinated in oil, lemon and chives

Serves 4

300g/11oz dried salt cod·fillet
40g/1½oz borlotti or other dried beans
120ml/4fl oz extra virgin olive oil
juice of 2 lemons
freshly ground black pepper
10 chive leaves, finely chopped
a bunch of rocket (or substitute sorrel)

Advance preparation

Leave the dried cod in cold water under a running tap for 48 hours (or change the water frequently), to remove all the salt and rehydrate it. Soak the dried beans overnight, then simmer for 1-1¼ hours until cooked but still firm. Drain them.

Marinate the salt cod

Drain the salt cod and dry it well, removing the skin, any discoloured flesh and any bones. Slice it very finely. Put the slices in a bowl, cover with a mixture of the oil, lemon juice, 2 grinds of pepper and half the chives. Leave to marinate for 24 hours.

Serve the salad

Use a slotted spoon to lift the salt cod strips on to 4 salad plates and arrange them. Insert the rocket leaves at regular intervals. Garnish with a scattering of beans and sprinkle very finely chopped chives on top.

My wine suggestion: an elegant Friuli wine, the Blanc de Rosis, or the sparkling rosé from the Cà del Bosco in Lombardy would go well with the salt-sweet flavour of this *baccalà*.

FARFALLE, BROCCOLETTI E VONGOLE

Pasta bows with broccoli and mussel sauce

Serves 4

200g/7oz pasta bows
300g/11oz fresh mussels, cleaned
150g/5oz calabrese florets
60g/2oz shelled fresh broad beans, from about
175g/6oz pods
1 garlic clove
a small piece of hot chilli pepper
3 tablespoons olive oil
75ml/2½fl oz white wine
salt and freshly ground black pepper
freshly chopped parsley

Heat a pan then put in the mussels and cover. Shake them over the heat for 1-2 minutes until opened then drain and discard the shells.

Cook the pasta and make the sauce

Cook the pasta in plenty of boiling salted water, adding the calabrese and broad beans too, for about 8 minutes, or until *al dente*.

Peel and finely chop the garlic and crush the chilli pepper. Toss them in a frying pan with the oil and the mussels. Stir in the white wine and keep hot.

When cooked, drain the pasta and the vegetables. Tip them into the hot sauce in the frying pan and toss for a couple of minutes over a high flame. Sprinkle with chopped parsley and serve.

My wine suggestion: this warm fresh Mediterranean dish begs for an attractive fragrant wine; in my Milan neighbourhood choose a Malvasia from Montù Beccaria or else a more seductive Chardonnay Gaia & Rey from Piedmont.

ROGNONE DI VITELLO CON FUNGHI PORCINI E CRESCIONE

Calf's kidneys with fresh ceps and watercress

Serves 4

400g/14oz calf's kidneys
6 tablespoons olive oil
400g/14oz fresh ceps, cleaned
30g/1oz butter
salt and freshly ground black pepper
1 garlic clove, finely chopped
parsley, finely chopped
75ml/2½fl oz fruity white wine
200g/7oz watercress

Remove the membrane from the kidneys and cut into thick slices. Cut out the cores. Heat 2 tablespoons oil in a frying pan over high heat and sear the kidney to seal for 1½-2 minutes on each side. Then remove and leave to drain in a sieve for about 10 minutes.

Slice the ceps then cook them for 5 minutes in 2 tablespoons olive oil and the butter. Turn them over from time to time with a spatula (or shake the pan regularly) and season with salt and pepper.

In a fresh pan heat 2 tablespoons oil over high heat and add the drained kidney slices. Cook for 3-4 minutes, turning them over, add the cooked mushrooms, garlic, chopped parsley and white wine. Season with salt and pepper.

Presentation
Wash the watercress and dry it in a cloth, then trim it to small sprigs. Arrange in a ring, on 4 warmed plates. Serve the kidneys and mushrooms in the centre, straight from the pan.

My wine suggestion: from among the many great red wines of Italy I would narrow the choice to two from Tuscany: the well-balanced Sodi di San Niccolò or the romantic Coltassala.

MOUSSE DI MELONE CON SALSA DI KIWI, FRAGOLE E ANANAS

Melon cream with kiwi, strawberry and pineapple sauce

Serves 4

500g/18oz melon flesh
100g/3½oz icing sugar, plus extra to taste
1 leaf gelatine
15 strawberries
3 kiwi fruit
½ small pineapple
fresh mint leaves

Purée the melon in a food processor or blender with the icing sugar. Pour the liquid into a bowl and set this in another containing crushed ice to chill. Soak the broken gelatine sheet in 2 tablespoons hot water, then dissolve over heat, stirring well to ensure there are no lumps. Stir into the melon liquid.

Pour into four small moulds about 150ml/¼pt capacity and chill in the refrigerator for a couple of hours until set.

Reserve 4 of the best strawberries for the decoration and prepare all the fruit. Reduce each one to a purée in turn, washing out the blender each time. Keep them in separate bowls. Taste each one and add icing sugar if needed.

Presentation
Turn out the mousses on to chilled dessert plates and decorate the tops with a strawberry and 2 mint leaves. Pour a little pool of each colour fruit on every plate.

My wine suggestion: so simple a dessert suggests a natural-tasting muscatel from Piedmont, sparkling and light or, from further south, the sunny, honeyed Greco di Bianco from Calabria.

Angelo Paracucchi

LOCANDA DELL'ANGELO

19031 Ameglia telephone: 187 64391

Paradoxically one of the gastronomes best known abroad as an ambassador of Italian cuisine is a convinced regionalist at home. 'The traditional dishes of Italian regional cooking included many more lessons than you might imagine' says Angelo Paracucchi. 'People won't be deceived for long by fried air with a fragrance of nothing.' His efforts to promote Italian cooking include demonstrating in Japan, America and Sweden, opening a restaurant in Seoul for Swissair and, nearer home, opening the Carpaccio in Paris in 1983. The popular presenter of a TV programme on cooking which ran for two years, he has been giving cookery classes round Italy for more than ten years. His recipes and practical tips appear monthly in the magazine Il Piacere.

Angelo Paracucchi was born in Umbria and many of his dishes demonstrate an affection for his native region and the one where he now lives. He has been the owner of the Locanda dell'Angelo since 1975, when he was forty-five; it was starred by Michelin within three years of opening. The architect Magistretti designed the restaurant, which is situated near the Carrara marble quarries, in the country between the mountains and the sea.

He knows as much about nutrition as he does cooking and skilfully combines the two. 'I have a great interest in cooking food which helps us to 'live'', he says, 'in other words, food which is perfectly suited to the moment in both its techniques and its flavour. I have become gradually more and more convinced that cooking is not so much an art as a science. It is always necessary to find the ideal balance between the aesthetic sense (how to prepare a certain dish) and the essence of the dish (the way it is done).'

MENU

RAVIOLI AI CARCIOFI
Ravioli with artichokes

FILETTO DI VITELLA AI BROCCOLI
Veal fillets with broccoli

SEMIFREDDO CON FICHI FLAMBEES
Ice cream with figs flambé

RAVIOLI AI CARCIOFI
Ravioli with artichokes

Serves 4

500g/18oz flour
3 eggs
100ml/3½fl oz water
60g/2oz butter
100g/3½oz sieved tomato (passata)
salt
60g/2oz freshly grated Parmesan

For the artichoke filling
8 globe artichokes
20ml/⅔fl oz extra virgin olive oil
1 garlic clove, chopped
1 sprig of marjoram, chopped
2 basil leaves, chopped
60ml/2fl oz white wine
60ml/2fl oz meat stock (page 68)
1 whole egg
1 egg yolk
20g/⅔oz freshly grated Parmesan
salt and freshly ground pepper

Make the pasta dough
Pour the flour on to a pasta board or work surface and make a well in the middle. Into this put the eggs and water. Using a fork, then your fingers later, pull the flour into the liquid, making sure that a smooth paste is formed. Continue until a dough is formed.
Knead the dough on a lightly-floured surface in the same way as bread. Push out the dough with the heels of your hand, then fold it back on top. Give the dough a quarter turn (so it is being stretched a different way) and then push it out again in the identical manner. Repeat for about 10 minutes until the dough is pliable and elastic. Wrap and rest for 10 minutes.

Make the ravioli filling
Trim the bottoms of the artichokes flat and pull off all the leaves – the outside ones are hardest to remove. Trim round with a knife. Blanch in boiling water for 1 minute then remove the chokes. Cut the artichoke bases into eight pieces. Heat the oil in a frying pan and add the artichokes, garlic, marjoram and basil; heat gently. Add the white wine then the stock. Boil

until the liquid has evaporated. Turn out the contents of the pan on to a chopping board and chop finely. Transfer to a basin and mix in the whole egg, egg yolk and the Parmesan and season. Leave until cold.

Roll out the pasta dough
Cut off half the pasta dough and pass it 5 times though a pasta machine (closing the rollers by only one notch each time); cover the strips until ready to use. Alternatively, roll it out on a lightly floured surface with a long rolling pin, rolling only lightly and always in the same direction and with an even rhythm, until it is 2mm/⅛in thick. Keep the pasta covered when not in use. Repeat with the remaining pasta.

Make the ravioli
On the pasta sheet arrange little piles of filling, about ½ teaspoon and about 4cm/1½in apart. Roll out the remaining pasta and cover the filling. Apply gentle pressure, working along the row between the fillings, first in one direction then the other, to eliminate all the air (which could cause the ravioli to burst on cooking.) Stamp out the ravioli with a biscuit cutter of 4cm/1½in diameter. Do not make ravioli ahead – it is better made as near to eating time as possible.

Make the sauce and serve
Cook the ravioli in plenty of boiling salted water for 3 minutes, until *al dente*.
Put the butter in a frying pan with the sieved tomato, salt gently and cook for 30 seconds.
In another big pan melt the butter. Add the drained, hot ravioli and sauté them gently with 2 tablespoons of their cooking water, sprinkling the Parmesan over them.
Put a little tomato sauce on each plate, top with ravioli and dribble more sauce over the top.

My wine suggestion: Villa della Signora from the estate of Poggio al Sole.

FILETTO DI VITELLA AI BROCCOLI

Veal fillets with broccoli

Serves 4

600g/1¼lb veal fillet, cut in 4 filets mignons
40g/1½oz broccoli florets
salt and freshly ground black pepper
40g/1½oz bacon
60ml/2fl oz extra virgin oil
1 garlic clove
60g/2oz butter
85ml/3fl oz white wine
2 tablespoons balsamic vinegar
2 tablespoons meat stock (page 68)

Boil the broccoli florets in salted water for 5 minutes. Cut the bacon into short strips. Heat 15ml/½fl oz of the oil in a frying pan and put in the bacon. Brown it slowly. Pour off all the fat from the pan. Add the garlic clove and 30ml/1fl oz oil. Add the broccoli florets and sauté for 4-5 minutes.

In another pan put 30g/1oz butter and 15ml/½fl oz oil. Heat till the butter foams and put in the veal *filets mignons*. Cook for 1 minute on each side and season with salt and pepper.

Complete and serve the dish

Arrange the drained broccoli on 4 warm plates and put the veal fillets on top. Pour out all the fat from the pan and return to the heat. Add the white wine, stirring to deglaze and boil to reduce the volume by half. Add the vinegar and the stock. Reduce for a moment more. Whisk in 30g/1oz butter, in dice, to enrich the sauce and pour over the meat.

My wine suggestion: San Giorgio from Lungarotti, which has an intense flavour with an excellent lingering aroma and good body.

Editor's note: balsamic vinegar is a speciality of Northern Italy, matured by law for a decade – sometimes longer – in a succession of casks of different wood. It is particularly mellow, tasting both sweet and sour, since it is made from grapes with a high sugar content. Originally it was used as a medicine, hence its name.

SEMIFREDDO CON FICHI FLAMBEES

Ice cream with figs flambé

Serves 4

60ml/2fl oz milk
160g/5½oz sugar
4 egg yolks
500ml/18fl oz double cream

For the flambéed figs

12 ripe figs
40g/1½ oz sugar
2 tablespoons water
40ml/1½fl oz kirsch

Make the ice cream

Bring the milk and sugar to the boil, stirring to dissolve the sugar. Put the yolks in a bowl that will stand over a pan of simmering water. Whisk hard then pour in the boiling milk mixture.

Set over hot water and whisk continuously until the mixture greatly increases in bulk and becomes thick and foamy. Remove from the heat and whisk until cold then chill briefly. Whip the cream in a bowl to very soft peaks. Add the zabaione and continue whisking.

Turn the mixture into a shallow 850ml/1½pt container and freeze immediately – this stops the zabaione separating. Move the ice cream from the freezer to the refrigerator about 15 minutes before you start the flambéed figs.

Flambé the figs

Peel the figs. In a shallow pan heat the sugar and water together. When the sugar is foaming, warm the kirsch in a ladle or small pan, set light to it and add to the sugar. Add the figs, turning to caramelise them well.

Presentation

Cut the ice cream into cubes and pile these in four sundae dishes. Put 2 hot figs in each dish. Crush the remaining figs into the sugar and kirsch mixture with a fork to form a sauce and pour this over the ice cream. The contrast of sugar-hot fruit and ice cream is delicious!

My wine suggestion: Moscato d'Asti from the Dogliotti estate; it has an intense and fruity perfume and a multiplicity of small bubbles.

Sergio Lorenzi

SERGIO

Lungarno Pacinotti 1, 56100 Pisa telephone: 50 48245

'I feel that I express something of myself through cooking, in the same way that a painter does', says Sergio Lorenzi. 'I take more pleasure in preparing the very best of dishes for other people to eat than in eating them myself'. A pressing need to earn money propelled him into catering at the age of thirteen, in 1950. It seemed a natural choice at the time, for other members of the family before him were good cooks. His apprenticeship and the climb up the kitchen ranks to chef de cuisine were pursued largely in the restaurants of Northern Italy, working under some of Italy's leading cooks of the era.

In 1970 he opened the Sergio, moving in 1976 to a more prestigious location in the centre of Pisa: an inn which has entertained every distinguished traveller from Shelley to Garibaldi. It backs on to the Piazza delle Vettovaglie, an ancient market square selling local specialities, a happy connection since the market rules his kitchen, and the menu is compiled on a daily basis. The restaurant was awarded a Michelin rosette in 1978.

Owning a restaurant in a historic centre has its disadvantages — like restrictions on building expansion. But it does reinforce a sense of tradition, one reason perhaps why he is the General Secretary of the Italian professional restaurateurs association, which links chefs offering the best Italian food in Italy and worldwide. His cooking is rooted in the region — he is president of the Tuscan chefs — but there is a great deal of his own personality and own innovation in it as well. 'I love tradition, but am not its slave', he says.

MENU

TIMBALLO DI RISO CON SCAMPI E SALSA DI CROSTACEI
Timbales of rice with Dublin Bay prawns and shellfish sauce

CINGHIALE IN DOLCE E FORTE CON PUREA DI MELE
Boar in sweet and sour sauce with apple purée

GRATIN DI ALBICOCCHE CON ZABAIONE AL MOSCATO D'ASTI
Apricot gratin with zabaione and Moscato d'Asti

TIMBALLO DI RISO CON SCAMPI E SALSA DI CROSTACEI

Timbales of rice with Dublin Bay prawns and shellfish sauce

Serves 4

250g/9oz risotto rice, such as Arborio
85g/3oz butter
2 small white onions, finely chopped
150ml/¼pt aromatic white wine
60g/2oz grated Parmesan
1.2kg/2¾lb Dublin Bay prawns, about 300g/11oz
after shelling, with claws and shells reserved
75ml/2½fl oz cognac
60ml/2fl oz double cream
salt and freshly ground black pepper
12 asparagus tips, or other vegetables in season
15g/½oz flour
choice of asparagus tips, courgette slices or green beans,
lightly steamed, to garnish

For the shellfish court bouillon
heads, claws and tail shells of the prawns
1 carrot, chopped
1 small onion, chopped
1 celery stalk, chopped
a bouquet garni of sprigs of myrtle, rosemary and
fennel, tied together

Make the shellfish court bouillon
Shell the prawns, reserving all the shells. Put 2L/3½pt water on to boil in a big pan. Add the heads, claws and tail shells, the chopped carrot, onion, celery and bouquet garni. Simmer slowly for 1 hour and then pass through a strainer; the liquid should have reduced by half.

Cook the risotto
Heat 15g/½oz butter in a pan and fry 1 chopped onion until brown. Add the rice and fry for a few seconds, stirring until well coated in butter. Pour in the white wine and 200ml/7fl oz reduced shellfish stock and cook, stirring every now and then, for 18 minutes until creamy, adding a little more shellfish stock if needed – different types of risotto rice absorb varying amounts of liquid. Add 30g/1oz butter and the grated Parmesan and stir to a smooth mixture.

Prepare the scampi stuffing
Heat another 30g/1oz butter and cook a second chopped onion until softened. Add the prawn tails and cook, turning gently for about 4 minutes. Add the cognac and cream and heat through.

Fill the timbales
Take 4 ramekins about 150ml/¼pt capacity and on the bottom put a single prawn. Boil the asparagus tips for 5 minutes (or cook another trimmed vegetable to make an attractive but simple pattern) and arrange them in the dish. On top put the risotto, pressing it in lightly, then make a well in the centre. Spoon prawns into the centre and add a little salt; there will be some prawns left over, as you must leave room for the remaining rice. Add rice to fill the mould and cover the tops with aluminium foil.

Make the shellfish sauce
Melt 15g/½oz butter in a pan and stir in the flour. Cook, gently stirring for 1 minute. Stir in 150ml/¼pt reduced shellfish stock and the remaining prawn and cream mixture that did not fit into the moulds; cook gently for 2 minutes. Taste and correct the seasonings.

Cook and serve the dish
Put the timbales in a bain-marie and pour in boiling water to come half way up the moulds. Cook gently in an oven at 180°C/350°F/gas 4 for 20 minutes while you steam some garnishing vegetables.

Spoon sauce on to 4 warmed plates. Unmould the timbales in the middle and garnish with fresh vegetables.

My wine suggestion: Cabreo-cru La Pietra, produced from the Chardonnay grape on the hills of Florence, yellow and with an intense oak fragrance from the oak casks in which it is matured.

CINGHIALE IN DOLCE E FORTE CON PUREA DI MELE

Boar in sweet and sour sauce with apple purée

The sweet-and-sour sauce with the surprising ingredient of chocolate is a classic way of cooking game in Tuscany.

Serves 4

*800g/1¾lb leg of boar, prepared and boned
75cl bottle Chianti classico riserva
a bouquet garni of sprigs of myrtle, rosemary and
fennel, tied together
6 juniper berries, crushed
4 cloves
60ml/2fl oz extra virgin oil
60g/2oz raisins
60g/2oz pinenuts
20g/²⁄₃oz cocoa powder
beurre manié made from 15g/½oz flour worked into
15g/½oz butter, if needed
salt and freshly ground black pepper
apple purée to serve*

Marinate the boar's leg ahead
Put the boar's leg in a deep dish and add the wine and tuck in the bruised herbs, juniper berries and cloves. Leave for at least 24 hours, turning occasionally.
Cook the boar and make the sour-sweet sauce
Remove the meat and pat dry with absorbent paper. Heat the oil in a large pan. Put in the boar's leg and colour the outside over medium heat, turning to brown all sides. Add the bunch of herbs and pour in the red wine and spices. Cover and simmer gently for about 2 hours, until done. Transfer the leg to a platter and keep warm. Add the raisins and pine nuts to the sauce. Stir the cocoa to a paste with a little water and add. Bring the sauce back to the boil: it should be thickened and smooth, but not greasy. If the sauce is not thick enough, stir in some beurre manié in little pieces and bring back to the boil, stirring. Taste and season with salt and pepper. Slice the boar and serve on warmed plates, garnished with a little warm apple purée. Pour the sour-sweet sauce over the meat.

My wine suggestion: Chianti classico riserva.

GRATIN DI ALBICOCCHE CON ZABAIONE AL MOSCATO D'ASTI

Apricot gratin with zabaione and Moscato d'Asti

Serves 4

*600g/1¼lb apricots
300ml/½pt Moscato d'Asti
120g/4oz sugar
3 egg yolks
1 egg*

Blanch the apricots in boiling water for 10 seconds each, peel them, cut in half and stone them. Poach in the Moscato with a little sugar: they should remain firm.
Remove the fruit with a slotted spoon and then boil the Moscato to reduce to 150ml/¼pt.
Put the egg yolks, egg and remaining sugar in a bowl set over simmering water and whisk hard. Add the reduced Moscato and continue whisking until you have a lovely big mass of frothy zabaione, much increased in size and thickening on the whisk.
Arrange the apricots on 4 plates and coat with zabaione. Brown quickly under a very hot grill and serve at once.

My wine suggestion: Moscato d'Asti, straw coloured and highly fruity, from the muscat grape.

Paolo Vai

CAVALLO BIANCO
Via Aubert 15, 11100 Aosta telephone: 0165 362214

'My aim is to create food which appeals to all the senses, enhancing the sense of taste, using the pure colours of nature' says Paolo Vai. Still a passionate painter, who regrets he has so little time for art, his first career was running a small graphic advertising company. He was born in the Val d'Aosta during the war. Though his grandfather owned what is now the Cavallo Bianco, the connection with catering seemed distant, until he married Corinne, whose father came from Monaco and was chef at the Café de Paris. In 1968 his grandfather wished to retire but had no obvious heir for the restaurant. Cooking seemed a more limited way of life than art when he made the choice, but Paolo Vai and his father-in-law took over the restaurant. An old coaching inn with wooden balconies on to a courtyard, in the heart of Aosta at the foot of Mont Blanc, it served one of the main routes into Italy. Supported by his saucier, Dante Chilietti, a haute cuisine chef, who had trained with Escoffier and worked in the great hotels of Monte Carlo and Deauville, he started to master his new career. His convivial brother Franco Vai manages the dining room. Paolo Vai began to recognise the artistic potential of cooking from his mentors – and also as a customer. Dining in many of Europe's great restaurants, he realised the emotions felt by a connoisseur of fine food. In his own kitchen he has created a light cuisine of great finesse, based on high quality regional produce. Michelin awarded the first rosette in 1976 and a second in 1984. Is he interested in regional food? 'Yes, for what we regard as being in the past can suddenly become modern again.' His ambition as a chef, though, is 'to come as close as possible to nature with a sensitive and loving relationship to it.'

MENU

SALADE DE FOIE GRAS
Foie gras salad

FARAONA FARCITA AL PROFUMO DI POLENTA E CARCIOFI
Stuffed guinea fowl with polenta and artichokes

BAVARESE AI FRUTTI DELLA PASSIONE
Passion fruit bavarois

SALADE DE FOIE GRAS
Foie gras salad

Another – and more economical – way this salad is served at the Cavallo Bianco is to sliver the foie gras and to scatter it over the top. Like this 50g/1¾oz foie gras will serve 4 people.

Serves 4

200g/7oz cooked foie gras, preferably Mortara
4 tomatoes
½ small red cabbage, or 1 radicchio di Treviso
olive oil for glazing
60g/2oz lambs' lettuce
4 warm slices of brioche to serve

For the apple salad dressing
½ green apple
1 lemon, squeezed
120ml/4fl oz extra virgin oil
1 teaspoon balsamic vinegar
salt and freshly ground black pepper

Make the apple salad dressing
Quarter, peel, core and roughly chop the apple half and put in the blender with the lemon juice, virgin olive oil, balsamic vinegar and salt and pepper to taste. Blend to a purée, then strain.

Assembly and presentation
Pour boiling water over the tomatoes in turn, wait 10 seconds then peel them. Quarter and seed 2 of them and chop the flesh coarsely. Slice the others.

Slice the red cabbage or the radicchio di Treviso very finely. Arrange on 4 plates and pour the apple salad dressing over.

Chill the foie gras before slicing very finely. Arrange these on top, rolling the slices over. Brush with olive oil to give them a glaze. Garnish one side of each plate with lambs' lettuce and a tablespoon of chopped tomato flesh – called *concassé* tomato. Arrange a few tomato slices on the other side.

My wine suggestion: Chardonnay Fratelli Gancia S.P.A. 1985, which comes from the Val d'Aosta – it's made by the charmat method, which induces a fizz.

Editor's note: The Romans may have invented foie gras, but as an Italian delicacy it is really confined to the north of the country, centring on Piedmont and Lombardy – Mortara is in the Po valley, west of Pavia.

Traditionally foie gras is produced by over-feeding geese with maize in the last weeks of life, inflating the liver to a quarter of the bird's weight. It also acquires the richness and silky texture that have made it so prized.

However, duck foie gras has become so popular that more are now produced in France than goose liver and Mortara is Italy's main centre. This type of farming is banned in Britain and America, though the Americans are the world's biggest importers of cooked foie gras.

A raw duck foie gras weights 450-500g/16-18oz. To prepare it for cooking, sever the little blood vessel between the two lobes. It should be at room temperature so it is easy to work with. Make an incision in the top and work this back with your fingers and a small and not too sharp knife. Underneath you will find a layer of veins. Pull these out gently and then the layer of veins beneath. Salting and standing for a period will draw out blood, like soaking in milk, but is not strictly necessary.

Slices of foie gras eaten hot need the minimum cooking, otherwise the expensive fat will weep away. More often whole foie gras are cooked in a terrine inside a bain-marie. Once cooled, the foie gras is served from the terrine with a spoon dipped in hot water.

Salade de foie gras at the Cavallo Bianco

Faraona farcita al profumo di polenta e carciofi

Bavarese ai frutti della passione

FARAONA FARCITA AL PROFUMO DI POLENTA E CARCIOFI

Stuffed guinea fowl with polenta and artichokes

Serves 4

1 guinea fowl
1 carrot, chopped
¾ onion, chopped
1½ garlic cloves, finely chopped
120ml/4fl oz Vin Santo (a sweet dessert wine –
Sauternes could be subtituted)
chopped thyme
chopped rosemary
chopped marjoram
1 egg
salt and freshly ground black pepper
30g/1oz butter
85ml/3fl oz meat stock (page 68) or water

For the vegetable accompaniments
150g/5oz polenta
salt and freshly ground black pepper
250g/9oz potato, peeled and sliced
60g/2oz butter
1 large globe artichoke base
oil for deep fat frying, plus 2 tablespoons oil
250g/9oz ceps
1 garlic clove, crushed with the flat of a knife

Cook the polenta ahead
Bring 200ml/7fl oz lightly salted water to the boil and sprinkle in the polenta, stir it rapidly to prevent lumps forming, then leave it to cook over medium to low heat for an hour, stirring.

Prepare and cook the guinea fowl
Cut off the legs and the wings. Remove the wishbone then take off both breasts, working down the carcass from the breast bone with a sharp knife. Strip the flesh from the wings, legs and carcass – there will be about 300g/11oz.
Arrange a base of chopped vegetables, using all the carrot, plus ½ onion and 1 garlic clove, in a baking dish and add the meat. Sprinkle with 40ml/1½fl oz Vin Santo and cook in an oven at 180°C/350°F/gas 4 for 12 minutes.
Mince in a food processor, adding enough chopped thyme, rosemary and marjoram for your personal taste, and the egg. Season well.

With the point of a kitchen knife make a long horizontal pocket in each guinea fowl breast. Open them up and beat them out very thinly. Mound stuffing on them (do not overfill them) and reform them. Tie them neatly with string. Season the outsides and rub with 15g/½oz butter. Melt another 15g/½oz butter in a small flameproof dish and add ¼ chopped onion and ½ garlic clove. Put in the breasts and sprinkle with the remaining Vin Santo. Roast in an oven at 180°C/350°F/gas 4 for 20 minutes.

Prepare the vegetables and make the sauce
Cook the potato in salted water until done, then drain, saving a little of the cooking water. Mash the potato, with a little water if necessary. Beat in the hot, cooked polenta and the butter to make a cream and season well and keep warm.
Cut the artichoke into thin strips. Heat oil for deep frying and fry them in a basket until just brown. Drain on absorbent paper and keep warm. Dice the ceps. Heat 2 tablespoons oil and cook them quickly with the garlic clove, then season; remove the garlic.
Remove the guinea fowl breasts from the dish when cooked and keep warm. Add the remains of the stuffing (about a quarter) and the meat stock or water to the juices. Bring back to the boil then press through a sieve.

Presentation
Put 2-3 spoonfuls of polenta cream on each plate and spread it out. Cut the guinea fowl breast into slices 1cm/½in thick and divide each one between two plates, arranging the slices like a fan on top of the cream or aligning them horizontally, according to your personal taste. Pour a little Vin Santo sauce over the meat on each plate. Put a spoonful of cooked ceps with a sprinkling of crisp artichoke strips on to the potato and polenta cream, arranging them at the base of the fan, or to balance the plate visually.

My wine suggestion: Cabreo from the Ruffino estate in Tuscany.

Editor's note: At 1kg/2¼lb, a guinea fowl may seem small, but there is as much meat on it as a duck of twice the weight. A duck could be substituted.

BAVARESE AI FRUTTI DELLA PASSIONE

Passion fruit bavarois

This is one of those attractive moulded creams, with a sophisticated fruit flavour, that combines so well with whatever pretty fruit you have available. Aim for a contrast in colour as well as texture and flavour.

Serves 6

1 egg
85g/3oz caster sugar
100ml/3½fl oz milk
2 leaves gelatine
5-6 passion fruit
your choice of fruit, such as kiwis, black seeded grapes,
and peaches

For the raspberry syrup
150g/5oz raspberries
2 tablespoons sugar
1 lemon

Make the raspberry syrup
Purée the raspberries in a blender with the sugar and a few drops of lemon juice, adding 2 tablespoons water to obtain a sauce of a good consistency. Rub the purée through a sieve to remove the pips and then chill.

Make the bavarois
Separate the egg and whisk the egg yolk with about 50g/1¾oz sugar. Bring the milk to the boil. Pour on to the sugar and yolk mixture, whisking hard all the time, then pour back into the pan. Stir over very low heat until the mixture has a slightly creamy consistency.

Break up the gelatine leaves, soak them for 5 minutes in 2 tablespoons hot water, then stir over heat until melted. Scoop the contents of the passion fruit into the blender, purée with a few drops of lemon juice, then rub through a sieve to remove the pips. Measure the liquid and make it up to 120ml/4fl oz with water. Stir this into the cooling custard with the dissolved gelatine. Place the bowl inside a larger one containing ice cubes to chill, stirring occasionally.

When the custard starts to show signs of setting, whisk the egg white until stiff then whisk in the remaining sugar to make Italian meringue. Fold the meringue into the custard. Spoon into 6 metal moulds, 75ml/2½fl oz capacity, or small ramekins and chill in the refrigerator for about 1 hour until set.

Presentation
Pour the raspberry syrup on to 4 dessert plates. Turn the bavarois creams out of their moulds into the middle – if the moulds were ornamental, touch the tips and middle with a little raspberry purée. Arrange your choice of fruit round the puddings – a simple pattern of half kiwi slices is quite effective.

Britain

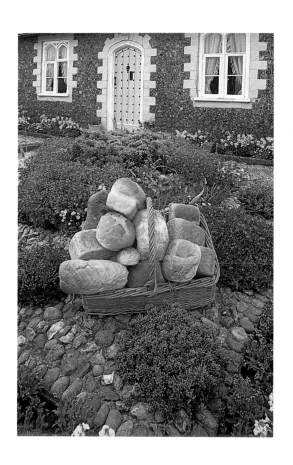

*Baking, roasting and boiling –
à l'anglaise used to mean
'plain cooked'. But new confidence
and invention are being applied
to traditionally splendid produce.*

Anton Mosimann

MOSIMANN'S
11B West Halkin Street, Belgrave Square, London SW1 telephone: 01 235 9625

An encounter with a lorry driver, for whom he cooked lunch on television, made Anton Mosimann Britain's best-loved chef. As head chef at the Dorchester for twelve years, he was already the most celebrated – the first British chef since Escoffier to have a world-wide reputation. His English, which he speaks with a soft lisp on the 'th,' was acquired during three years in Canada.

He was born in Switzerland – and a cook. Aged eight he used to cook for friends in his parents' restaurant in Nidau on the day it was closed. A good deal of determination soon showed; an apprenticeship at the Hotel Baeren in Twann which involved seven-day-a-week schooling gained him a diploma two years early. Next came the mastery of technique, at the Palace Hotel, Villars, in 1964, then Rome and St Moritz, where he worked for an old chef who had himself worked for Escoffier. He was the youngest chef ever to win the Chef de Cuisine diploma, the highest Swiss award. He then set about mastering patisserie.

In 1970 he was made head chef at the Swiss Pavilion in Osaka, acquiring an interest in things oriental and meeting his wife, Kathrin. He was hired by the Dorchester in 1976, subsequently becoming chef aged twenty-nine, inspiring and teaching the kitchen brigades of three restaurants, and gaining two Michelin rosettes for the Terrace Room in 1986. Slim and fit himself, his second book, Cuisine naturelle, *started as an artistic introspection into low fat, no-salt healthy food, but became a style in itself, irrespective of its goodness.*

A perfectionist in everything he touches, he is interested in traditional British dishes, adding a sense of adventure to their sensible methods and down-to-earth qualities. In 1988 he moved to an ex-chapel, the Belfry, to cook for club members, and plans more books and television.

MENU

SMOKED SALMON AND CUCUMBER
SALAD

CHICKEN HOT POT

BREAD AND BUTTER PUDDING

SMOKED SALMON AND CUCUMBER SALAD

Serves 4

1½ cucumbers
30g/1oz radishes
175g/6oz smoked salmon
juice of ½ lemon
2 tablespoons mayonnaise
salt and freshly ground black pepper
2 tablespoons whipped cream
2 tablespoons salmon caviar
4 sprigs of dill

Score the cucumber skin from end to end with a canelle cutter, or by pulling a fork down the skin. Cut 36 thin slices. Cut the ½ cucumber in half lengthways and scrape out the seeds with a teaspoon. Cut into thin lengthways strips and then cut across to make julienne about 4cm/1½in long.

Cut the radishes into matchsticks and the smoked salmon into thin strips. Put them all together in a bowl, and add the cucumber julienne.

Add the lemon juice and mayonnaise and toss gently, seasoning with salt and pepper. Stir in the whipped cream to bind.

Presentation

Lay the cucumber slices overlapping on 4 plates in a circle. Stand a biscuit cutter in the middle (about 7.5cm/3in diameter) and put in the smoked salmon mix. Remove the mould.

Garnish the top of each portion with salmon caviar and a sprig of fresh dill.

My wine suggestion: Chablis or a Montrachet.

CHICKEN HOT POT

Serves 4

2.2kg/4¾lb maize-fed or grain-fed chicken
2L/3½pt white chicken stock (page 96)
3 onions, each studded with 2 cloves
1 bay leaf
2 garlic cloves
a few white peppercorns
a bunch of herbs such as thyme, rosemary and parsley stalks
4 small carrots
1 celery stalk
20cm/8in white leek
4 small onions
1 small celeriac, peeled and quartered
salt and freshly ground white pepper
sprigs of parsley to garnish

Bring a large saucepan of water to the boil and add the chicken. Bring back to the boil, drain and allow to cool slightly.

In a large pan heat the chicken stock with the clove-studded onions, bay leaf, garlic cloves, peppercorns and herb bunch. Simmer for 20 minutes. Add the chicken and poach for 20 minutes.

Remove the chicken from the pan. Strain the stock, then remove the fat from the top by drawing strips of absorbent paper across the top. Return the stock to the washed-out pan. Remove the skin from the chicken.

Return the chicken to the stock, add the vegetables, bring to the boil and simmer for 10 minutes. Remove the chicken and vegetables and keep them warm.

Strain the stock back into a saucepan and boil rapidly to reduce by half. Adjust the seasoning to taste.

Presentation

Cut the chicken into eight and arrange in 4 warmed soup plates with the vegetables. Pour some stock over each one and garnish with the parsley sprigs. Serve at once.

My wine suggestion: a Côte de Beaune or something quite basic for this good peasant dish.

Smoked salmon and cucumber salad

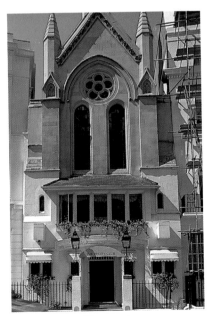

Mosimann's

Chicken hot pot

Bread and butter pudding

WHITE CHICKEN STOCK

*1 boiling fowl, blanched by putting it into a big pan of
boiling water, then bringing back to the boil, and
draining it
2L/4½pt water
60g/2oz white bouquet garni, made of a strip of onion,
white of leek, strip of celeriac and herbs, tied together
salt and freshly ground black pepper*

Put the boiling fowl in a large saucepan, fill up
with cold water and bring to the boil. Skim off
the scum. Add the bouquet garni and a little
seasoning.
Leave to simmer gently for 2 hours, occasionally
skimming and removing the fat. Strain the stock
through a fine cloth or sieve, allowing it to drip
through, then season again to taste.

BREAD AND BUTTER PUDDING

This famous English nursery pudding was
given a whole new lease of life when it
appeared on the menu at the Dorchester,
with subtle changes – cream instead of milk
for instance – that transformed it.

*Serves 4-6
500ml/18fl oz milk
500ml/18fl oz double cream
a little salt
2 vanilla pods, split lengthways
6 eggs
250g/9oz sugar
6 small bread rolls
60g/2oz butter, softened
20g/²/₃oz sultanas, soaked for ½ hour in water
40g/1½oz apricot jam
a little icing sugar to serve
double cream to serve (optional)*

Bring the milk, cream, salt and the vanilla pods
to the boil. Beat the eggs and sugar together and
pour the simmering milk down on them. Sieve
the mixture.
Cut the rolls into thin slices and butter them.
Arrange them in a buttered ovenproof soufflé
dish, 1.7L/3½pt capacity, scattering soaked
sultanas between each layer.
Pour in the milk mixture and dot the remaining
butter over the top.
Stand in a bain-marie, and pour in boiling water
to come halfway up the sides of the dish. Cook
carefully on the top of the stove for 35-40
minutes until the custard is set.

My wine suggestion: a glass of champagne –
something sophisticated to go with an ex-
nursery pudding.

John Burton-Race

L'Ortolan

Church Lane, Shinfield, Nr Reading, Berkshire telephone: 0734 883 783

Starred by Michelin when he was twenty-six, John Burton-Race had fourteen years behind the stove before he was thirty. He started thinking about being a chef as a child in Singapore. After catering school and periods at Quaglino's in London, Chewton Glen in New Milton and La Sorbonne in Oxford, he joined Raymond Blanc as second chef at Les Quat' Saisons. Here the excitement of the kitchen really bit him, working for a chef who cared little for training but believed everything happened anew in the kitchen. When Raymond Blanc moved to new premises, John, with his French wife Christine as maître d'hôtel, was given charge of the old one. It became Le Petit Blanc and soon secured a Michelin rosette.

John Burton-Race is not only a creative chef, but one driven by an idea of what might be achieved, always reaching forward. His recipes have been described as 'classically complicated': they certainly have an amazing number of ingredients. But the important thing is that at the end the tastes seem simple, magically right. He took the first opportunity to own his own restaurant. When Nico Ladenis left his Reading restaurant to return to London, the Burton-Races promptly bought it. Renamed L'Ortolan, it gained a Michelin rosette within four months of opening in 1987.

He describes his own cooking as 'in the contemporary classic mould, with the emphasis on light natural juices and less of the classical usage of cream and butter'. 'Taste is of the utmost importance', he says, 'rather than prettiness of presentation'.

MENU

SALADE DE RAIE ETUVEE AU SOJA
Salad of steamed skate in butter scented with soy

SUPREME DE PIGEONNEAU EN ROBE DE CHOUX AU MADERE
Pigeon breasts in cabbage leaves with Madeira sauce

TARTE SOUFFLEE A LA RHUBARBE AU COULIS DE FRAISES ET SORBET DE CITRON VERT
Rhubarb soufflé tart with strawberry and lime sorbet

SALADE DE RAIE ETUVEE AU SOJA

Salad of steamed skate in butter scented with soy

Serves 4

*2 skate wings, each 550g/1¼lb, outer fins removed,
and washed
2 carrots, cut in julienne strips
2 courgettes, cut in julienne strips*

For the flavoured butter
*60g/2oz butter, melted
garlic
lemon juice
cayenne
1 tablespoon chopped tarragon, blanched in
boiling water*

For the tarragon vinaigrette
*1 tablespoon white wine vinegar
1 tablespoon virgin olive oil
1 tablespoon corn oil
1 garlic clove, crushed under a flat knife
¼ teaspoon sugar
salt and freshly ground black pepper
2 sprigs of tarragon*

For the salad
*120g/4oz baby spinach leaves, trimmed
120g/4oz rocket leaves, trimmed
175g/6oz curly endive
2 shallots, finely chopped
1 bunch of chives, chopped
few drops of soy sauce
2 tomatoes, blanched, skinned, seeded and the
flesh diced
300ml/½pt reduced fish stock (page 161)
lemon juice*

Steam the skate wings
Lay out two pieces of cling film large enough to wrap up the skate. Flavour the melted butter to taste with garlic, lemon juice, cayenne and chopped, blanched tarragon and brush this over the cling film. Sprinkle with the julienne of vegetables and season lightly. Place the skate wings on top, brush them with more butter and seal the parcels: they must be completely air-tight.

Steam in a covered container for 5 minutes on each side or until tender. Remove from the pan Unwrap the fish, saving the julienne to use in the salad. Strain off the cooking juices and save them for the sauce.
Skin and fillet the skate. Keep the fish warm and covered to retain its moisture.

Prepare the salad and garnish
Wash and dry the salad leaves and reserve. Combine the ingredients for the tarragon vinaigrette, seasoning to taste. In a bowl mix 1 chopped shallot with some of the chopped chives. Add the vinaigrette with a few drops of soy sauce. Taste and check the seasonings.
Prepare a colourful garnish of the diced tomato flesh.

Prepare the lemon and soy sauce
Add the reserved cooking juices from the skate to a small pan with the fish stock. Boil to reduce the liquid by half. Then strain it, cool slightly and whisk in a tablespoonful of tarragon vinaigrette, to enrich the sauce. Finish it by adding 1 finely chopped shallot, about 2 tablespoons finely chopped chives and a few drops of soy sauce. Taste and correct the seasonings.

Presentation
Toss the salad in the prepared dressing and arrange in the centre of 4 plates. Place the warm skate, cut into slices, around the edge of each plate. Season the fish with a little lemon juice and sprinkle the reserved julienne of carrots and courgettes over it with the diced tomato on top. Flash in an oven heated to 220°C/425°F/gas 7 for 3 seconds. Spoon the warm sauce over the skate and serve.

My wine suggestion: normally with a vinaigrette it is not advisable to drink wine, but a Gewürztraminer would be rather nice.

SUPREME DE PIGEONNEAU EN ROBE DE CHOUX AU MADERE

Pigeon breasts in cabbage leaves with Madeira sauce

Serves 4

2 Norfolk squab pigeons, with livers and hearts
60g/2oz foie gras
4 shallots, coarsely sliced
2 cloves of garlic, peeled and cut in half
2 sprigs of thyme
1/3 bay leaf
3/4 teaspoon each port, Madeira and white wine
120ml/4fl oz chicken stock (page 250)
salt and freshly ground black pepper
300ml/1/2pt double cream
about 6 tablespoons clarified butter (page 23)
4 Savoy cabbage leaves 15cm/6in diameter

For the Madeira sauce
30g/1oz butter
4 shallots, chopped
1 garlic clove
sprig of fresh thyme
1/4 bay leaf
2 tablespoons white wine vinegar
4 tablespoons old dry Madeira
425ml/3/4pt clear chicken stock (page 250)
120g/4oz button mushrooms, sliced
1 tablespoon well-reduced brown bone stock (page 178)
1 tablespoon finely chopped truffle

For the garnish
4 small puff pastry 'saucepan' cases
175g/6oz mixed wild mushrooms
1 shallot, finely chopped
1/4 garlic clove, chopped
1 teaspoon chives, chopped
30g/1oz butter

Prepare the mousse

Remove the breasts and legs from the pigeons, discarding the skin. Keep the carcasses. Bone the legs and put the flesh in a bowl with the hearts, livers, foie gras, shallots, garlic, thyme and bay leaf. Just moisten with port, Madeira and white wine. Marinate for 12 hours.

Drain the meat in a colander over a small pan then bring the juices to the boil, skimming off impurities which rise. Boil until syrupy, then add the stock and reduce to 2 tablespoons syrup.

Pick the shallots, thyme, garlic and bay leaf from the meat and discard. Put the flesh in a food processor with 2 good pinches of salt and purée until very fine (about 1 minute). This must then be chilled, which can be done in the freezer for about 15 minutes. Add the cream, check the seasonings then press the mousse through a fine sieve. Finally stir in the reduced juices and chill.

Assemble the pigeon parcels

Fry the seasoned pigeon breasts in 2 tablespoons clarified butter for 30 seconds on each side to seal, then cool. Blanch the cabbage until tender – about 2 minutes – then drain and dry carefully with absorbent paper.

Spoon a little mousse on to one half of the leaves. Lay a breast on top and smooth over the remaining mousse with a palette knife. Fold the leaves over to enclose the meat completely. Press down on the edge and trim off overlapping leaf. Wrap in cling film until water-tight.

Prepare the Madeira sauce

Fry the carcasses in 30g/1oz butter until golden-brown, add the shallots, garlic, thyme and bay leaf and fry together for 2-3 minutes. Deglaze the pan with wine vinegar, cooking until dry, add the Madeira and reduce the liquid by half. Add the stock, bring to the boil, skim and simmer with the mushrooms for 1 hour.

Strain the stock, bring again to the boil and reduce to about 100ml/3½fl oz and a light consistency. Enrich the sauce with well-reduced bone stock (meat glaze), check the seasonings and keep warm.

Cook the pigeon breasts and garnish

Poach the parcels in boiling water for 10 minutes. Heat 2 tablespoons clarified butter and throw in the wild mushrooms, shallot, garlic, chives and 15g/½oz butter. Cook over high heat and season. Pile into the warmed pastry cases.

Presentation

Unwrap the breasts and slice into 5 pieces. Arrange in a semicircle on the plates with a puff pastry case at the top. Add the truffle to the sauce, whisking in the remaining butter, and spoon round the breasts.

My wine suggestion: a Volnay or a Fleurie.

TARTE SOUFFLEE A LA RHUBARBE AU COULIS DE FRAISES ET SORBET DE CITRON VERT

Rhubarb soufflé tart with strawberry and lime sorbet

Serves 4
500g/1lb rhubarb
500g/1lb strawberries
about 175ml/6fl oz stock syrup (page 253)
225g/8oz sugar
7g/¼oz butter
12 egg whites
2 tablespoons caster sugar plus icing sugar
4 tablespoons crème pâtissière (page 112)

For the sablé pastry
120g/4oz caster sugar
275g/10oz flour, sieved
225g/8oz butter
2 egg yolks

For the baked custard
300ml/½pt milk
1 vanilla pod, split
3 egg yolks
225g/8oz sugar
freshly grated nutmeg

For the lime sorbet and its decoration
6 limes, with zest thinly peeled
300ml/½pt stock syrup (page 253)
60g/2oz sugar
7g/¼oz butter

Make the sablé pastry tarts
Mix the sugar and flour, rub in the butter, add the egg yolks and mix to a smooth dough. Wrap in cling film; relax for at least 1 hour.
Roll out and line 4 ring moulds 10cm/4in across, making sure the sides are strong. Line with foil and beans; bake 7 minutes at 180°C/350°F/gas 4.
Make the baked custard filling
Bring the milk and vanilla pod to the boil. Mix the egg yolks, sugar and a little grated nutmeg and pour on the boiling milk, whisking all the time. Strain into a shallow ovenproof dish at least 20cm/8in across. Stand in a bain-marie and

cook in the oven at 200°C/400°F/gas 6 for about 40 minutes until set.
When cold, use a pastry cutter slightly smaller than the tarts to cut out 4 rounds to line the pastry cases. Arrange in the tarts.
Make the lime sorbet and lime julienne
Reserve the zest of 2 limes and cut the rest into tiny squares. Bring the juice to the boil, skim off any scum and strain. Add the lime zest squares. Add the syrup and turn into an ice cream maker or freeze in a freezer, beating several times.
Blanch the remaining zest, refresh in cold water and repeat this twice. Cut into thin julienne strips. In a small pan, boil the sugar, butter and 2 tablespoons water until reduced then add the julienne. Move the lime around in the syrup with a fork as it caramelises. Turn out on a plate to cool and separate the strands.
Make the strawberry coulis
Set aside 4 strawberries diced, and purée the rest, adding enough syrup to give a thickish sauce.
Prepare the rhubarb
Cut up half a stick of rhubarb into julienne shreds. There is no need to blanch it, but caramelise it, using 50g/2oz sugar, 7g/¼oz butter and 2 tablespoons water. Chop and cook the remaining rhubarb with 175g/6oz sugar but no water until tender. Purée then sieve.
Make the soufflés
Whisk the egg whites to soft peaks, then gently sprinkle with the caster sugar. Mix 4 tablespoons rhubarb purée with the crème pâtissière. Fold in the diced strawberries without crushing them. Stir in half the egg whites, then fold in the rest.
Assemble and bake the soufflés
Arrange a little caramelised rhubarb on top of the baked custard in each tart case. Carefully balance a metal ring on top of the previous ring. Fill with rhubarb soufflé. Bake at 180°C/350°F/gas 4 for 12 minutes or until done. Run a small sharp knife round inside the rings and remove.
Presentation
Dust the soufflés with icing sugar and score in a criss-cross pattern with a hot poker and arrange on the plates. Decorate each plate with pools of coulis and rhubarb purée, lime zest and a spoonful of lime sorbet.

My wine suggestion: an Eiswein – like the dessert it combines sweet and dry.

Pierre Koffmann

La Tante Claire

68-69 Royal Hospital Road, London SW3 telephone: 01 352 6045

In an era where chefs are also starring personalities, Pierre Koffmann is a great chef who does not want to go into the dining room. 'He just prefers to stay at the stove', says his wife, Annie Koffmann. Not a great talker at any time, he is very reluctant to come out front, for his talent flowers best in the kitchen. Born at Tarbes in the Pyrenees, his interest in food came from his mother and, more particularly, his grandmother, Camille, who was a great cook. After training at the local catering school, he went on to work in restaurants on the French Riviera, and in Lausanne and Strasbourg, none of them famous.

On his arrival in England he worked for the Roux brothers, first at Le Gavroche, then as head chef of the Brasserie Benoit (now Le Gamin in Old Bailey), where he met his wife. In 1972 he was asked to open and run the newly created Waterside Inn in Bray, where he gained one then two Michelin rosettes within two years.

An attempt to open a restaurant in the Pyrenees failed for lack of finance and he returned once more to London. Then in 1977 he opened La Tante Claire in Chelsea. It enjoyed an immediate success, and Michelin awards followed, the first rosette in 1978, the second in 1980. The expansion and refurbishment that this demanded was completed by 1985.

In his early years at La Tante Claire, the menu and his cooking moved from an emphasis on the cooking of South-west France towards the so-called nouvelle cuisine. He now sees the way forward as moving again towards those regional roots. The same recipes, he feels, can now be found everywhere, and what interests him is a cuisine that is purely personal.

MENU

GALETTE DE FOIE GRAS AUX ECHALOTES ROTIES
Duck foie gras with potato cakes and roast shallots

PIECE DE BOEUF D'ECOSSE AUX LEGUMES OUBLIES
Scotch steaks with old-fashioned vegetables

SUMMER PUDDING WITH BEAUJOLAIS

GALETTE DE FOIE GRAS AUX ECHALOTES ROTIES

Duck foie gras with potato cakes and roast shallots

Serves 4

4 slices fresh duck foie gras, 100g/3½oz each
12 shallots, all the same size
15g/½oz butter
salt and freshly ground black pepper
1 teaspoon oil

For the pomme darphin
1 large potato
4 tablespoons oil

For the Sauternes sauce
75cl bottle Sauternes
100g/3½oz cold butter, diced

Prepare the shallots and pancakes
Peel the shallots and put on a piece of foil large enough to enclose them. Top with the butter, season well and wrap them. Cook in the oven at 190°C/375°F/gas 5 until golden, calculating so they are ready when the foie gras is cooked: they will need about 20 minutes. Peel and wash the potato. Grate it finely on a mandolin then get rid of most of the water by squeezing it out in your hand.

Heat 1 tablespoon oil in a small 15cm/6in frying pan and add a quarter of the grated potato, spreading it out in the pan. Cook for 4-5 minutes on each side, pressing it down into the pan with a palette knife or fish slice, so it coheres to make a cake. Turn when crisp and golden on the underside and salt lightly. Keep warm and cook the remaining potato cakes in the same way.

Make the Sauternes sauce
Meanwhile make the sauce. Pour half the wine into a pan and boil to reduce to 2 tablespoons. Add the rest of the bottle and reduce by half. Whisk in the butter, a few pieces at a time, adding more before the first lot has melted.

Cook the foie gras
Season the slices of duck liver with salt and pepper then cook them briefly in a lightly oiled frying pan – for 1 minute on each side, until the slices are just pink in the middle.

Presentation
Arrange the potato cakes on hot plates, top each one with a slice of foie gras, arrange the shallots and pour the sauce round. Serve immediately.

My wine suggestion: a good Monbazillac.

Editor's note: The partnering of foie gras with a luscious sweet wine is in fashion once more. Until the end of the last century foie gras was often served at the end of a meal, where it could share the dessert wine.

PIECE DE BOEUF D'ECOSSE AUX LEGUMES OUBLIES

Scotch steaks with old-fashioned vegetables

Serves 4

4 fillet steaks, 175g/6oz each, 5cm/2in thick and tied round the middle
4 large Jerusalem artichokes
1 large swede
4 carrots
100g/3½oz pumpkin
salt and freshly ground black pepper

For the mustard cream sauce

1L/1¾pt clarified chicken stock (page 250)
100ml/3½fl oz single cream
made English mustard

Prepare the garnish

Wash and peel the vegetables, starting with the artichokes. Trim them to matching oval shapes. Cook in the chicken stock in a wide shallow pan until done but still crisp, about 20 minutes.

Meanwhile prepare the swede and carrots, cutting 2-3 identical shapes and sizes per person from both vegetables. Cook these in turn in the chicken stock until done but crisp and keep all the vegetables hot.

Poach the steaks and make the sauce

Poach the steaks in the chicken stock at a very gentle simmer for 8-10 minutes until cooked but still pink in the middle. Remove from the pan and keep warm.

Peel and add the pumpkin and let it boil until it falls to pieces in the stock, and the liquid has reduced to about 150ml/¼pt.

Add the cream and bring back to the boil. Purée the sauce in a blender, add mustard to taste then strain through a fine sieve.

Presentation

Remove the string from the steaks and season them lightly. Arrange them on hot plates, pour the sauce around them and divide the different vegetables between the plates.

My wine suggestion: a St-Emilion or St-Julien.

SUMMER PUDDING WITH BEAUJOLAIS

Serves 4

300ml/½pt beaujolais
400g/14oz red fruit: redcurrants, blackberries, blackcurrants
100g/3½oz sugar
200g/7oz mixed strawberries and raspberries
1 long rectangular brioche
double cream to serve

Marinate the fruit in beaujolais

Pour the beaujolais into a saucepan, add the redcurrants, blackberries and blackcurrants together with the sugar and cook over a very low heat for about 10 minutes (the fruit should remain whole). Add the strawberries and raspberries then leave to cool.

When cold, drain the fruit and reserve the juice.

Line the mould with brioche

Cut the brioche into even slices, about 1cm/½in thick. Soak them in fruit juice then use to line a loaf tin 850ml/1½pt in capacity. Keep enough brioche back to make the top of the pudding. Tip the fruit into the centre of the tin and cover with the remaining brioche slices. Cover the tin with a board that just fits inside the top and weight with a 1kg/2lb weight. Leave to stand in the refrigerator overnight.

Presentation

Turn the pudding out of the tin and cut 2 slices per person. Arrange on plates and serve with double cream.

My wine suggestion: any good champagne.

Michel and Albert Roux

THE WATERSIDE INN
Ferry Road, Bray-on-Thames telephone: 0628 20691

LE GAVROCHE
43 Upper Brook Street, London W1 telephone: 01 408 0881/499 1826

Two brothers, both with restaurants, is not uncommon: six Michelin rosettes between them makes them a phenomenon. Their start was unusual too. After an apprenticeship in patisserie (Michel was fourteen when he began), both Michel and Albert trained in the kitchens of private houses. Albert began at the British Embassy in Paris, where Michel joined him, before moving on to Mlle Cécile de Rothschild; he became her head chef.

It took twelve years for the brothers to achieve their ambition to own their own restaurant and they shrewdly chose England rather than France for the venture. Le Gavroche opened in 1967 with a high profile – a menu of 20-25 grande cuisine dishes.

Michel Roux's first medal came when he was a pastry apprentice. Increasingly others followed, including Best Pastry-cook of France in 1976. Of the two brothers, Michel tends to attract more attention, but Albert's restaurant, Le Gavroche, was the first to gain Michelin's highest accolade, in 1982. The award to the Waterside Inn followed three years later. The staff were originally all French, but now half are English.

The brothers have written two best-selling books, New Classic Cuisine *and* The Roux Brothers on patisserie. *They advise Marks and Spencer and British Airways on food. They own seven restaurants, including Le Poulbot and Le Gamin. Albert's latest interest is vacuum-packed food, served in the less expensive Rouxl Brittania chain of restaurants.*

MENU

FEUILLANTINE DE SAUMON ET LANGOUSTINES, CITRON VINAIGRETTE
Salmon and Dublin Bay prawns in aspic with lemon vinaigrette

SUPREME DE GROUSE VOILE AU PORTO
Breasts of grouse veiled in port

SOUFFLES CHAUDS AUX MIRABELLES
Hot mirabelle plum soufflés

ENSALADA DE BOGAVANTE DE ARZAK

Warm lobster salad, Arzak style

Serves 2

1 live lobster weighing 700g/1¹/₂lb
salt
60ml/2fl oz walnut oil
4 teaspoons sherry vinegar

For the pink mayonnaise
2 tablespoons freshly-squeezed orange juice
100ml/3¹/₂fl oz mayonnaise
1 tablespoon tomato ketchup
1 tablespoon single cream

For the salad
lettuce
escarole
watercress
white of leek
spring onions
chervil

Prepare and cook the lobster
Put the live lobster in a pan and cover with cold salt water and a lid. Bring to the boil. When boiling point is reached, turn down the heat and simmer for 5 minutes. Remove the lobster and let it cool slightly (lie it on its back to keep the juices in the shell). With a heavy knife, split the lobster in two across the tail top. Split the tail shell down the inside with scissors, cutting on the underside from the tail towards the head, and remove the shell, keeping the tail meat intact. Discard the stomach (which lies behind the eyes), but keep the liver from the head, chop and put in an ovenproof dish. Cut the tail flesh in neat rings and add to the chopped liver. Crack the claws carefully and remove the shell, trying to keep the flesh intact. Dress the lobster flesh with 2 tablespoons walnut oil and 2 teaspoons sherry vinegar.

Make the pink mayonnaise
Stir the orange juice into the mayonnaise and then the ketchup and cream alternately, tasting and watching the colour.

Presentation
Select enough lettuce, escarole and watercress to arrange attractively on two plates. Dress these in a bowl with 2 tablespoons walnut oil and 2 teaspoons sherry vinegar; add a little salt and toss. Then arrange on the waiting plates.
Flash the lobster in its vinaigrette briefly in the oven at 225°C/425°F/gas 9 for 2 minutes just to warm. Arrange the lobster slices neatly on the salad. Give the pink mayonnaise a stir, spoon over the meat and sprinkle with chopped leeks and a little spring onion. Garnish decoratively with the claws and a little chervil.

My wine suggestion: Txakolí Txomin Echaniz, which comes from Basque grapes, grown by the sea.

BEGUIAUNDI A LA PARRILLA CON SU TINTA Y PIMIENTOS DULCES

Grilled squid served with its ink and green peppers

Serves 4

4 squid, weighing about 400g/14oz each
3 shallots
3 tablespoons finely chopped parsley
300ml/¹/₂pt olive oil
4 green peppers
2 onions
1 sprig of rosemary

For the red wine and ink sauce
100ml/3¹/₂fl oz olive oil
1¹/₂ onions, chopped
2 green peppers, seeded and chopped
2 garlic cloves, finely chopped
2 tomatoes, sliced
2 sprigs of fresh rosemary
120ml/4fl oz red wine
the ink from the squid

Prepare the squid and leave to marinate
Use the tentacles to pull out the insides of the squid. Reserve the ink bags, being careful not to tear them. Cut off the tentacles above the eyes and reserve. Discard everything else from inside. Bend the squid body slightly to dislodge the

bony structure inside and pull it out. With salted hands rub off any skin. Trim the fins from either side of each squid and slit open the body down one side where the fins were attached.

Lay the bodies flat. With a knife held diagonally make a series of little cuts across the flesh then reverse the knife and cut again, leaving the flesh marked with diamonds. Repeat again on the other side.

Put the bodies and tentacles in a bowl with the chopped shallots, parsley and 250ml/9fl oz oil and leave to marinate for 12 hours.

Make the red wine and ink sauce

Heat 100ml/3½fl oz oil in a pan and add the chopped onions and peppers, finely chopped garlic, tomato slices and rosemary sprigs. Add the fins from the squid and leave to simmer gently until the onion is soft. Add the red wine and simmer slowly for 5 minutes.

Remove the squid fins and add the reserved ink. Then pass the liquid through a fine sieve into a clean pan.

Prepare the vegetable bed for the squid

Remove the stalks and seeds from the peppers and cut into fine julienne strips. Halve the onions and cut off both ends. Slice into similar julienne strips. Cook in boiling water for 3 minutes then drain very well and keep hot on a serving dish.

Grill the squid

Run a skewer through the inside of each squid and lay them on a hot grill, with the tentacles beside them, cut side towards the heat. When slightly browned, turn over and brown again just a little.

Presentation

To serve, place the squid on the green pepper bed and remove the skewers. Arrange the tentacles round them and pour the reheated sauce around the squid. Arrange a sprig of fresh rosemary on top.

My wine suggestion: a light red, since the sauce is made with red wine; we serve a Rioja Alta.

LECHE FRITA

Crisp-fried milk squares

Creamy on the inside, but crunchy outside, this traditional Basque pudding is now found all over Spain. It is sometimes served with jam or a fruit purée.

Serves 6

1L/1¾pt milk
50g/2oz cornflour
50g/2oz flour
200g/7oz caster sugar
1 vanilla pod, split
1 cinnamon stick
1 strip of lemon zest

For frying the squares
2 eggs, beaten
flour for coating
oil for frying
sugar for dusting

Prepare the squares ahead

Take enough milk from the measured quantity to make a paste with the cornflour, flour and sugar in a bowl. Heat the remaining milk with the vanilla pod, cinnamon stick and lemon zest and let it infuse for 10 minutes. Remove the vanilla pod, cinnamon and lemon zest. Stir a little hot milk into the paste then return to the pan. Put over low heat and simmer for 5 minutes, stirring constantly so that it does not burn or go lumpy.

Pour the mixture into a shallow bowl or tray so that it is about a finger's width deep. Leave until cold.

Fry the 'milk' and serve

Cut into squares, 2 per person. Dip into beaten egg then into flour, shaking off the excess. Heat the oil and fry the squares quickly until crisp and golden on each side. Dust with sugar and serve immediately.

My wine suggestion: a Trajinero de López Hermanos, from the Málaga region, made from the Pedro Xímenes grape, served very cold.

Josep Boix

Boix

Carretera Lérida-Puigcerdá, Martinet, 225724 Lérida telephone: 73 51 50 50

Josep Boix was born in the province of Lérida at Martinet, high in the Pyrenees, where his parents owned an inn; it had been in the family since the beginning of the century. His family background encouraged him to become a chef — one of his father's uncles had been chef at the Can Martin in Barcelona, one of the finest restaurants of its day. At the age of fourteen he started as an apprentice in Barcelona, at the Hostal de la Perdix, followed by the Hotel Colón. After his military service he married, and with his wife, Loles, opened the Hotel-Restaurant Boix in 1975. Her efforts and good taste in the dining room have been a tower of strength in a project for which they both evince great affection. The restaurant has large windows overlooking a little river and a cheerful outdoor terrace in what the owners charmingly describe as 'grand mountain style'.

Josep Boix's private passion is reading old cookery books. From these he feels he learns many secrets he didn't master in his youth. They also enforce his sense of belonging to the Catalan tradition, for he has always wanted to play a part in the renaissance of regional cooking. He credits some of his success to his local suppliers who can produce 'the rarest herbs, the freshest mushrooms and the best of seasonal vegetables'.

His greatest pleasure is 'when a new dish comes to fruition after days of preparation to make sure it is right in every way: taste, aroma colour and so on'. As a consequence, the restaurant Boix is rising in the national guides — 8/10 in Gourmetour, four suns from 1985 forward in the Guía del Viajero and the first Michelin rosette in 1983.

MENU

SALTEADO DE CIGALAS Y SETAS
Sauté of Dublin Bay prawns and wild mushrooms

PICHON A LA VINAGRETA
Pigeon served hot with vinaigrette, the old Catalan way

HELADO DE CANELA Y MANZANA
GOLDEN AL HORNO
Cinnamon ice cream with glazed Golden Delicious

SALTEADO DE CIGALAS Y SETAS

Sauté of Dublin Bay prawns and wild mushrooms

Serves 4

*12 large fresh Dublin Bay prawns (langoustines),
shelled
200g/7oz ceps
200g/7oz fairy ring mushrooms
200g/7oz chanterelles
200g/7oz St George's mushrooms (tricholoma)
2 tablespoons olive oil
white part of 4 spring onions, finely chopped
4 tablespoons goose fat
salt and freshly ground pepper
a few red leaves of radicchio to garnish
sprigs of parsley to garnish*

Wash the mushrooms in three changes of water and dry them gently. Heat the olive oil in a large pan and add the mushrooms. Sauté them over high heat until they become golden, adding the spring onion towards the end.
In another frying pan, fry the Dublin Bay prawn tails lightly in the goose fat, seasoning them with salt and pepper.

Presentation
Pile some of each type of mushroom on four plates and place three prawns on each one. Sprinkle a little goose fat on top. Garnish the plate with a few radicchio leaves, tucking in curly parsley sprigs.

My wine suggestion: Milmanda 1986 from Torres.

PICHON A LA VINAGRETA

*Pigeons served hot with vinaigrette,
the old Catalan way*

Serves 4

*4 young pigeons
salt and freshly ground black pepper
200ml/7fl oz olive oil
1 onion, sliced
750ml/1¼pt meat stock (see right)
200ml/7fl oz sherry vinegar
2 garlic cloves
1 bay leaf
10g/⅓oz black peppercorns
2 tablespoons meat glaze (page 251)*

*For the vegetables
1L/1¾pt water
100g/3½oz sugar
200g/7oz small pickling onions
200g/7oz new potatoes
olive oil
salt*

Clean the pigeons and season with salt inside and out, then truss them. Heat the oil in a casserole into which they fit snugly and put in the pigeons. Brown them, turning on all sides. Add the sliced onion, stock, vinegar, garlic, bay leaf and peppercorns. Cover the pan and simmer for about 2 hours until the pigeons are cooked and the stock reduced.
Put the water and sugar in a saucepan over low heat, stirring until the sugar has dissolved. Bring to the boil, add the pickling onions and cook for 15 minutes. Fry the new potatoes lightly in oil, shaking the pan so they do not stick.

Presentation
When the pigeons are cooked, remove from the casserole. Strain the sauce into a saucepan and add the meat glaze to this. Leave to reduce until a rich glaze is formed.
Meanwhile, untruss the pigeons and split them down the middle. Lay the halves on a large warmed platter. Arrange the glazed onions at one end of the dish and the fried potatoes at the other. Pour the sauce over the pigeons.

My wine suggestion: Campillo 1982 from Rioja.

CALDO DE CARNE

Meat stock

1kg/2¼lb veal bones, chopped
2 poultry carcasses
500g/18oz chopped veal
3 onions, chopped
2 carrots, chopped
1 leek, white part chopped
1 garlic clove, chopped
a handful of thyme
a handful of parsley

Wash the bones and poultry carcasses in cold water. Put everything in a big stockpot, cover with plenty of water and heat slowly, skimming off scum as it rises. Leave to simmer over a very low heat for 8 hours, then pass through a fine sieve.

Editor's note: Meat stocks vary considerably – bones are not obligatory, unless the stock is to be reduced later for meat glaze. A stock containing both bones and fresh meat is given on page 48. Alain Chapel bases his stock on 2kg/4½lb very fresh beef, cut from the top of the leg. This is simmered very slowly with 4 carrots, 3 leeks, 1 celery stalk, a garlic clove, 40g/1½oz coarse salt, 5g/⅙oz freshly ground black pepper in 5L/1gal water. Skim steadily until clear, simmering for 3 hours before straining.

HELADO DE CANELA Y MANZANA GOLDEN AL HORNO

Cinnamon ice cream with glazed Golden Delicious

Serves 4

4 Golden Delicious apples
60g/2oz granulated sugar
60g/2oz butter
60g/2oz caster sugar
30g/1oz ground cinnamon

For the cinnamon ice cream
250ml/9fl oz milk
15g/½oz ground cinnamon
5 egg yolks
75g/2½oz sugar
175ml/6fl oz double cream

Make the cinnamon ice cream
Bring the milk to the boil in a pan with the cinnamon. Meanwhile whisk the egg yolks and sugar together in a bowl. When the milk comes to the boil, pour it down on the egg yolks, whisking. Return to the saucepan and bring back to the boil, whisking all the while. As boiling point is reached, pour in the cream, whisking continually. Remove from the heat and cool.
When cold turn it into an ice cream machine – it will take about 35 minutes. Alternatively put in the freezer, beating several times before firm.

Prepare the glazed apples
Peel and core the apples and cut them into quarters, then simmer with the granulated sugar and water just to cover until cooked, about 15 minutes. Remove them immediately, pat them dry and cut each quarter into thin slices.
Arrange the apple slices on a baking tray generously greased with butter. Sprinkle the apples with a mixture of caster sugar and ground cinnamon and bake in an oven at 200°C/400°F/gas 6 for 5 minutes.

Presentation
Arrange the hot apple slices overlapping, in the shape of a cross, on each plate and then add a scoop of cinnamon ice cream to the centre.

My wine suggestion: a vintage champagne from Henry Abele.

Ramón Ramirez

EL AMPARO
Puigcerdá 8, 28001 Madrid telephone: 1 431 64 56

Ramón Ramirez is the holder of two Michelin rosettes, until recently Spain's highest award and shared by only five other Spanish restaurants. He was born in Málaga and a relationship with catering started only when he worked in England as a waiter for three years, to learn the language. He liked the business, but was unimpressed by the food — he thought he could do better. On his return to Madrid in 1976 he was appointed the kitchen manager at the Boqui, being opened by friends. He remained there until 1978.

At the beginning he learned by initiative and telephone calls to his aunt Gabrielle, a good cook and generous entertainer. However a visit to Les Prés d'Eugénie in 1977 so impressed him he became 'committed to modern cookery at the highest levels'. It was here he thought of opening El Amparo in Madrid, achieved in 1979. He also has a close friendship with Firmin Arrambide in French Basque country and regards him as a mentor. This led to an involvement with the Basque group, introducing nouvelle cuisine ideas and adapting them to the Spanish style. One of the young chefs who provided this impetus, Ramón Roteta, is working with him at El Amparo for two years.

His style has a definite Spanish base — Andaluz as well as Basque — and he has contributed substantially to making Spanish cooking known outside the country. In 1987, when he was thirty-three, El Amparo won its second Michelin rosette. With 19 out of a possible 20 from Gault Millau, it is acknowledged to be Madrid's second restaurant.

MENU

ROLLITOS DE LANGOSTO CON SALSA DE SOJA
Spring rolls with crawfish and soy butter

LUBINA AL TOMILLO Y COMPOTA DE TOMATE
Sea bass with thyme and a tomato compote

DATILES FRESCOS RELLENOS DE CHANTILLY CON MOUSSE Y HELADO DE ALMENDRA
Cream-filled dates with almond mousse and ice cream

Rollitos de langosto con salsa de soja

ROLLITOS DE LANGOSTO CON SALSA DE SOJA

Spring rolls with crawfish and soy butter

Serves 6

1.2kg/2½lb spiny rock lobsters or crawfish
2 carrots
2 leeks
6 spring roll wrappers, made with rice flour
20cm/8in square
oil for deep frying
parsley sprigs to garnish
optional vegetables to garnish:
broad beans and red pepper

For the soy butter
60ml/2fl oz soy sauce
120ml/4fl oz sherry vinegar
500g/1lb butter
salt and freshly ground black pepper
grated zest of 1 lemon

Prepare the spring rolls

Cut the carrots and leeks into small dice. Blanch in boiling water for 2 minutes then drain.
Shell the raw crawfish; this lobster-without-claws has all the meat in the tail. Cut the tails making 6 portions of about 60g/2oz.
Cut each spring roll wrapper into 4 squares. Divide a portion of crawfish between four, piling it across one corner of the wrapper, and add vegetables to each one. Roll to cover, turn the corners over the filling, and roll up.
Make the soy butter
Pour the soy sauce and sherry vinegar into a pan and boil until reduced by half. Beat the butter until soft and gradually beat in the warm liquid. Season with salt, pepper and grated zest.
Deep-fry the spring rolls and serve
Coat the base of 6 plates with soy butter.
Deep-fry the spring rolls in a basket in very hot oil, 6 at a time, for 2-3 minutes until golden. Drain on a cloth, then arrange the rolls in a star shape, garnishing with sprigs of parsley between each roll. In the restaurant we use small piles of fresh, podded broad beans in season, and garnish the spring rolls with diamonds of red pepper.

My wine suggestion: Albariño de Santiago Ruiz.

LUBINA AL TOMILLO Y COMPOTA DE TOMATE

Sea bass with thyme and a tomato compote

Serves 6

1.2kg/2½lb sea bass, cleaned
1kg/2lb tomatoes
2 small onions, chopped
olive oil for frying
salt and freshly ground black pepper
7 sprays of fresh thyme
chopped parsley

Blanch the tomatoes individually and quickly in boiling water then peel and cut in half. Remove the pips and cut into quarters.
Fry the chopped onions in a little olive oil over low heat. When they start to brown, add the tomato pieces. Leave for 10 minutes, then season with salt and pepper and one of the thyme sprays.
Remove the head and tail and fillet the sea bass, cutting each fillet into 3 portions. Season with salt. Fry in a flameproof dish over low heat, using very little oil and putting the fish into the pan skin side-up. Cook for 2 minutes. Turn skin side down and move to an oven at 180°C/350°F/gas 5. Cook for 4 minutes. In the restaurant we decorate the fish by holding a red-hot iron or skewer over it to make a diamond pattern.
pattern.
Meanwhile, cook 6 sprays of thyme briefly in hot oil.
Presentation
When the sea bass is ready, place it in the centre of a warmed platter and spoon the tomato sauce round it in a ring. Sprinkle with chopped parsley. Arrange the thyme sprays one on top of each piece of fish.

My wine suggestion: El Rosal.

DATILES FRESCOS RELLENOS DE CHANTILLY CON MOUSSE Y HELADO DE ALMENDRA

Cream-filled dates with almond mousse and ice cream

Serves 6

36 fresh dates
42 perfect raspberries or strawberries

For the almond ice cream
500ml/18fl oz milk, warmed
4 egg yolks
150g/5oz caster sugar
100g/3½oz ground almonds
60ml/2fl oz Amaretto
60ml/2fl oz whipping cream

For the cream chantilly
100ml/3½fl oz whipping cream
60g/2oz caster sugar

For the almond mousse
60g/2oz butter
100g/3½oz ground almonds
100g/3½oz sugar
2 eggs
60ml/2fl oz Amaretto

Make the almond ice cream
Warm the milk. Beat the egg yolks and sugar in a bowl until light and fluffy, then pour in the hot milk. Set the bowl over simmering water and stir until the custard thickens, being careful not to let it boil. Add the ground almonds and Amaretto and let it cool, stirring occasionally. When cold, whip the cream and stir in. Freeze in an ice cream machine, or in a freezer, beating several times before stiff.

Stuff the dates and make the mousse
Peel and stone the dates. Whip the cream with the sugar. Use a piping bag fitted with a starred nozzle to pipe the cream into the dates. Centre a berry in the cream on each one.
Make the mousse by creaming the butter with the ground almonds and sugar in a mixer. Add the eggs and Amaretto and mix well. Spread the almond mousse over the base of the 6 plates.

Presentation
Slip the plates under a medium grill, about 30cm/12in from the grill, for about 2 minutes. The mixture will brown and acquire something of a cakey texture: the plates will be very hot. Quickly arrange the dates on each plate in the form of a star, scooping almond ice cream into the middle of each one, and topping with another berry. Serve at once.

My wine suggestion: Celebration Cream sherry by Domecq.

Lubina al tomillo y compota de tomate

El Amparo

El Amparo

Dátiles frescos rellenos de chantilly con mousse y helado de almendra

José Monje

Via Veneto

Ganduxer 10, 08021 Barcelona telephone 3 200 72 44

José Monje is maître d'hôtel of Barcelona's leading restaurant; he believes his vocation is as great as that of any chef. As a child of twelve he left his village in the Lérida Pyrenees, to travel to the nearest city, Barcelona. Here he worked in a restaurant in the Plazo de Colón, filling refrigerators and washing dishes, beginning a career dedicated to Spanish food. A succession of dining rooms and kitchens followed until 1967, when the Via Veneto was launched. On opening day he was there as waiter and he is still there — in a different rôle! He is executive chef and became sole proprietor in 1980. The restaurant is decorated in the belle epoque style, appropriate in a city famous for its Modernist buildings. 'Like the cooking', he says, 'it is not unnecessarily sophisticated.'

Ostentatious dishes have disappeared in favour of authentic local cuisine, dishes that a smart restaurant would have disdained a dozen years ago — made with attention to detail and the very best produce that raise them to an art. He believes that 'the cooking should not cloak or overload the distinctive flavours of the ingredients'. Success was marked in 1969 by the award of a Michelin rosette and, in 1984, by the National Gastronomy prize. The kitchen is now in the talented hands of José Muniesa. He was spotted by his employer and sent for training to the best Basque chefs, to Switzerland and to Jacques Pic in Valence. He became head chef, aged twenty-five, in 1986. They work in enthusiastic union.

MENU

ERIZOS DE MAR DE CADAQUES GRATINADOS
Purée of sea urchins served from the grill

SALMON FRESCO ASADO AL HORNO CON MADERA DE PINO A LA MANTEQUILLA DE ESTRAGON
Salmon oven-smoked over pinewood with buttery tarragon sauce

BUNUELOS DE HOJALDRE RELLENOS DE CREMA CATALANA
Fried puffs filled with Catalan cream

ERIZOS DE MAR DE CADAQUES GRATINADOS

Purée of sea urchins served from the grill

Serves 4

72 sea urchins
15g/¹/₂oz butter
3 shallots, finely chopped
500ml/18fl oz double cream
salt
cayenne pepper
120ml/4fl oz brandy

Open the sea urchins by cutting each one round the middle with strong scissors. Scoop out the pink flesh with a teaspoon. Reserve 24 of the best looking half shells so they can be filled.

Melt the butter in a pan and fry the shallots gently until soft. Add the sea urchin flesh and leave for a minute or two, then pour in the cream and season with salt and cayenne. Leave for another minute over very low heat, then pass through a fine sieve.

Presentation

Arrange the best half shells on a baking tray. Warm the brandy, set it alight and pour into the waiting shells. Put the tray of shells into the oven (heated to 200°C/400°F/gas 6) and heat them for 3 or 4 minutes – this will just aromatise them.

Fill the shells with the sea urchin purée and put under a hot grill to heat through and just colour on top.

My wine suggestion: white Raimat Chardonnay, which comes from 'la terra firma', the Catalan wine growing region of Lérida, and is made exclusively from Chardonnay.

SALMON FRESCO ASADO AL HORNO CON MADERA DE PINO A LA MANTEQUILLA DE ESTRAGON

Salmon oven-smoked over pinewood with buttery tarragon sauce

Serves 4

4 fresh salmon steaks, 250g/9oz each
butter for greasing
a selection of steamed vegetables
oil for frying
a few saffron strands to garnish

For the salmon marinade
20g/²/₃oz sugar
100g/3¹/₂oz salt
100g/3¹/₂oz green pepper, finely chopped
2 bay leaves, crumbled
1 sprig of thyme

For the tarragon butter sauce
1 shallot
250g/9oz cold butter, cut into dice
250ml/9fl oz dry white wine
2 tablespoons finely chopped tarragon leaves
250ml/9fl oz fish stock (page 161)

About 6 hours beforehand, make the marinade and turn the salmon steaks in it.

Start the sauce

Chop the shallot very finely, sauté in a little butter until soft then add the white wine and tarragon leaves. Boil to reduce the liquid by two-thirds.

Add the fish stock and leave to reduce again for about 10 minutes: there should be about 150ml/¼pt. Strain out the shallot and tarragon and return to a clean pan.

Pine-smoke the salmon

Put a small container with pinewood sawdust into the oven and warm it while the oven heats to maximum temperature.

Wipe the pieces of salmon with a cloth and place on a baking tray lightly greased with butter. Bake the salmon in the oven for 10 minutes. Without actually catching fire, the aroma of pinewood will give the fish a pleasant flavour. Remove the skins from each piece of fish and keep the fish warm. Roll up the fish skins for garnish, neatening the edges where necessary.

Prepare the garnish and sauce

Steam small vegetables in season while the fish is cooking. Fry the rolls of fish skin in plenty of oil until very crisp, then drain on absorbent paper. Make the sauce. Put the reduced liquid over very low heat and whisk in the remaining butter, a little at a time, adding more lumps before the last ones lose their texture, so the sauce becomes very smooth and velvety.

Presentation

Divide the tarragon butter sauce between 4 plates and place the salmon steaks on top. Arrange steamed vegetables round them and top each steak with a crisp roll of skin and a couple of saffron strands.

My wine suggestion: drink the Chardonnay with both these courses.

BUNUELOS DE HOJALDRE RELLENOS DE CREMA CATALANA

Fried puffs filled with Catalan cream

These pastries are reminiscent of doughnuts, puffed in hot oil. The filling is a rich cinnamon custard and they are gorgeously presented on plates ringed with chocolate.

Serves 4
250g/9oz made weight puff pastry
1L/1¾pt olive oil for deep frying
250g/9oz milk chocolate
100g/3½oz icing sugar

For the Catalan cream
375ml/13fl oz milk
½ cinnamon stick
½ vanilla pod, split
strip of lemon zest
30g/1oz cornflour
5 egg yolks
120g/4oz sugar

Make the Catalan cream

Reserve 150ml/¼pt milk, then bring the rest to the boil with the cinnamon stick, vanilla pod and strip of lemon zest. Meanwhile make a paste from the cornflour and reserved milk and beat in the yolks and sugar.

Pour the hot milk on to the yolks, then return to the saucepan, stirring continuously with a wooden spoon over low heat until it returns to the boil. Remove from the heat, strain and leave until cold.

Make and fry the pastry puffs

Roll out the puff pastry to a thickness of about 4mm/⅛in and use a pastry cutter to cut circles about 4cm/1½in across. Heat the olive oil until very hot and fry the pastries, a few at a time, turning them gently until golden and really puffed up. Drain on a cloth and slash them on one side.

Presentation

Serve the pastries freshly fried, slightly warm or cold. Using a piping bag, fill each one with cold Catalan cream.

Cover the centres of four plates with the remaining custard and then paint the rims of the plates with melted milk chocolate – it makes life easier to do this before you start frying.

Place four *buñuelos* in the centre of each plate and sift icing sugar over them.

My wine suggestion: Grand Cru Cava of Juvé y Camps; made by the champagne method in Sant Sadurní de Noia, the celebrated Catalan region, Grand Cru is only made in exceptional years.

Pedro Subijana

AKELARRE

Barrio de Iguerdo, 20008 San Sebastián telephone 43 212 052

A Basque by birth, Pedro Subijana had decided on a chef's career by the age of seventeen, when he entered catering school in Madrid. Six years later the top pupil became a teacher himself; he is still interested in the next generation of cooks and is a consultant for the Basque School of Catering. After military service cooking for the Governor of Guipúzcoz, he became chef at the Mesón de Idiáquez in Tolosa – and married.

With a wife to take charge of the dining room, the couple embarked on a joint project: the Frontón Galarreta restaurant in Hernani. But the lure of Madrid, where the restaurant Zalacaín was just opening, proved too strong and he joined the team there. A year later he became head chef at the Hotel Irache in Estella, leaving in 1975, when a partnership was formed with the owners of the Akelarre restaurant in San Sebastián. He returned to his birth place, to run the restaurant whose reputation he has made.

One of the chefs most identified with Basque cooking and the new movement to rejuvenate Spanish cooking, he worked small 'stages' with Paul Bocuse and then with the Troisgros brothers. 'As time went on, I began to detest those anti-cuisine architectural displays in which the taste of the dish counts for nothing.' Aged twenty-nine, he won his first Michelin rosette and a year later, in 1979, the National Gastronomy prize for best chef. In 1980 he bought out his partners, to concentrate on the Akelarre. The Club des Gourmet recognised his achievement there by voting him the best chef in Spain, and a second Michelin rosette followed in 1983.

MENU

ENSALADA TEMPLADA CON PASTA, ANGULAS Y PIPARRAS
Warm salad with pasta, baby eels and pickled peppers

MERLUZA EN SALSA VERDE
Hake in green sauce

CANUTILLOS FRITOS CON INTXAURSALSA
Fried pastry horns with Basque walnut cream

ENSALADA TEMPLADA CON PASTA, ANGULAS Y PIPARRAS

Warm salad with pasta, baby eels and pickled peppers

Serves 4

200g/7oz elvers (minute threadlike baby eels)
1 garlic clove
1-2 tablespoons olive oil
8 piparras (small slim peppers, not hot), pickled in light vinegar
100g /3½oz tagliatelle
1-2 tablespoons clarified butter (page 23)
freshly ground black pepper
a few drops of lemon juice
a few drops of cider vinegar

A earthenware dish is traditional in the Basque country for elvers, (which are bought very briefly blanched). Rub the pot on the inside with the cut garlic clove. Throw in the elvers and season with a sprinkling of olive oil.

Cut the pickled peppers into small pieces about 1cm/½in square and mix with the elvers. Dress with a little vinegar from the pickle jar.

Cook the tagliatelle until *al dente* and drain. Toss it with a little clarified butter and season with ground pepper and a few drops each of lemon juice and cider vinegar.

Presentation

Spoon the dressed elvers into the centre of the dish. Arrange the dressed pasta round the outside and serve while it is still warm.

My wine suggestion: a light red wine, such as Remelluri 1983.

Editor's note: Angulas are a famous Basque speciality, so slim they seem like silver spaghetti. They can be caught in other countries too, but are rarely sold commercially, except in Spain, where they are very briefly blanched before sale. Occasionally they are found frozen, but these are less good. The dish could be attempted with lightly-cooked whitebait, if they are tiny enough, and different pickled pepper.

MERLUZA EN SALSA VERDE

Hake in green sauce

Serves 4

4 fillets of hake, about 120-150g/4-5oz each, with skin
16 hake cheeks (from either side of the head)
salt and a pinch of sugar
250ml/9fl oz water
100ml/3½fl oz oil plus 1 tablespoon
1 spring onion, chopped
1kg/2lb new peas in the pod (about 200g/7oz shelled)
3 garlic cloves, sliced
16 good-sized clams
1 tablespoon Txakolí or dry white wine
a handful of parsley, chopped and well chilled

Season the hake with salt and refrigerate.

Bring the water to the boil, season it with salt, sugar, a tablespoon of olive oil and the spring onion. When it boils, add the peas and simmer for 10 minutes, then remove from the heat.

Cook the hake

Put an earthenware pot – traditional for this dish – over an indirect heat (such as a trivet or heat-diffuser) or on the side of the hob. Pour in the oil and when it is warm, add the garlic. After a few seconds, when the garlic is nicely golden, pour off the oil and remove the garlic.

Return half the oil to the pot and set on a gentle heat again. Add the pieces of hake, skin side down, and the hake cheeks and clams, fitting them round the fish.

Hold the pot with both hands and carefully but constantly shake it in a circular movement, raising the temperature at the same time. Then turn over the hake, the hake cheeks and clams and continue shaking, adding the rest of the oil.

Add the peas and finish the sauce

Continue shaking, maintaining the heat, and add the drained peas (saving the liquid). The sauce will have thickened and become smooth. Add 2 small tablespoonfuls of the cooking water from the peas and another of white wine.

Bring to the boil, taking care that the fish does not stick. Sprinkle the dish with lots of **parsley**.

My wine suggestion: Txakolí, a dry white from a grape that grows by the sea locally.

CANUTILLOS FRITOS CON INTXAURSALSA

Fried pastry horns with Basque walnut cream

Intxaursalsa is a Christmas Eve dessert in the Basque country, so it gives this dish a special festive air.

Serves 6
120ml/4fl oz milk
60ml/2fl oz oil
a few drops of vinegar
a small pinch of salt
250g/9oz flour
flavourless oil for deep-frying

For the walnut cream
500ml/18fl oz milk
100g/3½oz sugar
½ cinnamon stick
small strip of lemon zest
100g/3½oz shelled walnuts
30g/1oz fresh bread without a crust, slightly toasted
85ml/3fl oz single cream

For the confectioners' custard
2 egg yolks, or 1 egg
60g/2oz sugar
20g/⅔oz flour or cornflour, or a mixture of the two
250ml/9fl oz milk
a piece of vanilla pod
a strip of lemon zest
15g/½oz butter, in tiny pieces

Prepare the walnut cream
Bring the milk to the boil with the sugar, cinnamon stick and lemon zest. Grind the walnuts to powder in a mortar or with a rolling pin on a marble table. (In a food processor be careful not to overgrind, or they turn oily.)
Add the walnuts to the milk and simmer for 30 minutes.
Grate the bread and add the crumbs. Simmer for a further 30 minutes.
Finally add the cream and simmer again for 5 minutes. Leave until cold, but remove the cinnamon stick and lemon zest before serving.

Make the confectioner's custard
Put the yolks in a bowl and beat them with a wooden spoon, adding the sugar and flour and/or cornflour. Beat in a little of the milk to make a smooth paste. Bring the remaining milk to the boil with the vanilla pod and lemon zest. Stir into the paste a little at a time. Return to the saucepan and cook over medium heat, stirring constantly. A wooden spoon is better for this job than a metal one (especially if the pan is made of aluminium), which could give an off taste and colour to the custard.
When thick, remove from the heat, pour into a bowl and leave to cool. Dot the surface with butter to stop a skin forming. Give the custard a thorough stirring, incorporating the butter, before chilling in the refrigerator.

Make the pastry and model the horns
Put the milk, oil, vinegar and salt in a bowl. Add the flour a little at a time and mix in until the dough is smooth but not hard. Wrap it in cling film and leave to rest in the refrigerator for 30 minutes. Oil about 20 metal cornet moulds.
Roll out the dough as thinly as possible on a lightly floured surface. Cut strips measuring 2cm/¾in across by 20cm/8in long. Starting at the tip of the cone, wrap the strips round the mould, just overlapping the pastry with each new layer.

Fry the pastry horns
Heat oil for deep frying. When very hot put the pastry horns in a basket, a few at a time. Fry until golden all over and very crisp, but this is not a flaky pastry, so they will not float or puff up. In hot oil they will take 3 minutes.
Remove in the basket, drain well on a cloth to free from oil. Carefully removing the metal moulds when cool enough to handle. Fry the next batch.
Use a piping bag to fill the fresh pastry horns with cold confectioners' custard.

Presentation
Serve the custard-filled *canutillos* accompanied by the cold walnut cream. They are rather rich, but one can probably eat 3 without indigestion.

My wine suggestion: Santo Domingo de Gonzáles Byass – a typical muscat, serve it chilled.

Benjamín Urdiain

ZALACAÍN

Alvarez de Baena 4, 28008 Madrid telephone 1 261 1079

Only one chef in Spain holds three Michelin rosettes. The man who made this breakthrough for Spanish cooking modestly thinks of himself as advancing a tradition of regional food. Benjamín Urdiain was born to a farming family in Ciordia-Navarra in the lush green Navarre countryside, south of the Basque region, in a town proud of its good cooks. His start was local but his training was purely classical. At the age of sixteen he went to France to learn cookery and acquired his enthusiasm for the profession. For several years he trained in various establishments in south-west France and ended up in Paris, where he worked in the kitchens of the Plaza Athenée.

On his return to Spain he worked in a couple of Basque restaurants. Then in 1973 he moved to Madrid at the request of a childhood friend, Jesús María Oyarbide, who was opening a new restaurant with the Basque name of Zalacaín. He is still executive chef of the restaurant, carrying it to fame by gaining two Michelin rosettes in 1978.

A man in love with his profession, who reads anything to do with his job, his own cooking nevertheless has strong local ties. He is convinced that the way forward for Spanish cuisine is to look for inspiration to the traditional village foods of peasant cooking, often neglected as too humble, and changing season by the season. His reward has been the National Gastronomy prize in 1981, and the third Michelin rosette in 1987.

MENU

**GAZPACHO AL VINAIGRE DE JEREZ AL
ESTILO DE ZALACAIN**
*Gazpacho with sherry vinegar
the Zalacaín way*

**HOJA DE COL RELLENA DE OCA A LAS
TRUFAS**
Cabbage leaves stuffed with goose and truffles

**GRATINADO DE MANDARINAS Y
FRAMBUESAS AL JEREZ**
Gratin of mandarin oranges and raspberries with sherry

Gazpacho at Zalacaín

Hoja de col rellena de oca a las trufas

Gratinado de mandarinas y frambuesas al jerez

GAZPACHO AL VINAIGRE DE JEREZ AL ESTILO DE ZALACAIN

Gazpacho with sherry vinegar the Zalacaín way

Originally an iced Moorish soup, transformed by the introduction of tomatoes, every province in Spain has a summer version of *gazpacho*. Here is mine, which contains mayonnaise and sherry vinegar.

Serves 8

1.5kg/3lb ripe tomatoes
200g/7oz onions
200g/7oz green peppers
400g/14oz cucumber
1 small garlic clove
200g/7oz crustless bread
1 small red pepper
½ lemon
2 tablespoons sherry vinegar
350ml/12fl oz olive oil
350ml/12fl oz cold water
15g/½oz salt
60ml/2fl oz mayonnaise
salt and freshly ground black pepper

For the garnishes, a choice from:
bread with the crusts removed and cut into small cubes
oil for frying (optional)
onion, finely chopped
green pepper, finely chopped
tomatoes, blanched, peeled, seeded and the flesh finely chopped
cucumber, peeled, seeded and the flesh finely chopped

Prepare the vegetables and marinate them
Chop the tomatoes (with the skin and seeds) and the onions and put them in a very large bowl. Remove stalks and seeds from the green pepper and chop and add to the bowl.
Skin the cucumber, slice in half lengthways and scoop out the seeds with a teaspoon and discard. Chop and add to the bowl.
Chop the garlic finely, the bread more coarsely and treat the red pepper like the green one. Squeeze the lemon juice over them all.

Add the sherry vinegar, the olive oil and water and salt and leave to macerate for 12 hours.

Prepare the garnishes
The amount and number of the garnishes is a matter of taste, but at the Zalacaín we offer a choice of the following: bread cubes (which may be fresh or fried till crisp and drained); chopped onion, green pepper, tomato flesh and cucumber. All are arranged in separate bowls and chilled before serving, then are presented on a serving tray so each guest may make a choice.

Complete the iced soup
Purée the whole mixture in a blender or food processor and add the mayonnaise. Press through a sieve to give a smooth texture and remove skins and pips. Check the seasonings and chill thoroughly. The soup must be served very cold. The recipe makes about 2L/3½pt, but servings are generous in Spain. The soup will also keep well for a second day.

My wine suggestion: don't serve a wine – it would be spoiled by the vinegar. Drink water instead.

HOJA DE COL RELLENA DE OCA A LAS TRUFAS

Cabbage leaves stuffed with goose and truffles

Serves 6

300g/11oz raw goose flesh off the bone
4 eggs
100g/3½oz truffles, chopped
200ml/7fl oz goose stock (page 109)
200ml/7fl oz whipping cream
½ teaspoon salt
6 green cabbage leaves
10g/⅓oz butter
white pepper
extra truffle to garnish (optional)

Stuff the cabbage leaves

Mince the goose flesh then mix in the eggs, 40g/1½oz of the truffle, 100ml/3½fl oz of goose stock and the cream to make a wet mixture. Season with salt.

Grease six moulds about 150ml/¼pt capacity. Trim the cabbage leaves at the stalk end and blanch quickly in rapidly boiling water. Drain well. Fit them into the moulds, leaving enough hanging over the edge to fold over the top. Spoon in the goose mixture and fold over the leaves gently to cover the tops.

Bake and make the truffle sauce

Stand the moulds in a bain-marie and pour in boiling water to come halfway up the sides. Bake in an oven heated to 120°C/235°F/gas ½ for 15 minutes.

Mix the remaining goose stock with the chopped truffles and bring gently to the boil.

Presentation

Turn each stuffed cabbage leaf out on to a warm plate and pour the sauce over the top.

My wine suggestion: Contino 1981.

GRATINADO DE MANDARINAS Y FRAMBUESAS AL JEREZ

Gratin of mandarin oranges and raspberries with sherry

Serves 6

300g/11oz peeled mandarin segments
480g/17oz raspberries
200ml/7fl oz whipping cream
30g/1oz caster sugar
100ml/3½fl oz confectioners' custard (see below)
60ml/2fl oz fino sherry

Whip the cream with the sugar then stir into the confectioners' custard. Add the sherry and stir, taking care to keep the mixture light and not to lose the air in it.

Arrange the orange segments attractively on serving plates – we do this in 3 circles of differing size – and cover with the cream.

Heat the grill at maximum power for a good 10 minutes. Just before serving, put in the plates and grill until golden. Decorate with raspberries.

My wine suggestions: Pedro Xímenes – a grape and a luscious wine from the south.

CREMA PASTELERA

Confectioners' custard

250ml/9fl oz milk, boiling
1 vanilla pod, split
4 egg yolks
75g/2½oz sugar
30g/1oz flour, sifted

Bring the milk to the boil with the vanilla pod. Cream the yolks and sugar together and gently fold in the flour; mix to a smooth paste. Whisking rapidly, add the hot milk. Return to the saucepan and cook over a low heat without boiling, whisking until smooth and creamy – the mixture thickens in patches. Cool, stirring occasionally.

Editor's note: crème pâtissière in French, *crema pasticcera* in Italian, this custard never curdles and is firm enough to support fruit, or pipe.

Germany

*Sausage and sauerkraut,
beer and boiled dumplings –
now the hearty German kitchen
has been updated. A new
elegance and lightness has
transformed traditional food*

Peter Wehlauer

Burg Windeck
Kappelwindeckstrasse 104, 7580 Bühl-Baden telephone: 7223 23671

A butcher's boy turned cook, a trained hotel manager and now a starring chef, Peter Wehlauer started his varied training in 1959, aged nineteen. He was lucky enough in his first job, at the Schweizer Hof in Berne, to learn from Ernesto Schlegel, one of Switzerland's great chefs and gourmets, who had a decisive influence on him. The Palace hotel in Corfu followed, a spell learning hotel management, then back to cooking, as head rôtisseur at the Breidenbacher Hof in Düsseldorf. He spent seven years as head chef of the Miramare Beach hotel in Rhodes. During this time he did 'stages' at the Dorchester in London, the Meurice in Paris and the Carlton in St Moritz. Another role model was Alfred Walterspiel, who was famed for introducing French cooking to München in the 1920s. Peter Wehlauer married his great-niece Marianne, herself well versed in the hotel business. He returned to Germany, as chef at the Parkhotel Wehrle, at Triberg, but decided in 1978 it was time to own his own restaurant, and became proprietor of the Burg Windeck at Bühl. A gabled building on the old castle site, the view made it a popular tourist destination. Here he developed his own style, his creative imagination applying the principles of nouvelle cuisine *to old recipes. Two Michelin rosettes were awarded in 1982 and the following year the coveted Silver Owl, for particular merit in German* nouvelle cuisine. *'Cooking and eating is part of German culture,' he says and he has made several trips to China and the United States, demonstrating.*

MENU

WACHTELMOUSSE MIT KARTOFFEL-TRÜFFEL-SALAT
Quail mousse with potato and truffle salad

MIGNONS VOM KALBSFILET MIT LAUCHKRUSTE UND BLATTSPINAT MIT MORCHELN
Veal mignons in a leek crust with spinach and morels

WARMER ZWETSCHGENTARTE MIT ZIMTEIS UND ARMAGNACSABAYON
Warm plum puffs with ice and Armagnac sabayon

For the almond mousse
*60g/2oz butter
100g/3¹/₂oz ground almonds
100g/3¹/₂oz sugar
2 eggs
60ml/2fl oz Amaretto*

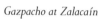

WACHTELMOUSSE MIT KARTOFFEL-TRUFFEL-SALAT

Quail mousse with potato and truffle salad

Serves 5

5 quails
salt and freshly ground black pepper
40g/1½oz butter
250ml/9fl oz brown chicken stock (page 250)
100ml/3½fl oz white port
100ml/3½fl oz Armagnac
3 leaves gelatine
75g/2½ oz pâté de foie gras
75ml/2½fl oz whipping cream
a selection of leaves from lettuce, cabbage lettuce, frisée,
lambs' lettuce and watercress
vinaigrette to dress (see below)

For the potato and truffle salad
10 small salad or new potatoes
1½ tablespoons cider vinegar
85ml/3fl oz olive oil
salt and freshly ground black pepper
2½ teaspoons tiny dice of shallots
2½ teaspoons diced leek white, the same size as the shallot
50g/1¾oz fresh Périgord truffle

Make and chill the quail mousse
Season the quails with salt and black pepper from the mill. Heat the butter and fry the quails, turning them until coloured on all sides and cooked through – 8-10 minutes.
Strip all the meat from the bones and keep the meat warm. Return all the bones to the pan and add the brown stock. Boil to reduce to 100ml/3½fl oz, then strain out the bones. Let the stock settle then skim off all fat.
Break up the gelatine leaves and soak in a little water for 5 minutes. Add the gelatine to the hot stock, stirring well until dissolved.
Add the quail meat to the stock with the white port and the Armagnac. Press the mixture through a sieve.
Sieve the pâté de foie gras into the quail mousse then mix it in, stirring well. Whip the cream to soft peaks and fold into the mousse.
Rinse out a mould 15 x 8 x 7cm/6 x 3½ x 3in with cold water and put in the mousse, tapping it on the work surface to make sure it has settled into the corners. Chill for at least 2 hours.

Make the potato salad and marinate
Use a small knife to 'turn' the potatoes – trimming them all to an identical shape and size. Boil in salted water until cooked but still firm. Drain and slice while still warm. Mix the vinegar and oil and season well. Dress the potatoes while still warm and leave to marinate.

Presentation
Ease a knife inside round the mould then turn out the quail mousse and cut 5 slices. In the restaurant we use a 10cm/4in high cutter, 5cm/2in diameter, which gives little high towers of mousse, which look very elegant. Dress your chosen salad leaves with vinaigrette and arrange on 5 plates. Centre the quail mousse on each salad.
Sprinkle the *brunoise* – tiny dice – of shallots and leeks over the potato salad then carefully grate fresh truffle on top. Mix all the ingredients gently, then arrange the potato and truffle salad on the mixed leaves.

My wine suggestion: Britzinger Rosenberg 1985 from one of Baden's classical white Burgundy grapes; this year the grapes were picked as Spätlese, and it is a big-bodied, aristocratic wine of stimulating acidity.

VINAIGRETTE

120ml/4fl oz olive oil
2 tablespoons white wine vinegar
salt and freshly ground black pepper
½ teaspoon Dijon mustard (optional)

Whisk all the ingredients together with a fork to emulsify them. Use only a small amount of vinegar in the dressing of salads that are to be served with wine.

MIGNONS VOM KALBSFILET MIT LAUCHKRUSTE UND BLATTSPINAT MIT MORCHELN

Veal mignons in a leek crust with spinach and morels

Serves 5

10 filets mignons of veal, each 75g/2½oz
salt and freshly ground black pepper
Dijon mustard
1 leek
flour to coat
120g/4oz butter
spinach baked with morels to serve
gratin dauphinoise, to serve

For the Madeira sauce
200ml/7fl oz brown bone stock (page 178)
100ml/3½fl oz dry Madeira
30g/1oz butter, diced

For the spinach baked with morels
100g/3½oz fresh morels
60g/2oz butter, half of it diced
1 tablespoon finely chopped shallot
100ml/3½fl oz Noilly Prat
100ml/3½fl oz white chicken stock (page 96)
120ml/4fl oz whipping cream
1 tablespoon hollandaise sauce (page 157)
1kg/2lb spinach, washed and trimmed
salt and freshly ground black pepper
juice of 1 crushed garlic clove

Make the spinach and morel dish

Wash the morels carefully and trim. Heat 30g/1oz butter in a pan large enough to hold the morels and fry the shallot until softened. Add the Noilly Prat and reduce to about 1 tablespoon. Add the white stock and the cream (keeping back 1 tablespoon cream for finishing the sauce). Add the morels and simmer for 2 minutes.

Remove the morels from the sauce with a slotted spoon and keep them warm. Season the sauce to taste and whisk in 30g/1oz diced butter. Fold in the hollandaise and 1 tablespoon whipped cream. From this point the sauce must not boil again, or it will curdle. Return the morels to the sauce.

Blanch the spinach in a large pan of lightly salted boiling water and drain well. Season with salt and pepper to taste and the crushed garlic clove. Put it in a heatproof dish.

When nearly ready to serve, pour the morels and cream sauce over the top of the spinach and put under the grill until very hot.

Cook the filets mignons of veal

On one side of the veal make a series of parallel cuts, several millimetres deep and repeat in the other direction to make diamonds. Season well and coat with mustard.

Dice the white of leek, making a *brunoise* — tiny cubes about 3mm/⅛in square. Scatter ½ tablespoon diced leek on to the cut side of each mignon and press in well. Coat with flour.

Heat the butter and fry the mignons, leek side down for 2-3 minutes until the coating is crisped. Turn the veal mignons over and then bake them in the oven at 200°C/400°F/gas 6 until cooked through, about 6 minutes.

Make the Madeira sauce

Put the brown bone stock and Madeira in a pan and boil until reduced to 200ml/7fl oz. Whisk in the butter dice.

Presentation

Serve 2 filets mignons on each plate, crusty side up, surrounded by a pool of Madeira sauce and accompanied by baked spinach with morels and a gratin dauphinoise.

My wine suggestion: Affentaler 1983, a red Spätburgunder; this is Baden's red wine *par excellence,* with a robust Burgundy bouquet and marked woody flavour, distinguished by a fine dryness.

WARMER ZWETSCHGENTARTE MIT ZIMTEIS UND ARMAGNACSABAYON

Warm plum puffs with ice and Armagnac sabayon

Serves 5

*350g/12oz made puff pastry
flour for dusting
500g/1lb plums, preferably Zwetschgen
1½ tablespoons melted butter
3 tablespoons caster sugar mixed with a good pinch
cinnamon
icing sugar*

For the marzipan cream
*250ml/9fl oz milk
30g/1oz marzipan, crumbled
10g/⅓oz caster sugar
10g/⅓oz cornflour
2 egg yolks*

For the cinnamon ice cream
*500ml/18fl oz milk
2 sticks of cinnamon
85g/3oz caster sugar
3 egg yolks*

For the Armagnac sabayon
*5 egg yolks
5 teaspoons sugar
100ml/3½fl oz Armagnac
3 tablespoons whipped cream*

Make the marzipan cream

Heat the milk with the crumbled marzipan and stir together. Beat the sugar, cornflour and egg yolks together with a wooden spoon until smooth. Strain in the boiling milk then return to the pan. Bring to the boil, stirring, then cool in a bowl inside another one containing water and ice. (There will be a little leftover marzipan cream from this recipe.)

Make the cinnamon ice cream

Heat the milk with the cinnamon sticks. Beat together the sugar and yolks. Strain in the boiling milk and skim the liquid. Return to the pan and cook over low heat, preferably over simmering water, stirring until the custard will coat the back of the spoon. Leave to cool, then freeze in an ice cream maker, or alternatively, freeze in a freezer, beating several times before the ice cream is stiff.

Make and bake the plum puff pastries

Roll out the puff pastry on a lightly floured surface to 4mm/⅙in thick and cut 5 discs with a 12cm/5in crinkle-cut biscuit cutter.

Prick each one with a fork, then coat with a spoonful of marzipan cream.

Stone the plums neatly and cut into crescent-shaped slices. Cover the puff pastry rounds with a closely-packed layer of plum slices, arranging them in circles.

Sprinkle a few drops of melted butter over each one then sprinkle with cinnamon sugar. Bake in an oven at 220°C/425°F/gas 7 for about 8 minutes, or until nicely puffed and hot.

Make the Armagnac sabayon

Put the egg yolks, sugar and Armagnac in a bowl which fits over a pan of simmering water. Whisk until the mixture thickens and greatly increases in volume; when ready it should hold the marks of the whisk. Fold in the whipped cream.

Presentation

Spoon the warm Armagnac sabayon over 4 warmed plates. Dust the pastries with icing sugar and centre them, with a scoop of cinnamon ice cream on each one.

My wine suggestion: Käfersberger Andreasberg 1976, a Beerenauslese wine from Ortenau.

Gerhard Gartner

GALA

Monsheimsalle 44, 5100 Aachen telephone: 241 1530 13

'A whole calf's head, served by my mother, an excellent cook' is the childhood memory that stirs Gerhard Gartner most: he would like to see a greater awareness of traditional German recipes. Yet he was one of the first to introduce nouvelle cuisine to Germany, adapting it to German needs, and his Restaurant Gala is now one of German's top ten.

He always knew he wanted to be a chef. His grandfather cooked at London's Savoy and his uncle was equally celebrated at the Hotel Billo in Moscow. An apprenticeship in Münich at the Sonnenhof was followed by work in Frankfurt, Brussels, Münich and, outside Europe, in Izmir in Turkey. During the five years he spent at the Amsterdam Hilton – the group's youngest executive chef – he prepared the wedding banquet for Queen Beatrix and won a gold medal for the Dutch team at the 1968 Cookolympiade in Frankfurt.

In 1970, when he was thirty-one, he took over the Hotel Meindelei in Bayrischzell; it soon attracted a Michelin rosette. Eight years later he moved to Aachen, buying the restaurant in the gardens of the classical casino. The Gala is named after Salvadore Dali's wife and eight of the artist's paintings on goatskin hang there. The interior is art nouveau – the tables by Charles Rennie Mackintosh, the chairs by Hoffmann of the Viennese Workshops, while thousands of glass beads make up the modern chandeliers.

Gerhard Gartner is a champion of fine German cuisine. There is a boldness and youthful originality about his cooking; the dishes are logical in their composition and both beautiful and natural in arrangement. The second Michelin rosette was awarded in 1982.

MENU

ZANDERFILET MIT JASMINBLUTEN
Fillets of zander with jasmine blossom

KALBSLEBERSTEAK MIT ROTER ZWIEBELMARMELADE UND SENFSAUCE
Calf's liver with red onion marmalade and mustard sauce

TRAUBENCREPES ALEXANDRA
Caramelised grape pancakes Alexandra

ZANDERFILET MIT JASMINBLUTEN

Fillet of zander with jasmine blossom

Serves 2

2 zander fillets, each 150g/5oz (or substitute perch,
see note, page 177)
100ml/3½fl oz fish stock (page 161)
3 jasmine blossoms
15g/½oz smoked bacon
30g/1oz celery
60g/2oz cucumber, halved, seeded and peeled
15g/½oz butter
salt and freshly ground black pepper
a few drops of garlic juice
100ml/3½fl oz brown bone stock (page 178)
1 teaspoon Noilly Prat
20g/⅔oz beurre manié, made by mashing equal
quantities of butter and flour to paste
3 tablespoons hollandaise sauce (see right)
a few chives, finely chopped

Poach the fish and fry the garnish

Lay the fillets flat in a pan in which they just fit and pour in the cold fish stock. Add the jasmine flowers. Bring the liquid to simmering, then cover, turn down the heat and poach gently until you judge them just to be cooked and lightly glazed – the time will depend on their thickness. Drain, reserving the fish stock, and keep the fish hot.

Finely shred the bacon, celery and cucumber to make a julienne. Sauté in the butter until cooked but still crisp. Season with salt, pepper and garlic.

Make the sauce

Strain the fish stock into a saucepan, add the brown bone stock and boil until reduced to 175ml/6fl oz. Add the Noilly Prat and stir in the beurre manié in little pieces, bring gently back to the boil, stirring, and cook for 1-2 minutes.

Fold in the hollandaise sauce. Do not allow the sauce to boil from this point on, or it will separate.

Presentation

Transfer the zander fillets to 2 warmed plates, sprinkle with the bacon and vegetables and top with the sauce. Garnish with finely chopped chives.

My wine suggestion: Oberemmeler Karlsberg, a dry Riesling from the Saar – even recent vintages are extremely elegant.

HOLLANDAISE SAUCE

120g/4oz unsalted butter
2 egg yolks
salt
lemon juice to taste

Clarify the butter by heating it until it froths. Let the butter cool until the scum subsides, then pour the oil from off the top of the sediment. In a bowl that will fit on a pan of simmering water whisk the yolks until creamy and thick enough to hold the marks of the whisk. Off the heat whisk in the warm butter, a little at first as you would for mayonnaise, then faster as the sauce thickens. Season to taste with salt and lemon juice.

KALBSLEBERSTEAK MIT ROTER ZWIEBELMARMELADE UND SENFSAUCE

Calf's liver with red onion marmalade and mustard sauce

Serves 2

*350g/12oz calf's liver, cut in one thick slice
from the centre of a small liver, trimmed
15g/½oz butter
cooked noodles, to serve
parsley, finely chopped*

*For the onion marmalade
3 large red onions, finely sliced
30g/1oz butter
salt and freshly ground black pepper
1 tablespoon wild-flower honey
350ml/12fl oz red Lemberger wine
1 lemon*

*For the mustard sauce
500ml/18fl oz brown bone stock (page 178) or other
well-flavoured stock
500ml/18fl oz double cream
1 tablespoon medium-hot mustard
½ teaspoon strong mustard
500ml/18fl oz dry white German wine
30g/1oz butter, diced*

Make the red onion marmalade
Cook the sliced onion in the butter over a low heat until transparent – do not let it colour. Season with salt and pepper and stir in the honey and wine.
Cover and transfer to the oven at 150°C/300°F/gas 2. Cook until the sauce has the consistency of marmalade – about 45 minutes. Check occasionally that it is not burning. Season to taste with lemon juice.
Make the mustard sauce
Stir all the ingredients for the mustard sauce together in a saucepan. Over low heat reduce the liquid by one-third. Just before serving, whisk in the cold, diced butter.
Cook the liver briefly
Heat the butter in a frying pan and slowly seal the calf's liver in butter over low heat, about 1 minute each side. Turn off the heat and leave the liver to continue cooking in the pan; the liver should be pale pink all the way through, which takes about 5 minutes. (This method is not practical on solid plate or coiled ring electric cookers.)

Presentation
Slice the liver thinly and arrange in overlapping slices on 2 warmed plates. Serve with red onion marmalade and mustard sauce, accompanied by noodles, topped with parsley.

My wine suggestion: Neipperger Schlossberg; unique to Württemberg, this deep coloured wine comes from the Lemberger grape.

TRAUBENCREPES ALEXANDRA

Caramelised grape pancakes Alexandra

My daughter Alexandra is head waitress at the Gala, and this grape pancake, with its aroma of grape spirit, is named for her.

Serves 6

1kg/2lb black or white dessert grapes
9 tablespoons melted butter
250g/9oz icing sugar, sifted
150ml/¼pt crème fraîche (page 250)
200ml/7fl oz Trester, marc or grappa
single cream to serve
caster sugar to serve

For the pancake batter
250g/9oz flour, sifted
5 eggs
250ml/9fl oz milk
2 tablespoons melted butter
60ml/2fl oz whipping cream

For the tonka bean ice cream
¼ tonka bean, grated (see note)
750ml/1¼pt milk
6 egg yolks
150g/5oz sugar

Start the tonka bean ice cream ahead
Grate the tonka bean and add to the milk in a pan; bring to simmering. Whisk the egg yolks well with the sugar, then slowly add the hot milk, whisking continually. Return the mixture to the pan.

Set the mixture over very low heat – or over simmering water – and whisk continually until it thickens, without allowing the mixture to boil. Strain into a bowl and leave until cold.

If you prefer a softer ice cream, add 1-3 extra yolks and an extra 15g/½oz sugar. Transfer to an ice cream maker, or alternatively, freeze in a freezer, beating several times before the mixture is stiff. For a richer ice cream, fold in 60ml/2fl oz lightly whisked whipping cream before the ice cream is fully frozen.

Make the pancake batter
Put the flour in a bowl, make a well in the centre, add the eggs and beat the yolks and whites together. Work the flour systematically into the eggs, a little at a time to avoid lumps. Beat until smooth then beat in the melted butter – this helps to prevent the pancake sticking to the pan. Strain the batter and let it stand for 10 minutes.

Just before frying, beat in the whipping cream.

Fry and caramelise the grape pancakes
Peel, seed and halve the grapes before frying.

A non-stick or Teflon-coated pan is essential; choose one with a 22cm/9in base and put over medium heat. Swirl with ½ tablespoon melted butter and pour in about 175ml/6fl oz batter. Cover the surface generously with grapes and sprinkle with about 2–3 tablespoons icing sugar. Cook until the underside is set, then use a fish slice to turn the pancake, just lifting the edge and slipping in 1 tablespoon melted butter. The sugared grape side will caramelise.

Finally, pour about 20ml/⅔fl oz crème fraîche round the edge of the pancake, followed by about 30ml/1fl oz of the alcohol. Shake the pan with a circular movement, to stop the pancake sticking, and let the liquid bubble until it is caramelised.

Transfer the pancake flat to a warmed plate and keep warm. Wash and dry the pan and make the remaining pancakes the same way.

Presentation
Serve the pancakes hot, sprinkled with caster sugar. Top each one with a ball of tonka ice cream and pass single cream in a jug.

My wine suggestion: Schloss Vollrads, a Rheingau Beerenauslese Riesling.

Editor's note A tonka bean is the seed of a South American tropical tree. It has a pungent, sweet smell rather like vanilla, and vanilla seeds – scraped from the pod – could be substituted if you cannot find it.

Eckart Witzigmann

AUBERGINE

Maximiliensplatz 5, München 2 telephone: 89 59 81 71

Acknowledged Germany's greatest chef, and the first to be awarded three Michelin rosettes, Eckart Witzigmann proved that this distinction was not unattainable outside France.

He was born in Austria, where he was apprenticed at the Hotel Straubinger. Other kitchens followed. At the Hof Ragaz in Bad Ragaz in Switzerland he got to know Paul Simon, who was his first mentor; the two are still friends. A series of 'stages' mark his rapid professional rise, beginning in Illhaeusern with the Haeberlins, where he made the decisive move towards nouvelle cuisine, *on which he has left such an impression. A year spent with Paul Bocuse was followed by experience with the Troisgros brothers and Roger Vergé.*

He was fascinated by the idea of very simple, yet top-quality, products combined with suitable methods of preparation and he tried evolving this line of cuisine in his next posts: the Opernkällaren in Stockholm, the Erbprinz in Ettlingen, Germany, the Café Royal in London, the Villa Lorraine in Brussels and the Jockey Club in Washington.

While he was in America he was approached by Fritz Eichbauer, who wanted München to have a fine restaurant for the 1972 Olympic Games. He devoted seven years to the Tantris, building it up to a two-star restaurant. He left in 1978, to open his own restaurant, Aubergine, in München; it acquired Michelin's legendary award within a year.

His influence on German cooking has been enormous – about a third of top chefs have trained either at the Tantris or the Aubergine. His first book My Tantris Recipes *was followed by three more, the most recent being* Olympiadiet, *written with Professor Keul.*

MENU

STEINBUTTROSETTE MIT KAROTTEN AUF
LAUCH-TRUFFEL-BUTTERSAUCE
*Turbot rosettes with carrot on a leek, truffle and
butter sauce*

CREPINETTEN VOM LAMMSATTEL
Lamb chops stuffed with ham and spinach

MOHNCREME MIT ROTWEINBIRNEN
Poppy seed cream with pears in red wine

STEINBUTTROSETTE MIT KAROTTEN AUF LAUCH-TRUFFEL-BUTTERSAUCE

Turbot rosettes with carrot on a leek, truffle and butter sauce

Serves 4

400g/14oz turbot fillet
salt and freshly ground black pepper
a little lemon juice
100g/3½oz blanched carrots
150ml/¼pt fish stock (see right)
steamed green beans

For the leek, truffle and butter sauce
150g/5oz young green top of leeks
30g/1oz shallots, finely chopped
100g/3½oz cold butter, diced
40g/1½oz black truffles
30ml/1fl oz Noilly Prat
30ml/1fl oz white wine
200ml/7fl oz well-reduced fish stock (see below)
1 tablespoon whipped cream

Prepare the turbot and carrot shapes
Carve the turbot with a very sharp knife at an angle to make thin slices. Season with salt and pepper and sprinkle with lemon juice. Bend the slices round to build up a rosette. The middle of one slice should cover the gap where the ends meet in the slice below. Make 4 rosettes.
Cut the carrots into triangles and arrange the shapes between the individual petals.
Make the leek, truffle and butter sauce
Choose leek tops that are green, but still very tender. Blanch in boiling salted water for 5 minutes, drain and cut into 3mm/⅛in squares.
Fry the finely chopped shallots in 20g/⅔oz butter until transparent. Dice the truffles finely, add and sauté briefly, adding the Noilly Prat and white wine. Add the fish stock and boil to reduce to half the quantity.
On very low heat, or off it, whisk in the cold butter, a few dice at a time, adding more before the last has melted, so that the sauce retains a texture. Taste and season if necessary, then stir in the blanched diced leeks. Add a tablespoon of cream before serving.

Poach the turbot rosettes
Arrange the turbot fillets in a shallow pan in which they just fit neatly. Add the fish stock and bring to simmering, basting the tops of the rosettes frequently with fish stock, so they do not dry out. Cook for 2 minutes only from the point at which bubbles start to rise in the stock. Lift from the stock immediately.
Presentation
Pour the butter sauce on to 4 warmed plates and arrange the turbot rosettes in the middle. Arange the beans round the rosettes like spokes of a wheel.

My wine suggestion: Chassagne Montrachet 1983 'Les Chenevottes' from Dom M. Morey; a rich and broad wine, balanced by a healthy acidity.

FISH STOCK

1kg/2lb fish bones
1 stalk celery, chopped
60g/2oz white of leek, chopped
60g/2oz onion, chopped
30g/1oz mushrooms, chopped
thyme
bay leaf
parsley stalks
pinch of salt
5 peppercorns, crushed
1L/1¾pt water

Put everything into a stockpot and simmer slowly without a cover. After 20 minutes pour through a muslin or a fine sieve.
Skate bones can be used, but don't cook them at too hot a temperature (or too long), or the stock will be slimy.
For extra flavour, start by cooking the finely chopped vegetables in a little butter.
Don't use wine in the basic preparation; it could give a bitter taste. Also, it is better to add the wine when making the sauce, for one can then add an exact dose and the aroma is better.

Editor's note: To make concentrated fish stock – known as *fumet* – boil again after straining to reduce by half the volume. Be sparing with the salt if the fish stock will be reduced.

Steinbuttrosette mit Karotten auf Lauch-Trüffel-Buttersauce

Crépinetten vom Lammsattel

CREPINETTEN VOM LAMMSATTEL

Lamb chops stuffed with ham and spinach

Serves 4

1 saddle of lamb, 4 chops each side
60g/2oz caul (see note far right), soaked in cold water for 1 hour
salt and freshly ground black pepper
1 tablespoon olive oil
20g/²⁄₃oz butter
a sprig of thyme, or rosemary, and/or a garlic clove, crushed (optional)
4 Savoy cabbage leaves
your choice of carrots, salsify and parsnips
chervil to garnish
potato galettes to serve

For the lamb stock
1.5kg/3¹⁄₂lb lamb bones
2 tablespoons oil
8 shallots, roughly chopped
1 carrot, roughly chopped
150g/5oz celery stalk, roughly chopped
15 unpeeled garlic cloves
1-2 bay leaves
1 sprig of thyme
1 sprig of rosemary
2L/3¹⁄₂pt water

For the ham and spinach stuffing
30g/1oz butter
15g/¹⁄₂oz small cubes of bread without crust
30g/1oz boiled ham, diced finely
20g/²⁄₃oz cooked spinach, well drained and pressed of all juice
1 garlic clove, finely chopped
salt and freshly ground black pepper
a pinch of nutmeg
a pinch of thyme leaves
5g/¹⁄₈oz chervil

Prepare the lamb saddle

Chine the saddle of lamb, using a sharp pointed knife, and separate into chops. Trim away the fat, leaving the bone exposed about 7.5cm/3in. Your butcher will do this. Flatten the eye of meat slightly by beating it.

Make lamb stock for the sauce

Chop up the bones and put into hot oil in a roasting tin with the shallots. Cook until coloured, turning them then add the diced vegetables and garlic cloves. Cook for 5 minutes, then turn into a stock pot. Deglaze the roasting tin with a little water and add to the stock pot. Add the herbs and water and boil for 3-5 hours, skimming off impurities. I do this in an oven at 220°C/425°F/gas 7.

Strain the stock, then reduce if necessary – you need about 200ml/7fl oz. Let it stand, then skim off all fat from the surface.

Prepare the stuffing for the lamb parcels

Heat 10g/¹⁄₃oz butter in a small pan until it is frothy, then add the bread cubes and fry until crisp and brown. Tip into a sieve, retaining the butter.

Dice the ham finely, chop the cooked spinach coarsely and the garlic finely. Fry them lightly in the butter used for the croûtons. Mix them all together and season with salt, pepper, nutmeg and thyme. Chop the chervil finely and mix in.

Wrap the parcels in caul and cook

Spread out the caul on a damp surface. Spread with a tablespoon of the stuffing, the same size as the eye of the chop. Season a piece of lamb with salt and pepper and place it on top.

Cover the top of the meat with the same amount of mixture and, using a sharp knife, cut the caul to roughly the correct size, so that it can be wrapped neatly to enclose the meat completely. Repeat the steps with the other chops.

Put the olive oil and butter in a copper pan, or one with a very thick base, and 22cm/9in diameter. Heat until frothy and light brown in colour. A sprig of thyme or rosemary, and a lightly crushed clove of garlic can be added at this point, if you like.

Put in the lamb parcels and fry until the caul is crisp, about 5 minutes on each side. Then keep the parcels warm – in a low oven with the door open for 5 minutes.

Make the sauce

Pour away the fat from frying and add the lamb stock to the pan, stirring to deglaze. Make absolutely sure that the roasting juice is not burnt. Reduce the stock, tasting, until the flavour is right, then season.

Presentation

Put cutlet frills on the chops and arrange pairs at the bottom of each plate. Lay a Savoy cabbage leaf above. On this lay your choice of vegetables, garnished with chervil sprigs. Pour the sauce round the chops.

My wine suggestion: Château Cos d'Estournel 1971, a substantial St-Estèphe wine, full of character, with a fine bouquet.

Chef's note: The caul will have to be ordered specially from your butcher. A thin membrane from inside a pig, it is beaded with fat, which makes it look like lace. It melts and bastes the stuffing it encloses while cooking, and also crisps attractively on the outside.

MOHNCREME MIT ROTWEINBIRNEN

Poppy seed cream with pears in red wine

Serves 4

2 pears
250ml/9fl oz red wine
60g/2oz sugar
1 stick of cinnamon
zest orange
1 vanilla pod
20ml/²⁄₃fl oz pear schnaps, such as poire William
toasted almonds to serve
whipping cream to decorate (optional)
mint leaves (optional)

For the poppy seed cream

30g/1oz freshly ground poppy seeds
2 tablespoons red wine
1 whole egg
1 egg yolk
2 leaves gelatine
100g/3¹⁄₂oz white couverture chocolate
20g/²⁄₃oz honey
250ml/9fl oz double cream

Macerate the pears in red wine syrup
Heat the red wine, sugar, cinnamon stick, orange zest, vanilla pod and schnaps together in a pan, stirring to make sure the sugar dissolves. Bring to the boil.

Peel, core and slice the pears, put them in a bowl and pour the hot syrup over them. Leave to macerate for several hours, so that they can take on colour.

Make the poppy seed cream
Put the poppy seeds, which must be freshly ground, in a small pan with the red wine and boil for 1 minute; this tempers their harsh taste. Strain and reserve the poppy seeds.

Put the egg and egg yolk in a bowl which will fit over a pan containing simmering water. Soak the gelatine leaves in 4 tablespoons water, then stir to dissolve over hot water. Break up the white couverture and melt over hot water.

Whisk the eggs over hot water until starting to thicken on the beaters. Add the softened gelatine, the melted couverture and honey. Stir in the poppy seeds (but not the wine) and remove from the heat.

When the mixture has cooled down – do not let it get cold and set – whisk the cream to soft peaks and fold in. Spoon into a mould and chill to set.

Presentation

Use a spoon to put 2 scoops of poppy seed cream on to 4 dessert plates. Arrange the red pear slices attractively on the side, pouring a little syrup round them and scattering with almonds.

In the restaurant we pipe a pretty pattern with cream on the opposite side – swirls of white accompanied by swirls of pink cream, coloured with a little of the fruit syrup, then draw a knife point through the middle. Top with mint if you wish.

My wine suggestion: Bracchetto d'Acqui, a very light, likeable red wine with a natural sparkle. Made from a fine, very delicate grape it goes extremely well with poppy and cinnamon.

Mohncreme mit Rotweinbirnen at the Aubergine

Christian Begyn

SCHWARZER ADLER

Bad Bergstrasse 23, 7818 Vogstburg-Oberbergen telephone 7662 715

'I've never eaten better tripe than my father's' says Christian Begyn. Hot escalopes of foie gras, roast goat at Easter and great bowls of forest mushrooms were part of the country setting from which Christian Begyn came. Born in Colmar in Alsace, his mother raised goats and chickens and his father, who was a butcher, taught him to make tripes à la mode de Caen. *His father was also a hunter who brought back from the forest all sorts of mushrooms in addition to game. This background of good food, simply cooked, led him on to cookery as a fine art. Born at the crossroads of Europe, Christian Begyn is one of a number of Alsatians who have been influential in educating and refining German cooking. Soon after his fourteenth birthday he became an apprentice to René Fulgraphe, at the Restaurant du Musée in Colmar, who taught him his culinary technique. At the Auberge d'Hautrive in Switzerland Robert Lachaise taught him sauce-making and skill at pâtés. He went on to Epernay, to study the cuisine of the Champagne region and then to Aubère in the Vosges where he learned a discipline of a different sort – diet cuisine. After finishing military service, in 1970 he became head chef at Franz Keller's Gasthof Schwarzer in Oberbergen, an inn with traditions back to the 15th century. His new employer sent him to Paul Bocuse for training. A year later the restaurant acquired its second Michelin rosette. He describes his style as 'classical fine cooking, but lighter than in former times.' An authority on the gastronomy of the Black Forest and a wine grower, Franz Keller senior is well known for his advocacy of a dry range of German wines, fresh and elegant, from the Müller-Thurgau, Ruländer and Weissburgunder vines.*

MENU

BODENSEE-AAL IN GRAUBURGUNDER
Eels in Pinot Gris

SCHAUFELE MIT GRUNEM LINSENSALAT
Smoked blade of pork with lentils

SCHWARZWALDER HEIDELBEERTORTE
Black Forest bilberry tart

BODENSEE-AAL IN GRAUBURGUNDER

Eels in Pinot Gris

Serves 4

2 eels, about 500-600g/18-20oz together
salt and freshly ground black pepper
85g/3oz butter
100g/3½oz shallots, finely chopped
150g/5oz mushrooms, cleaned and chopped
250ml/9fl oz dry Pinot Gris
250ml/9fl oz double cream
2 sprigs of thyme
1 bay leaf
2-3 sprigs of parsley
2 tomatoes, blanched, peeled, seeded and the flesh chopped to garnish
4 puff pastry fleurons (see right) to garnish
chervil sprigs or finely chopped chives

Prepare the eels

Ask your fishmonger to skin and fillet the eels. All the fat from under the skin should be removed, as it is very unpleasant if left. However the meat is white with a very fine flavour.

Cook the eels in wine and cream

Cut the fillets into 7.5-10cm/3-4in lengths and season with salt and pepper. Fry them in a large saucepan in butter, turning until they are a light brown all over. Add the finely chopped shallots and mushrooms. Cook for 2-3 minutes, stirring once or twice, then add the Pinot Gris, cream, thyme, bay leaf and parsley.

Simmer over a low heat for about 10 minutes, depending on the size of the eels.

Finish the sauce and serve

Remove the eel pieces from the pan with a slotted spoon and arrange on a warmed serving dish.

Remove the thyme, bay leaf and parsley from the sauce. Reduce the quantity, if necessary by boiling; there should be about 175ml/6fl oz. Pour over the eel and serve very hot. Garnish the eel with sprigs of chervil or finely chopped chives. For a starter course, garnish the dish with warmed tomato dice and puff pastry *fleurons*. The eel may also be served as a main dish, accompanied by plain boiled potatoes or home-made noodles.

My wine suggestion: Pinot Gris 1986 Franz Keller. One of our proprietor's wines, the acidity of the Alsatian white wine goes very well with eels, bringing out the flavour of this traditional Baden dish.

Editor's note: Puff pastry *fleurons* are a pretty decoration and easy to make. Despite the name of 'flower', the commonest shape is a half-moon. Roll out puff pastry and take a 'bite' out of the side with a crinkle-edged biscuit cutter. Then take another behind the first. Brush the tops only with egg-and-salt glaze and bake at 220°C/425°F/gas 7 for 5-6 minutes until puffed and coloured. They will decrease in size as they rise. Keep in an air-tight tin and warm before serving.

SCHAUFELE MIT GRUNEM LINSENSALAT

Smoked blade of pork with lentils

Serves 6
800g-1kg/1¾-2¼lb smoked blade of pork
a bay leaf
1 onion
2 cloves

For the lentil salad
300g/11oz small green lentils
salt and freshly ground black pepper
2 tablespoons grapeseed oil
2 teaspoons wine vinegar
2 shallots, finely chopped
chopped chives

Cook the smoked pork blade
Put the blade of pork in a saucepan and add the bay leaf and the onion, studded with the cloves. Add water to cover and bring to simmering for 10 minutes. Then reduce the heat to a temperature of 70-80°C/160-170°F – on a solid fuel cooker, draw the pan to the side of the stove. Let the meat simmer very gently, so that it remains juicy and does not become stringy. Depending on the weight of meat used, it will take a total time of 45-60 minutes to cook.

Cook the lentils and make a salad
Boil the lentils in plenty of slightly salted water for 20-30 minutes until cooked, but not breaking up. Drain them well. While they are still hot, put them in a salad bowl and dress with the oil, vinegar and shallots, seasoning well. It is very important not to make the salad too vinegary, or this would not go well with the rosé wine recommended to accompany it.

Presentation
Carve the meat and arrange on a warmed plate with the lentils, sprinkling them with chopped chives.

My wine suggestion: Pinot Noir Rosé 1986; its bouquet and character make it well suited to accompany the delicate rustic flavour of this dish.

SCHWARZWALDER HEIDELBEERTORTE

Black Forest bilberry tart

Serves 4-6
300-400g/11-14oz bilberries or blueberries
lightly whipped double cream to serve

For the shortcrust pastry
200g/7oz flour, plus extra for rolling
100g/3½oz butter, diced, plus extra for greasing
1 teaspoon sugar
a pinch of salt
50ml/1¾fl oz cold water

For the custard
1 egg
120ml/4fl oz double cream
2 tablespoons sugar
½ vanilla pod

Make and chill the pastry
Mix the flour, butter, sugar and salt and work together; you can do this in a food processor, adding the water at the end. Alternatively, rub in the butter until it resembles fine breadcrumbs. Make a well in the middle and add the water and knead to a dough. Wrap this and chill in the refrigerator for 1 hour.

Make and bake the tart
Grease a push-bottom flan tin 18-20cm/7-8in diameter. Roll out the pastry 3mm/⅛in thick on a lightly floured surface. Move the pastry to the flan tin on the rolling pin and unroll and fit into the tin. Prick the pastry base all over with a fork, then add the washed berries.
Mix the egg, cream and sugar together, then scrape the tiny seeds from inside the ½ vanilla pod with a knife into the cream. Mix and pour this cream over the berries.
Bake in an oven at 200°C/400°F/gas 6 for 35-40 minutes, or until the custard is lightly set.
Let the tart rest in the tin for 5 minutes then remove the outside ring and serve, still warm. It will taste even better accompanied by cream.

My wine suggestion: in the Baden area connoisseurs of this dish like to drink a well-aged kirsch with it, though some believe it should be accompanied by bilberry wine.

Dieter Müller

SCHWEIZER STUBEN
Geiselbrunnweg 11, 6980 Wertheim-Bettingen telephone 9342 3070

Gault Millau Chef of the Year in 1987 and the holder of 19.5 out of a possible 20 points — Dieter Müller has scaled one of the high peaks of European cuisine.

He was born at Müllheim in Baden and has spent most of his life in the region. He began cooking with his brothers and sisters, and went on to work for his parents in the family restaurant. After an apprenticeship served at the Hotel Bauer in Baden and several major Swiss restaurants, and a period at the Miramare Beach in Corfu, he moved to Wertheim in 1973. His brother Jörg had been head chef at the Schweizer Stuben for a year.

With two Müllers in the kitchen, the restaurant gained first one Michelin rosette, in 1973, then the second, in 1977. In 1982, almost ten years after he arrived, his brother left for the island of Sylt to run his own restaurant, the Nösse, and Dieter took over. In his hands the restaurant became one of Germany's very best. He published a cookbook Kulinarische Jahreszeit *in 1986, reflecting the belief his proprietor shares that 'the great gift to cooking is the seasons — waiting for the products of nature to be at their best.'*

The owner of the Schweizer Stuben, is Adalbert Schmitt, a manufacturer willing to invest money in his passion for good food and drink. His son, Andreas, is restaurant manager and one of the best known in Germany.

MENU

FRANKISCHER BACHSAIBLING IN WEISSWEINSAUCE MIT GEFULLTER ZUCCHINIBLUTE
Franconian char in white wine sauce with stuffed courgettes

KALBSNIERE IM FETTMANTEL MIT GRUNEN BOHNCHEN, ROSTI UND BASILIKUMSENFSAUCE
Calf's kidneys cooked in their fat with green beans, potato cake and basil-mustard sauce

TOPFENGRATIN MIT ERDBEEREN UND RHABARBER
Gratin of strawberries and rhubarb

FRANKISCHER BACHSAIBLING IN WEISSWEINSAUCE MIT GEFULLTER ZUCCHINIBLUTE

Franconian char in white wine sauce with stuffed courgettes

Serves 4
2 char, each 400g/14oz (or substitute trout)
200ml/7fl oz dry white wine
1 shallot, chopped
60g/2oz leek, white part chopped
60g/2oz celery stalk, chopped
1 sprig of thyme
a little lemon juice
salt

For the stuffed courgettes
60g/2oz skinned char fillet
½ egg white
salt and freshly ground black pepper
60ml/2fl oz double cream
a little lemon juice
10ml/⅓fl oz sherry
1 tablespoon diced carrot and leek
2 firm courgettes, unpeeled

For the white wine sauce
500ml/18fl oz fish stock (page 161)
100ml/3½fl oz dry white wine
60ml/2fl oz double cream
60ml/2fl oz crème fraîche
60g/2oz cold butter, diced
salt
a little lemon juice
40ml/1½fl oz champagne
1 tablespoon whipped cream

Prepare the fish and poaching liquid
Gut the fish, fillet and remove the bones with a pair of tweezers. Make the poaching liquid by putting the white wine, shallot, leek, celery, thyme and lemon juice into a pan with 1L/1¾pt water and simmering for 10 minutes.

Stuff the courgettes
Finely chop the skinned char fillet and mix it with ½ egg white, seasoning with salt and pepper. Chill thoroughly in the freezer, chilling the double cream at the same time (but keeping the two of them separate).

Mix the two finely in the blender. Press the farce through a sieve, then round out the taste with salt, lemon and sherry.

Briefly cook the diced vegetables in salted water, drain, refresh and cool under running water and drain well. Stir into the farce.

Rinse the courgettes but do not peel them. Remove the seeds by pushing an apple corer through them. Use a piping bag with a large nozzle to pipe the farce into the courgettes.

Poach the stuffed courgettes in simmering, salted water for about 8 minutes until done.

Make the white wine sauce
Put the fish stock and white wine in a pan and boil until reduced to 150ml/¼pt. Add the double cream and crème fraîche and boil to reduce again. Whisk in the diced butter, a little at a time, adding more just before the last lot melts. Season with salt and lemon. Just before serving, fold in the champagne and a tablespoon of whipped cream.

Poach the char fillets briefly
Season the char fillets with salt and lemon, then poach in the simmering stock for 3 minutes; the fish must not be over-cooked.

Presentation
Pour the sauce on to 4 warmed plates and arrange a fish fillet on each one. Halve the courgettes horizontally, then slice thinly from the outside towards the middle, so each slice is edged with dark skin and with farce. Arrange the courgette slices at the thinner end of the fillet in a fan shape, to make a tail, and serve immediately.

My wine suggestion: Würzburger Pfaffenberg 1986, a dry white wine from the white Burgundy grape, picked as a Spätlese.

KALBSNIERE IM FETTMANTEL MIT GRUNEN BOHNCHEN, ROSTI UND BASILIKUMSENFSAUCE

Calf's kidneys cooked in their fat with green beans, potato cake and basil-mustard sauce

Serves 4

2 calf's kidneys, complete with their suet coating, about 250g/9oz each (these may have to be ordered from your butcher ahead)
salt and freshly ground black pepper
40g/1½oz clarified butter (page 23)

For the basil-mustard sauce
2 shallots
50g/1¾oz cold butter, diced
500ml/18fl oz brown bone stock (page 178)
200ml/7fl oz good red wine
a pinch of cornflour
1 tablespoon coarse Dijon mustard
2 teaspoons balsamic vinegar (page 80)
small bunch of fresh basil, leaves chopped
diced flesh of 1 blanched, peeled, seeded tomato (optional)

For the green beans
200g/7oz French beans
1 sprig of savory
20g/⅔oz butter
½ slice of pork belly, cut into 4 thin fingers
salt

Roast the kidneys in their suet

Trim the suet to a thin, uniform layer and season with salt and pepper. Heat the clarified butter in a flameproof dish and fry the kidneys, turning them until the fat is coloured all over.

Roast in the oven at 200°C/400°F/gas 6 for about 18 minutes until cooked, basting frequently with the juices that run from them.

Cover with foil and leave to rest for about 5 minutes before carving.

Cook the beans

Cook the beans with the savory in boiling salted water, very briefly: do not allow them to go soft. Drain and refresh them in ice-cold water, then drain again.

To serve, heat the butter in a frying pan and add the pork belly slices, spreading them out. Place the beans on top and cook at low heat. When the pork is cooked and the beans hot, toss together and season.

Make the basil-mustard sauce

Dice the shallot coarsely and fry lightly in 30g/1oz hot butter. Top up with the brown stock and red wine. Boil to reduce the sauce to 150ml/¼pt, then press through a sieve, return to the pan and boil again briefly.

Make a paste with the cornflour and a teaspoon water, add a litle hot sauce, stir back into the pan and cook gently. Stir in the mustard and balsamic vinegar and season with salt and pepper.

Before serving, whisk in 20g/⅔oz cold butter in dice, adding the second batch just before the first has melted. Flavour with chopped basil leaves. If you like, diced tomato can be added too.

Presentation

Slice open the suet and extract the kidneys then slice them thickly. Arrange on 4 hot plates and pour the basil-mustard sauce over them. Arrange the beans on one side, with a strip of pork on each portion, and add half a *rösti* potato cake to each plate.

My wine suggestion: Bürgstadter Centgrafenberg, a Spätburgunder Qualitätswein from Rudolf Fürst.

ROSTI

Potato cake

300g/11oz potatoes (these must not be floury)
30g/1oz clarified butter (page 23)
salt

Peel the potatoes and cut into thin sticks. Rinse off the starch, drain and dry well. Heat a non-stick or Teflon pan with the clarified butter and fry half the potatoes without stirring, pressing them down occasionally with a fish slice so they stick to form a cake. Season with salt. When the bottom in cooked, about 10 minutes, turn over and fry the other side. The *rösti* should be cooked through, with a golden-brown crust. Keep warm while you fry the second *rösti* the same way.

TOPFENGRATIN MIT ERDBEEREN UND RHABARBER

Gratin of strawberries and rhubarb

Serves 4

200g/7oz rhubarb
250ml/9fl oz white wine
85g/3oz sugar
1 vanilla pod
200g/7oz strawberries
icing sugar to serve

For the gratin topping
250g/9oz Quark cream cheese, 40% fat content
2 egg yolks
40g/1½oz icing sugar
30g/1oz cornflour
1 tablespoon rum
a little grated lemon zest
1 teaspoon vanilla sugar (see note)
2 egg whites
60g/2oz sugar

Prepare the fruit

Wash the rhubarb, peel and cut into pieces about 4cm/1½in long. Heat the white wine sugar and vanilla pod in a pan and add the rhubarb. Let it bubble up briefly. Then leave on one side to cool in its own juice. Hull and halve the strawberries.

Make the gratin topping

Put the Quark, egg yolks, icing sugar, cornflour, rum, grated lemon zest and vanilla sugar in a bowl and use an egg whisk to mix them well. Whisk the egg whites with the sugar until very stiff and fold them into the Quark mixture.

Assemble and brown the gratins

Butter 4 cold, deep dishes and divide the Quark cream among them. Dry off the rhubarb pieces on absorbent paper and put about 5-6 pieces in each dish. Lay the halved strawberries in the spaces between.

Put in the top of the oven at its hottest setting and bake until the gratin is golden-brown. Remove from the oven, dust with icing sugar and serve.

Editor's note: The best-quality vanilla pods are long – at least 18cm/7in – and black with a white frosting. To make vanilla sugar, which is both easy to cook with and economical, keep the pod buried in a jar of caster sugar, which it will impregnate with its delicious scent.

When a vanilla pod is infused in a liquid, chefs normally split it lengthways, releasing a fine spray of dark seeds which contain the maximum amount of flavour. These seeds can also be scraped out with a knife point, to give flavour to pastry and biscuits. Their fragrance and intensity is far superior to that of vanilla extract, which is made from the pod.

Austria

Coffee, cafés and gossip, morning
papers and afternoon cakes with
cream, that's traditional Vienna.
Here French elegance meets central
Europe, for a new cuisine — creative
yet traditionally inspired.

Ernst Huber

GASTHOF ZOLL
Arlbergstrasse 118, 6900 Bregenz telephone: 5574 31 705

There has been a Gasthof Zoll on the road to Arlberg since 1746. Here a bridge crossed part of Lake Constance – zoll means 'toll' – and the old building still appears on the menu card. The present modern building is the home of Ernst Huber and his wife Gerdi, who bought it in 1975 and refurbished it. Born in this region Ernst Huber spent many years as chef in Switzerland, France and Italy, rising to head chef in Dornblick.
He then bought the Gasthof Zoll, which has been described by the specialist magazine Vif *as 'the best restaurant round Lake Constance'.*

His mother was a major influence on his cooking, for she was 'an outstanding cook, particularly good at the plainer style of home cooking which is becoming so popular at present.' The inn is run as a friendly family business, based on local produce – fish from the lake, venison, mushrooms, local poultry and lamb. Its style is 'a blend of traditional cooking and the opportunities afforded by the wider choice of foodstuffs available today. The most important rule is that the products must be completely fresh and the result must be a perfect piece of handiwork.' The menu is revised at least once a week.
In the first Austrian edition of the Gault Millau guide in 1979, it gained a toque, *soon to rise to three, and a Michelin rosette in 1981. In 1984 Gault Millau chose Ernst Huber as Austria's Chef of the Year. Ernst's son Heino joined the team in 1983, aged twenty-five, and has added a further little touch to the cuisine from his training at Witzigmann's in Münich, Harry's Bar in Venice and Faugeron and Taillevent in Paris.*

MENU

BODENSEEFISCHSUPPE MIT SAFRAN
Fish soup from the Bodensee with saffron

BRIESRAGOUT MIT FRISCHEN PFIFFERLINGEN UND MAJORAN
Sweetbread ragout with chanterelles and marjoram

MANDELTULPE MIT FRISCHEN FRUCHTEN UND SCHOKOLADENCREME GEFULLT
Almond tulips filled with fresh fruit and chocolate

BODENSEEFISCHSUPPE MIT SAFRAN

Fish soup from the Bodensee with saffron

The Bodensee, or Lake Constance, is so vast that in summer its horizons are lost in the heat haze – an inland sea. The restaurant is at the foot of the lake, where the Alps almost come down to the water, and lake fish are a speciality.

Serves 4

*100g/3½oz mixed carrots, onions, celeriac
and fennel
2.5L/4pt water
750g/1¾lb gutted fish
250ml/9fl oz white wine
60ml/2fl oz Noilly Prat
6 black peppercorns, crushed
6 mustard seeds
1 bay leaf
2 tablespoons each chopped dill, chervil and parsley
a few drops Pernod
1 tablespoon lemon juice
salt*

For the forcemeat and garnish
*150g/5oz lake trout fillets
150g/5oz zander fillets (see note)
120ml/4fl oz double cream
salt and freshly ground black pepper
pinch of cayenne pepper
8 saffron strands to garnish
fresh dill, chervil and parsley to garnish*

Make the fish soup
Put all the ingredients for the fish soup except the Pernod, lemon juice and salt into a pan and simmer uncovered for 30 minutes. Strain and add a few drops of Pernod, lemon juice and seasoning to taste.

Make the good things to float in it
Take half the fish fillets and purée in a food processor, working in the cream. Season generously. Model into small fish dumplings with 2 teaspoons.

In a separate pan of salted water, poach the fish dumplings for 2-3 minutes, removing them with a slotted spoon; they will float when cooked.

Poach the remaining fish fillets in the soup for 5-6 minutes until done.

Presentation
Spoon the fish fillets and fish dumplings into each bowl and pour in the soup. Float a couple of saffron strands and fresh dill, chervil and parsley in each bowl.

My wine suggestion: Rheinriesling Spätlese 1983, Kollwentz, Burgenland.

Editor's note: The zander is a common East European sporting river fish. The largest member of the perch family, and also related to the pike (another name is pike-perch), it is a predator, like them. It has been introduced into British rivers and has multiplied rapidly. Perch could be substituted, but not pike, whose flesh is impossible to fillet because of the mass of bones.

BRIESRAGOUT MIT FRISCHEN PFIFFERLINGEN UND MAJORAN

Sweetbread ragout with chanterelles and marjoram

Serves 4

500g/18oz calf sweetbreads (page 252)
salt and freshly ground black pepper
1 tablespoon lemon juice
85g/3oz butter
85g/3oz shallots, very finely chopped
200g/7oz chanterelles, cleaned
400ml/14fl oz dry Madeira
fresh marjoram
200ml/7fl oz reduced brown bone stock (see right)
2 tablespoons double cream

For the potato croûtons
2 cold baked potatoes, 250g/9oz each
60g/2oz butter

Prepare the sweetbreads ahead
Rinse the sweetbreads then cover in cold water and leave to soak, preferably under a dripping tap, for at least 1 hour. Drain, put in a pan, cover with cold water, add salt and the lemon juice and bring slowly to the boil, skimming the scum. Boil for 2 minutes and remove. Plunge into cold water. When cold remove the pieces one at a time and pull away the thicker pieces of membrane from between the sections. Chill till needed – cook the same day.

Make the ragout
Melt the butter in a frying pan and add the shallots; cook gently until beginning to soften. Add the sweetbreads, turning them occasionally until starting to taken on a golden sheen. Add the chanterelles, shaking the pan regularly to turn them over. Remove from the pan with a slotted spoon and keep warm.
Add the Madeira to the pan – Sercial is best – and boil briefly to reduce by about a third. Make up the quantity with the well-reduced brown bone stock. Reduce to about 250ml/9fl oz.

Finish the dish
Stir in the double cream and return the sweetbread, shallot and chanterelle mixture to the pan. Season to taste and sprinkle with fresh marjoram leaves.

Make the potato croûtons
Peel the potatoes and cut into small cubes, discarding unevenly-shaped ones. Toss in hot butter until crisp then season and serve with the sweetbreads.

My wine suggestion: Zweigelt 1985, E & M Müller, Weststeiermark.

BROWN BONE STOCK

1kg/2lb veal bones, chopped
100g/3½oz carrots
100g/3½oz onions
1-2 tomatoes, quartered
50ml/1½fl oz red wine
1 bay leaf
6 peppercorns, crushed
4 juniper berries, crushed
parsley, sage and rosemary

Put the chopped bones in a roasting tin and cook in the oven at maximum heat, turning them occasionally, until they start to brown. Add the chopped vegetables and tomatoes and let these brown too. Add the red wine and stir to scrape up the sediment. Transfer to a stockpot and add water to cover, the bay leaf, peppercorns and juniper berries. Bring slowly to the boil, skimming as necessary.
Cover and simmer 3-4 hours, adding more water if needed to keep the bones covered. Strain and stand to let the fat rise. Remove the fat and boil to reduce again to about 300ml/½pt stock.

Editor's note: Ernst Huber likes a rather gamey brown bone stock, with its juniper berries, sage and rosemary, to balance the blandness of the sweetbreads in this recipe. The tomatoes are another optional touch – often associated with the Mediterranean south. If you are making the stock for other recipes, omit them all.
Nor is it always necessary to deglaze with red wine. Frédy Girardet, for example, uses a much plainer stock; he adds a leek, a shallot and a garlic clove to the basic vegetables and flavours with the traditional bouquet garni. Brown bone stock is not strongly flavoured. Raymond Blanc says he uses it mainly to add texture.

MANDELTULPE MIT FRISCHEN FRUCHTEN UND SCHOKOLADENCREME GEFULLT

Almond tulips filled with fresh fruit and chocolate

Serves 4

200g/7oz mixed strawberries, raspberries, bilberries and
redcurrants or blackberries in season
4 teaspoons Grand Marnier
12 fresh mint leaves
icing sugar to dust

For the almond tulips
200g/7oz marzipan
1 egg yolk
1 egg white
2 tablespoons flour
100ml/3½fl oz milk
4 tablespoons sugar
melted butter for greasing
flour for sprinkling

For the filling
75g/2½oz plain chocolate
2 teaspoons single cream
1 egg
1 teaspoon caster sugar
175ml/6fl oz whipping cream

Macerate the red fruit

Sprinkle the prepared fruit with the Grand Marnier and leave to macerate.

Make the almond tulips

Start by putting the baking tray in the freezer. Mix all the ingredients together in a bowl with a whisk to a smooth paste, then work this through a sieve with a wooden spoon.

Brush the baking sheet with butter and sprinkle – as thinly as you can – with flour.

Use a piece of cardboard to cut a stencil. In the middle draw a circle or a leaf shape of the size you need – this will be determined by the glasses you plan to serve the *Mandeltulpen* in. Cut out the centre of the cardboard neatly.

Put the stencil over the prepared baking sheet and dollop a little almond mixture in the middle. Spread it out thinly with a palette knife, filling the stencil neatly. Make more tulips, but not more than 4 to a tray.

Bake the biscuits at 180°C/350°F/gas 4 for 2-4 minutes, until just browning round the edges. Remove one by one from the tray with a fish slice and immediately bend them to fit into the glasses. Let them remain there until crisp and set. If baking ahead, keep them in an airtight tin.

Make the chocolate cream

Break up the chocolate and melt it in a bowl over hot water, stirring till smooth. Remove from the heat and stir in the single cream.

Put the egg and caster sugar in a small heatproof bowl which will balance over a pan of simmering water. Whisk over the heat until very foamy. Whisk in the chocolate and stir well. Let this cool, whisking occasionally, then fold in the whipped cream.

Presentation

Serve the almond tulips in glasses – in the restaurant we have a special glass called a *Tulpenglas* – an open goblet like a tulip – which gave these biscuits their name. Pile in the marinated fruit alternately with the chocolate cream. Decorate each one with mint leaves and dust with icing sugar.

My wine suggestion: Roter Veltliner Ausbruch 1983; a rare white grape gives this dessert wine its name, a speciality from the Mantlerhof vineyard at Gedersdoft near Krems.

Helmut Osterreicher

STEIRERECK

Rasumofskygasse 2, 1030 Vienna telephone: 222 713 51 68

His cuisine reflects Austria: small wonder since that is the meaning of his name. The restaurant Steirereck is in the heart of Vienna, and one of the best in the city. It is a family business and the owners, Margarethe and Heinz Reitbauer are dedicated to gastronomy, putting all their knowledge and boundless energy into building up the restaurant's reputation: 'always on the job, never stopping, determinedly developing the concept of the top restaurant – and no resting on the laurels.' As their son Heinz is training to enter the kitchen, this tradition will be maintained into the next generation.

Helmut Osterreicher's career at the Steirereck started in 1978, when he answered an advertisement. He was twenty when 'I took my first steps in the new Viennese cuisine.' As head chef he believes in team work, where each member of the team is given the job to which he is best suited. And his team is good: his sous-chef, Anton Schrei, was lured away from Sacher, where they had worked together. His own interest is in creating new sauces.

Had he a tip? 'Go easy on the salt and always use top quality vinegar for seasoning.' Helmut Osterreicher believes in constant further training, in seminars, and he has a great appetite for specialised literature, for 'cooking is a continual process of learning what the ingredients can achieve.' He is particularly keen to cultivate traditional Austrian dishes; 'I try to perfect them and at the same time make them more interesting.' The restaurant was awarded a Michelin rosette in 1985.

MENU

ZANDER UND FLUSSKREBSE IN BASILIKUMNAGE
Zander and river crayfish in basil cream

GEMSE MIT ROTWEINSAUCE
Chamois served three ways with red wine sauce

HIMBEERCHARLOTTE MIT MANDELMILCH
Raspberry charlotte with almond cream

ZANDER UND FLUSSKREBSE IN BASILIKUMNAGE

Zander and river crayfish in basil cream

Serves 4

700g/1½lb zander (or substitute perch, page 177)
30g/1oz butter
120ml/4fl oz dry vermouth
1.5L/2½pt extra fish stock
24 crayfish, about 60g/2oz each with the heads

For the fish stock
500g/1lb fish bones and trimmings
250g/9oz onion, chopped
2 celery stalks, chopped
1 bay leaf
6 parsley stalks, bruised
6 black peppercorns, crushed
strip of zest and juice from 1 lemon
250ml/9fl oz dry white wine

For the white wine and basil cream
45g/1½oz butter
4 tablespoons chopped shallots
250ml/9fl oz white wine
60ml/2fl oz Noilly Prat
500ml/18fl oz double cream
2 tablespoons crème fraîche (page 250)
12 basil leaves, chopped
salt

For the garnish
8 small broccoli florets
4 new carrots
4 ovals of seeded courgette
8 strips yellow pepper
1 tomato, blanched, peeled, seeded and cut into 8
paprika
chives
4 basil sprigs

Prepare the zander
Fillet the fish: you will need 250g/9oz neatly cut fillets. Collect the scraps of flesh from head and tail and the bones to give about 100g/3½oz chopped fish for thickening the soup.

Make the fish stock
Rinse the fish bones and trimmings and put in a pan with all the stock ingredients, pouring in the wine and about 1L/2pt water to cover. Simmer for 30 minutes, skim occasionally then strain.

Make the white wine broth and garnish
Pour the stock into a small pan and boil to reduce to 500ml/18fl oz for the broth.

Melt the butter and fry the chopped shallots until soft. Pour on the white wine and Noilly Prat and boil to reduce by a quarter. Add the fish stock and boil down again for about 10 minutes until you have 500ml/18fl oz. Add the cream and boil again to reduce by half.

Add the reserved fish flesh and the crème fraîche and bring to the boil. Sieve into a clean pan and reheat, stirring in the chopped basil leaves. Steam the garnishing vegetables.

Cook the zander and crayfish
Heat the butter and vermouth in a small flameproof dish. Cut the zander fillets into strips about 5mm/¼in wide. Cook these briefly in the butter and vermouth, in a covered pan – they should still look slightly glassy inside.

Bring the fish stock to the boil and cook the crayfish whole for 3 minutes, then drain. Protecting the hand that is holding them with a cloth, twist off their heads. Peel the legs on one side upward over the back, removing part of the shell, then pinch the tail fins firmly and pull out the cooked tail flesh. Remove the vein – with a needle if necessary.

Presentation
Pour the wine and basil broth into 4 soup plates and arrange the zander and crayfish tails on top. Scatter with the warm vegetables and sprinkle with a little paprika and chive leaves. Top each one with a basil sprig; serve immediately.

My wine suggestion: Riesling Kabinett 1985, Ried Zöbinger Heiligenstein, from Maria Retzl at Zöbing: the wine is dry, almost steely and distinctly spicy.

Editor's note: Freshwater crayfish – *écrevisses* in French – are found in streams through chalk and limestone throughout Europe. In Sweden eating *kräftor* is a summer pastime; in Britain it is illegal to catch them, for they are a threatened species. Their saltwater cousins, Dublin Bay prawns – *langoustines* – could be substituted.

Zander und Flüssekrebse in Basilikumnage

Gemse mit Rotweinsauce

Himbeercharlotte mit Mandelmilch

Pear schnaps at Steirereck

GEMSE MIT ROTWEINSAUCE

Chamois served three ways with red wine sauce

Serves 4

*4 small chamois chops (see note), from the best end,
about 40g/1½oz each, fat trimmed from the bone
salt and freshly ground black pepper
40g/1½oz butter
400g/14oz made puff pastry
flour for dusting
2 chamois loins, about 15cm/5in long and
150g/5oz each
8 spinach leaves, trimmed
beaten egg to glaze
meat cut from the top outside of the chamois leg, then
trimmed to about 150g/5oz
raspberry jellies to serve*

For the forcemeat
*100g/3½ oz chamois scraps from the leg
4 juniper berries, crushed
6 sprigs of fresh thyme, rubbed
salt and freshly ground black pepper*

For the port and red wine sauce
*120ml/4fl oz red port
120ml/4fl oz red wine
250ml/9fl oz brown venison stock (page 109)
1 tablespoon cranberry jelly or purée
a few juniper berries*

Prepare the parcel filling

Season the 4 chops and fry them lightly on both sides in 20g/⅔oz butter. Leave to go cold.
Mince the meat for the forcemeat, including the juniper berries and season with the leaves rubbed from 2 sprigs of thyme, salt and pepper.

Make the pastry parcels

Top the cold chops with a walnut-sized ball of forcemeat, then flatten. Roll out the pastry to a square about 25cm/10in and cut into four. Lay a chop with a bone pointing to the corner, so that the pastry folds over the eye of meat at its widest point. Dampen the edges with cold water and press to seal, then trim away unwanted pastry – the bone projects. Stand on a greased baking sheet and chill until needed.

Stuff the loins

Slit the loins lengthways almost through, then open up and beat to flatten them. Season lightly and sprinkle with the remaining thyme leaves and forcemeat.
Blanch the spinach leaves by pouring boiling water on them and draining. Dry on absorbent paper then lay over the forcemeat. Roll up the sirloins like a Swiss roll. Place on a greased sheet of foil and roll up, crimping the edges together so the parcel is waterproof.

Cook the chamois

Poach the loin parcels in simmering water in a bain-marie on top of the stove for about 6 minutes. Keep wrapped in foil in a warm place.
Glaze the pastry parcels with egg wash – egg and salt beaten together. Bake in the oven at 220°C/425°F/gas 7 for 10 minutes.
Season the leg meat well and rub the outside with 10g/⅓oz butter. Place in a small greased flameproof dish and roast in the oven with the pastries for 8-10 minutes. Reserve the pastry parcels and roast leg on a warm dish.

Make the port and red wine sauce

To the dish used for the leg, add the port, red wine and venison stock. Work in the cranberry jelly or purée, boiling until the liquid is syrupy and has reduced to 250ml/9fl oz. Pass through a sieve and season to taste with fresh thyme and pepper. Add a few juniper berries; these look attractive, but are not to be eaten.

Presentation

Carve the roast leg lengthways into small slices and carve the stuffed loins across into 4 slices each. Arrange on warmed plates. Put a cutlet frill on each exposed bone and add a pastry parcel to one side of each plate and a raspberry jelly at the top. Pour a little sauce round the roast meat; pass the remainder in a jug.

My wine suggestion: Blaufränkisher Barrigue 1985, from Weingut Hans Igler, Deutschreutz, Burgenland.

Editor's note: The chamois is a small goat-like antelope found in the mountains of central and southern Europe. The dish could be prepared with kid, or with venison from a young roebuck, which is the same size – *chevreuil* in French.

HIMBEERCHARLOTTE MIT MANDELMILCH

Raspberry charlotte with almond cream

Serves 8

400g/14oz raspberries
2 egg yolks
40g/1½oz caster sugar
40g/1½oz vanilla sugar (page 173)
grated zest and juice of ½ lemon
3 leaves gelatine
200ml/7fl oz Himbeergeist (raspberry eau-de-vie)
2 egg whites
100ml/3½fl oz whipping cream
flavourless oil for greasing
about 70 lady fingers or boudoir biscuits
48 raspberries to decorate
mint sprigs to decorate

For the almond custard
100ml/3½fl oz milk
100ml/3½fl oz cream
30g/1oz lump sugar
20g/⅔oz vanilla sugar (page 173)
60g/2oz flaked almonds
3 egg yolks

For the raspberry sauce
120g/4oz raspberries
icing sugar

Make the raspberry mousse
Reserve 150g/5oz raspberries then purée and sieve the remainder; there should be 120ml/4fl oz purée. Whisk the egg yolks with 20g/⅔oz sugar, the vanilla sugar and the grated lemon zest until frothy.

Break up the gelatine, cover with 4 tablespoons cold water, and leave to soak. Put the raspberry purée into a small pan and stir in the gelatine, lemon juice and Himbeergeist and bring to the boil, stirring until the gelatine has dissolved. Cool a minute or so, then whisk into the yolk mixture. Continue whisking until the mousse is cold.

With clean, dry beaters, whisk the egg whites until soft peaks form, sprinkle with 20g/⅔oz sugar and whisk until stiff. Whip the cream and fold into the raspberry mousse. Carefully fold in the meringue mixture and the reserved berries. Lightly grease 8 moulds about 200ml/7fl oz, with sloping sides with flavourless oil. Line with the biscuits baked side outward, then fill with raspberry mousse. Chill until set.

Make the almond custard
Heat the milk with the cream, lump sugar and vanilla sugar. Meanwhile toast the almonds in the bottom of a low oven or in a dry frying pan, watching that they do not catch.

Add the toasted almonds to the hot milk and simmer for 10 minutes to flavour it.

Whisk the egg yolks then pour the hot milk (and almonds) down on the yolks, whisking all the time. Pour back into the pan and cook over very low heat, and preferably over simmering water, stirring all the time, until the custard coats the back of a spoon. Remove from the heat and leave until cold. Strain before using.

Make the raspberry sauce
Rub the berries through a sieve to remove the pips. Sweeten to taste with icing sugar.

Presentation
Cut off the projecting biscuits flush with the top of the mould. Run a knife round inside the moulds and turn out the raspberry charlottes. Pour a little raspberry purée round each one, then almond cream. Pipe a line of purée on to the cream, then decorate it by pulling a knife point through the purée. Arrange fresh berries and mint sprigs round the plate.

My wine suggestion: Muscat-Ottonel Auslese 1983, Franz Schindel, Mörbisch, which has a delicate grapey aroma.

Editor's note: Lady fingers are usually homemade in Austria, where they are known as Rothschild biscuits. A similar broad sponge finger can be bought in Italian delicatessens, or the crisper, sugar-coated boudoir biscuit can be used.

Switzerland

The land of hotels and chocolate,
school for the world's chefs,
the Swiss are master of all their
neighbours' skills but paradoxically
have no Michelin guide — their good
restaurants appear in the red books
of neighbouring countries.

Alfred Girardet

GIRARDET

1 Rue d'Yverdon, 1023 Crissier telephone: 21 27 01 01/21 634 0505

Frédy Girardet is distinguished from his fellows by more than talent. Unlike many other celebrated chefs, he has not followed the traditional path through apprenticeship in great restaurants. He has never worked for anyone else. His famed restaurant is within easy reach of France, yet is without Michelin rosettes. Despite the temptations of stardom, he is not to be wooed away from family life and he rarely leaves his own restaurant.

He was born in Lausanne, where he received a basic training, then went to help his father in his modest hotel in the village of Crissier. At the age of twenty, in 1957, he found himself head of the family, aware of his responsibilities, but with no real enthusiasm for his work. Not until 1968, during a stay in France, where he met Paul Bocuse and the Troisgros brothers (whose photograph now hangs beside his father's) did he experience the revelation of what cuisine could be, and see the way out of the boredom of bistro life.

By 1974 he was beginning to be known outside the region – Gault Millau awarded him their Clé d'Or the following year – and he rapidly attained an international reputation. Two years later the restaurant finally took over the whole of the town hall at Crissier.

Is Frédy Girardet the best chef in the world? His peers say that they know none better. A deep respect for his profession, its produce and flavours underlies a cooking that is, he says, 'wholesome, generous and impulsive' with 'a sensible harmony between the produce and its cooking'. His simple words conceal cooking of the most exquisite sensibility.

MENU

MATELOTE DE HOMARD ET LANGOUSTINES AU POMEROL
Lobster and Dublin Bay prawns with Pomerol

RABLE DE LIEVRE ROTI AUX EPICES, SAUCE CREME, AVEC CHATAIGNES FONDANTES
Roast spiced saddle of hare with cream sauce and fondant chestnuts

SOUFFLE A LA PISTACHE
Pistachio soufflé

MATELOTE DE HOMARD ET LANGOUSTINES AU POMEROL
Lobster and Dublin Bay prawns with Pomerol

Serves 4
2 live lobsters, each 400g/14oz
salt and freshly ground black pepper
2 medium-sized Dublin Bay prawns
8 young leeks, 1cm/½in diameter
15g/½oz butter

For the Pomerol sauce
1 lobster shell
2 shallots
¼ bay leaf
pinch of sugar
300ml/½pt Pomerol
20g/⅔oz butter
salt and freshly ground black pepper

For the mousseline sauce
2 shallots
100ml/3½fl oz dry white wine
1 sprig of dill
2 egg yolks
40g/1½oz softened butter
salt and milled white pepper

Prepare the shellfish
Bring a large saucepan of salted water to the boil. Plunge in the lobsters, bring back to the boil, count 3 minutes, then take them out and plunge them into cold water to arrest the cooking. Remove the claws and return to cook for another 3 minutes, then take them out and cool.

Shell the tails completely. Split them in half lengthways. Hammer the claws open and take out the flesh. Shell the prawn tails and remove the black gut. Wrap all the flesh in cling film and reserve in the refrigerator.

Make the Pomerol sauce
Take one lobster shell (the other is not used) and split the head lengthways. Carefully remove and discard the stomach, which lies behind the eyes. Crush the shell well. Finely chop the shallots for both sauces.

Place in a saucepan the crushed lobster shell, half the shallots, ¼ bay leaf, a pinch of sugar and the Pomerol. Boil to reduce the liquid to 100ml/3½fl oz; then strain.

Prepare the leeks; start the mousseline
Trim the leeks to 5cm/2in only of green, then clip the green like a paper frill. Boil for 5-7 minutes in salted water. Drain and rinse, then peel off the outer 2-3 layers, reducing them to 5mm/¼in diameter. Make a diagonal cut removing part the white base and reserve them ready in a small oven dish. Slice the remaining uncooked green leek in fine (1mm/1⁄16in) strips. Put in a small pan with the butter and some salt. Cook over high heat for 1-2 minutes.

Put the rest of the chopped shallot in a small pan with the white wine. Boil for 3 minutes then sieve out the shallot, returning the liquid to the pan. Chop the dill finely.

Assembly
Half an hour before serving remove the shellfish from the refrigerator and heat the oven to 200°C/400°F/gas 6. Put 15g/½oz butter on the half lobster tails and claws, and season them all and lay in an oven dish.

Gently warm the reduced white wine, add 2 egg yolks and whisk over simmering water. When the mixture begins to thicken, add 40g/1½oz softened butter, still whisking. Season with salt and pepper, incorporate the dill and remove from the heat.

Reheat the lobster in the oven for 3 minutes. Reheat the white leek in the oven and the chopped leeks in the pan.

Cook the seasoned prawn tails in 20g/⅔oz hot butter for 1 minute, turning them over. Boil up the reduced red wine, whisk in 20g/⅔oz butter and correct the seasonings.

Presentation
Pour a spoonful of Pomerol sauce into the centre of each plate, spreading it out a little. Slant 2 prawn tails across the sauce to the bottom right of the plate. Arrange 2 white leeks above and parallel to them and a neat mound of green leek between the two.

Cut the lobster tail into 3 slices, reassemble it and slant it across the bottom left of the plate. Place one claw above it and spoon some mousseline sauce between the lobster and the prawn. Scatter some green leek round the edge.

My wine suggestion: Château Pétrus.

RABLE DE LIEVRE ROTI AUX EPICES, SAUCE CREME, AVEC CHATAIGNES FONDANTES

Roast spiced saddle of hare with cream sauce and fondant chestnuts

Serves 4

*1 large hare's saddle, about 600g/1¼lb, or 2 smaller
ones, cleaned, plus the trimmings
3-5 good sprigs of thyme
¼ carrot, in 1cm/½in cubes
½ onion, in 1cm/½in cubes
30g/1oz celery, in 1cm/½in cubes
1 small garlic clove, unpeeled
a long root from a bunch of parsley, cut in 6
10 juniper berries, lightly crushed
60g/2oz butter
1 teaspoon oil
salt and freshly ground black pepper
1 dessert apple, sliced and lightly caramelised*

For the fondant chestnuts

*20 chestnuts, preferably small wild ones
6 sugar lumps
150ml/¼pt brown bone stock (page 178)
3 pieces of celery, 5 x 2.5cm/2 x 1in*

For the spice mixture

*⅙ juniper berries
⅓ coriander seeds
⅓ pink peppercorns (baies roses, page 250)
⅙ black peppercorns*

For the cream sauce

*100ml/3½fl oz whipping cream
1 tablespoon Sauternes
few drops of lemon juice*

Prepare the hare and flavourings

Slash the hare deeply down each side of the spine, leaving about 3cm/1¼in uncut meat at either end. Slip a sprig of thyme into each gash, wrap the joint in cling film and chill, remembering to bring into room temperature at least an hour before cooking.

Chop the hare trimmings. Wrap and chill. Cube the carrot, onion and celery, add the garlic clove, parsley root, 1 thyme sprig and juniper berries. Wrap and chill. Grind the spices coarsely in the correct proportions.

Make the fondant chestnuts

Make big cuts all over the shell, plunge into boiling water, remove and peel. Even the skin will rub off in a cloth while hot.

Melt the sugar lumps in a saucepan over gentle heat until they caramelise. Immediately add the stock and same amount of water. Add the celery and chestnuts and cook without stirring until the juice is syrupy and the chestnuts creamy in texture. Discard the celery.

Cook the hare

Heat the oven to maximum and season the hare, then sprinkle all over with 6 pinches of the spice mixture.

Heat the butter and 1 teaspoon oil in a roasting tin over a high heat. Fry the hare trimmings, stirring, for 3 minutes, until brown. When the butter begins to darken, add the vegetable and juniper mixture prepared for flavouring. Make a space in the pan and brown the fillets on the saddle(s) for 1 minute on each side, supporting the hare against the side of the pan, one side then the other.

Turn the hare saddle(s) upward and roast for 10 minutes. Baste once or twice, then open the oven, stand the roasting tin on the door and let the meat rest for 6-7 minutes, basting frequently with the butter it was cooked in, to keep the flesh moist. Move to a dish and keep warm.

Make the cream sauce

Place the roasting tin over medium heat, add 300ml/½pt water and stir to deglaze. Boil until reduced to a mere film of liquid. Add the cream, boil hard for 2 minutes, then pour through a fine sieve into a small saucepan. Add the Sauternes and correct the seasoning, sharpening the flavour with a few drops of lemon juice.

Presentation

Use a spoon to detach the fillets from the saddle. Then cut them diagonally into thin slices and divide these between 4 warmed plates, fanning them out. Place a few rewarmed fondant chestnuts at the base, with a couple of slices of caramelised apple and a small spoonful of sauce on each side.

My wine suggestion: Château Yquem.

SOUFFLE A LA PISTACHE

Pistachio soufflé

Serves 2

40g/1¹/₂oz pistachio nuts, shelled
75g/2¹/₂oz caster sugar
butter for the soufflé dish
1 egg yolk
2 egg whites

For the pistachio custard
100ml/3¹/₂fl oz custard (see right)
10g/¹/₃oz pistachio nuts, shelled
1 drop bitter almond essence
5 drops cherry brandy

Make the pistachio custard
Make the custard then measure the correct quantity. Add the whole pistachios, a drop (no more) of bitter almond essence and 5 drops of cherry brandy. Turn the custard into a blender and purée, then return to a saucepan.
Prepare and cook the soufflé
Select 5 pistachio nuts for decoration, split and reserve them. Grind the remaining nuts with half the sugar.
Butter a 12cm/5in soufflé dish and heat the oven to maximum heat. Prepare a bain-marie, with 3-4cm/1¼-1¹/₂in water, just simmering.
Whisk the pistachio and sugar mixture together with the egg yolk until creamy.
Whisk the egg whites with the remaining sugar, working in plenty of air; they should not be too stiff. Work in one-third of the pistachio-yolk mixture with the whisk, then gently fold in the rest. Turn into the greased soufflé dish – it should not be filled to the top.
Start cooking the soufflé in the bain-marie on top of the stove with water at minimum boil, for 6-7 minutes. Then put it in the bottom of the oven for 12 minutes or so, until well risen. Half way through, scatter the pistachios on top. Warm the custard.
Presentation
Present the soufflé in its dish with the pistachio custard in a sauceboat. Serve on two plates, surrounding each portion with custard.

My wine suggestion: continue with the Château Yquem.

CREME ANGLAISE

Custard

200ml/7fl oz milk
1 vanilla pod, split lengthways
2 egg yolks
2 tablespoons sugar

Bring the milk with the vanilla pod to boiling. Beat the yolks and sugar and pour the hot milk down on to them. Pour back into the pan, removing the vanilla pod. Then cook over a very low heat, preferably over simmering water, until the custard coats the back of a spoon. Strain into a bowl.

Hans Stucki

STUCKI BRUDERHOLZ

42 Bruder Holzallee, 4059 Basle telephone: 6135 82 22

Hans Stucki has always wanted to be a cook since he was little. Rösti for the whole family — potato pancake (there is a recipe on page 172) — is the first dish he remembers cooking. Both sides of the family were restaurateurs and his parents owned a café-restaurant, the Cheval Blanc at Ens, in the Canton of Berne; he was the third son. Aged sixteen in 1945, he entered the Beau-Rivage Palace as apprentice, and then went on to work at the Souvretta House in St Moritz, the Splendid in Lugano, the Dolder in Zürich, the Carina Carlton in Morcote, and the Trois Rois in Basle and others.

When he married, he and his wife Suzanne leased the Bruderholz, which they bought eleven years later, transforming it into one of Switzerland's best known restaurants. In a quiet residential suburb of Basle, it is traditional in style, standing in its own garden. In 1975 the restaurant received its first Michelin rosette and started to rise in the Gault Millau guide. 'The house is more traditional, the cuisine more modern' Hans Stucki says, 'in the French style, not the German.' In 1977 he received the Gault Millau Clé d'Or — two years after Frédy Girardet — followed by a second Michelin rosette.

Was he, then, an advocate of nouvelle cuisine? *'Definitely no kiwi on the lobster! Too much* nouvelle cuisine *and the dining room would empty in a minute. That is not to say there should be no development, no progress, but it must be modified by good sense. Taste always comes first; secondly you can think about decoration.' He manages the combination so well that in 1988 the Bruderholz rated 19 out of 20 in the Gault Millau guide.*

MENU

FILET DE TURBOTIN GRILLE AUX RACINES DE PERSIL
Grilled turbot fillets with parsley roots

CANARD ROTI AUX ENDIVES
Roast duck with chicory

SOUFFLE AU CHOCOLAT AU COULIS D'AGRUMES
Hot chocolate soufflé with citrus sauce

FILET DE TURBOTIN GRILLE AUX RACINES DE PERSIL

Grilled turbot fillets with parsley roots

Serves 4

4 fillets from a small turbot, about 60g/2oz each
2 Hamburg parsley roots, about 100g/3¹/₂oz each (see note)
60g/2oz butter
salt and freshly ground black pepper
1 red pepper
flat parsley
400ml/14fl oz well-reduced fish stock (page 161)
1 tablespoon olive oil

For the provençal butter
60g/2oz butter, softened
10ml/¹/₃fl oz virgin olive oil
1 garlic clove
20ml/²/₃fl oz cognac
2 large basil leaves
¹/₄ bunch flat parsley, leaves only
salt and freshly ground black pepper

Preparations

Peel the parsley roots using a paring knife, then pass lengthways through a mandolin to cut into very thin slices of about 1mm/¹/₁₆in. Weigh out 120g/4oz of these slices, put in a pan with just sufficient water to cover and 15g/¹/₂oz butter and a little salt. Cook them for 3 minutes, drain, and keep in an airtight container if you are preparing them ahead.

Mix together all the ingredients for the provençal butter in a blender. Chill in a small container if working ahead.

Peel the pepper, using a small sharp knife. This is not essential – it is a fiddly operation – but is worth the effort, as pepper skin is rather indigestible. Remove pith and seeds and cut the pepper into strips, then 2mm/¹/₈in cubes. Measure out 4 tablespoons pepper. Chop the parsley until you have enough for 4 good pinches. Pour the fish stock into a saucepan and boil on high heat to reduce to one-quarter.

Cook the dish

Heat the grill to high. In the restaurant we use a charcoal grill for this. However, if you are using a domestic grill, with top heat, the diamond effect, described below, can be achieved by 'dry-frying' on a very lightly greased, ridged, hot dry frying pan under it.

Put 30g/1oz butter in a pan, add the sliced parsley root, season with salt and pepper and stir until heated through. Add the chopped parsley and red pepper, stir and remove from the heat.

Return the fish stock to the heat, adding 20g/²/₃oz butter and the provençal butter. Boil vigorously to emulsify the butter, then remove from the heat. Whisk up the sauce with an electric whisk.

Brush the fish fillets with oil and season both sides. Place on the hot bars of the grill (or ridged dry-fry pan) for ¼ minute. Then swing them through a quarter turn, to give what is called *quadrillage* – a diamond pattern underneath.

Leave for a further ¼ minute then turn them over and repeat on the other side. After a total of 1 minute cooking, remove from the grill.

Presentation

Arrange the parsley root on one side of 4 large heated plates, pour the sauce over the rest of the plate and place the fish fillets on the sauce. Garnish with a few flat parsley leaves and serve at once.

My wine suggestion: Chardonnay du Valais 1986 Provins, a Swiss wine or, from France, Alsatian Riesling, Meursault or Pouilly Fumé.

Editor's note: The turnip-rooted parsley resembles a large pointed carrot underground and it is a very popular vegetable in some countries, especially Germany, Scandinavia and Belgium. It is easy to grow from seed, but if it proves difficult to buy, you can replace it in this recipe with baby turnips or young carrots. Unexpectedly it has an extremely subtle, delicate flavour.

CANARD ROTI AUX ENDIVES

Roast duck with chicory

Serves 4

*2.5kg/5½lb duck, preferably Challans duck
(page 29)
150g/5oz butter
4 potatoes, about 60g/2oz each
salt and freshly ground black pepper
8 small, dense heads of chicory
1 tablespoon oil
100ml/3½fl oz water
4 small pinches of sugar
½ lemon
grated zest from 1 orange*

Prepare the vegetables

Clarify the butter; heat it until it froths then subsides. At the bottom of the pan the casein separates as white particles. Let it cool a few moments, then pour off the liquid butter, leaving the sediment in the pan. This is clarified butter, which can be heated to a high temperature without burning.

Peel and finely slice the potatoes on a mandolin, as though you were making crisps. Put them in a bowl and season with salt and pepper. Pour in 3 tablespoons clarified butter and use your hands to turn them over and over until they are evenly coated in butter and seasoning. Grease 4 small ramekins 8cm/3in diameter with clarified butter and put in the sliced potato, packing them as tightly and neatly as you can.

Cut off the solid section at the base of each chicory head and separate the leaves, discarding any that are damaged.

Roast the duck and the potato cakes

Heat the oven to maximum 1½ hours before you plan to serve the duck. Remove as much fat as possible from the duck's vent, season the bird inside and out and truss it. Heat the oil in a roasting tin until very hot on top of the stove, put in the duck on its side and turn it on to the other side after 1 minute (to get rid of some of the fat). Transfer to the first side and put in the oven.

After 10 minutes, turn on to the other side, pouring off the fat. After a further 10 minutes, turn it on to its back, for a final 5 minutes.

Remove the duck from the oven and turn down the oven heat to 200°C/400°F/gas 6, ready to cook the potato cakes. Leave the oven door open for a minute or two as well, to let it cool down.

Wrap the duck in foil – it is essential that it stands for 30 minutes to allow the meat to soften and tenderize. In the plate-warming compartment of the oven the temperature will be just right. Turn it over at least once during this time, to distribute the blood evenly.

Bake the potato cakes for 20 minutes (timing them so they will be ready when the duck is).

Make the sauce and cook the chicory

Pour off all the fat from the tin in which the duck was roasted. Put the tin over the heat and pour in 100ml/3½fl oz water, stirring to deglaze. Bring to the boil, remove from the heat and return the pan, so it reboils several times and reduces to 4 concentrated tablespoonfuls.

Meanwhile, divide the remaining clarified butter between 2 large, non-stick frying pans. Heat and add the chicory leaves, frying them for about 1 minute until they begin to brown. Season with salt and pepper, sugar and a squeeze of lemon juice, and grate the zest from the orange over them, using a nutmeg grater.

Presentation

Carve the duck, either cutting the meat off the bone into escalopes – which is more difficult – or simply cutting it into four portions (removing the backbone).

Arrange the chicory leaves in a circle round the edge of four heated plates. Turn the potato cakes out of the ramekins. Turn over, so they are browned side up and arrange on the left of each plate and place a quarter of the duck in the centre. Spoon a little gravy over the duck and serve immediately.

My wine suggestion: Merlot del Ticino 1985 Vinattieri, a Swiss wine, or French St-Emilion, Pomerol or Côte de Beaune.

SOUFFLE AU CHOCOLAT AU COULIS D'AGRUMES

Hot chocolate soufflé with citrus sauce

Serves 4

3 eggs
butter and sugar for the ramekins
40g/1½oz sugar
120ml/4fl oz buttermilk or whey
10g/⅓ oz cocoa powder (not drinking chocolate
powder, which is sweet)
icing sugar and cocoa, to decorate

For the citrus sauce
150g/5oz kumquats
100g/3½oz sugar
200ml/7fl oz squeezed blood orange juice
1 tablespoon Grand Marnier

Make the citrus sauce

Put the unpeeled kumquats in a small saucepan, add 75g/2½oz sugar and water to cover and cook for about 15 minutes, until just tender.

Meanwhile put the remaining sugar into a small pan with a tablespoon of water and cook until it caramelises. When it is nicely brown, off the heat, add the blood orange juice and Grand Marnier. Return to the heat, stirring to dissolve the caramel, and then boil to reduce to a syrupy consistency.

When the kumquats are cooked, drain the liquid from them into the orange syrup. Cut the kumquats into 5mm/1/8in cubes and add them to the orange sauce.

Prepare the soufflés

Grease 4 ramekins, 4cm/1½in deep and 8cm/3in diameter, with butter. Tip in a little sugar, swirling it around to cover the insides, then tip out the excess.

Separate the eggs, adding 40g/1½oz sugar to the yolks and whisk them with an electric whisk until the mixture is pale in colour. Add the buttermilk or whey and the cocoa and whisk in. Keep in a cool place if preparing ahead.

Bake the soufflés

Pour about 2.5cm/1in hot water into a roasting tin and place on the bottom shelf of the oven, heating it to 200°C/400°F/gas 6.

Whisk the egg whites until stiff, give the cocoa mixture a stir, then pour it into the egg whites. Fold in gently using a spatula, lifting the mixture from the bottom and revolving the bowl a quarter turn every now and then. Pour the mixture into the ramekins, smoothing over the top and wiping any spills from around the edges. Stand the ramekins in the hot bain-marie and cook in the oven for 20 minutes.

Presentation

Turn the soufflés out on to warm dessert plates, then turn them the right way up. Dust the tops with mixed icing sugar and cocoa. Pour the warmed kumquat sauce round them and serve immediately.

My wine suggestion: Petite Arvine Vendange-tardive, Mont d'Or 1983 – or a Gewürztraminer or Sauternes.

Gérard Perriard

CENTENARIO
Lungolago 15, 6600 Locarno Muralto telephone: 93 33 82 22

The youngest of eleven children, Gérard Perriard's parents owned a farm and his mother cooked in their café-restaurant, on the shores of Lake Neuchâtel. It gave him a familiarity with the business – and a love of lakesides. But his parents were elderly, and he was the only child with any aptitude for cooking: the business was sold.

Aged fifteen he started studying catering at the local Hôtel du Lac. After military service came two years at the Restaurant Kimsthalle in Basle, where he rose to be chef de partie and got married. Seven years followed at the lakeside Hôtel La Palma at Locarno, in southern Switzerland. An attempt to leave led to the offer of a second kitchen at the hotel, of which he should be chef. While this was being organised he worked 'stages', first at Taillevent in Paris, then with Frédy Girardet. Here he had a vision of what might be achieved. 'I was master of classic cuisine, but here another door opened. Cuisine based on the market, imaginative, light – the real cuisine'. This is what he wanted to achieve for himself. The new kitchen at Hôtel La Palma was inaugurated in 1978 and within two years he had gained two Michelin rosettes.

He was ambitious, however, to work for himself and in 1981 the Centenario was opened in partnership with Giorgio Giner, now maître d'hôtel. A family house in the Tessinoise style on the road along the lake, dating back to the early eighteenth century, it hadn't been occupied for years. A year after opening it gained a Michelin rosette.

'My style of cooking has the traits of my character,' says the chef, a love of 'joy, youth, sobriety, freshness and elegance.' A second Michelin rosette was awarded in 1984.

MENU

SALADE TIEDE DE LANGOUSTINES A L'HUILE DE NOIX
Warm Dublin Bay prawn salad with walnut oil

CARRE D'AGNEAU ROTI AU BASILIC
Roast best end of lamb with basil

FIGUE CHAUDE AU MERLOT
Hot figs in Merlot with vanilla ice cream

SALADE TIEDE DE LANGOUSTINES A L'HUILE DE NOIX

Warm Dublin Bay prawn salad with walnut oil

Serves 4

16 Dublin Bay prawn tails, shelled
crisp curly endive
12 mange tout, trimmed
salt and freshly ground black pepper
8 leaves of tarragon
8 sprigs of chervil
8 sprigs of dill or fennel
8 chive leaves
paprika

For the nut oil vinaigrette
4 tablespoons walnut oil
1½ tablespoons lemon juice

Arrange curly endive on each of 4 salad plates. Blanch the mange tout briefly in boiling salted water, making sure they retain their crispness; leave to cool then separate the two halves. Remove the seeds – to maintain their perfect appearance – and arrange on the endive.

Cook the shelled prawn tails in boiling salted water for 1-2 minutes – they should remain transparent. Drain them, slice them in half lengthways and arrange on the salad.

Make the vinaigrette dressing beating together the oil and lemon juice with a fork and adding seasonings to taste. Pour over the salad on the plates, garnish with the herbs and sprinkle with a little paprika. Serve immediately.

My wine suggestion: Il Mattirolo, a white wine from Mendrisiotto, which is pale straw coloured, dry scented, and with a fruity flavour in which the Chasselas grape predominates.

Editor's note: These sea creatures, with their long, elegant, lacy-edged claws, are striped in pink and red when they are fished from the water, unlike prawns which only blush when cooked. Nowadays much of Europe has learned to call them *scampi,* after the Italians.

In Britain they have changed their name four times in a generation. In the 1950s they were new and strange and recommended by the author Elizabeth David as 'Norway lobsters'; shellfish from these cold northern waters have an excellent flavour. Rechristened Norway prawns, which suited their size better, they then switched again to become Dublin Bay prawns, because the fishing boats sailing south put off their supply of the perishable shellfish in Dublin Bay.

As the head and claws, which contain almost no meat, make up over half of the shellfish, these are frequently removed before sale. The French name, *langoustine,* is used when they are imported from France, when they are more likely to be sold complete with their elegant heads.

*Salade tiède de langoustines
à l'huile de noix*

Carré d'agneau rôti au basilic

CARRE D'AGNEAU ROTI AU BASILIC

Roast best end of lamb with basil

In spring when the lambs are really tiny, you can serve a whole best end of four chops as a portion. When the lambs are bigger, two chops each will be sufficient.

Serves 4

4 small best ends of neck of lamb, each consisting of 4 chops and weighing about 500g/18oz
salt and freshly ground black pepper
30g/1oz butter
3 tablespoons olive oil
4 shallots, chopped
2 garlic cloves, finely chopped
2-3 medium-sized tomatoes
16 basil leaves
60ml/2fl oz red wine
seasonal vegetables to serve: choose from asparagus, green beans, young carrots, cauliflower sprigs and sliced courgettes

Prepare and cook the lamb

Ask the butcher to remove the backbone and to trim the neckbones so that they stand only 3cm/1¼in clear of the meat. Trim the back fat to 1cm/½in thickness.

Bring the lamb to room temperature for 2 hours before roasting – with a brief roasting time it is crucial that it should not go chilled into the oven. Check that the fat cover on the chops does not extend too high up and that the bones project only a discreet length beyond the fat. Season the joints all over.

Heat the butter with 2 tablespoons olive oil and brown the joints on the fat side, and swiftly on both ends. Put in the oven at 190°C/375°F/gas 5 and roast for 15 minutes: the meat should still be pink in the centre. Remove from the oven and let the joints rest for 5 minutes.

Prepare the sauce and garnish

Meanwhile sweat the shallots and garlic gently in 1 tablespoon of oil until soft. Blanch the tomatoes for 10 seconds each in boiling water, peel them, cut in half and discard seeds and juice. Chop the flesh into neat dice – this is called *concassé* tomato – you need 4 tablespoons to add colour to this sauce.

Heat the diced tomato through with the shallots without cooking them. Cut the basil leaves into strips, adding them to the pan and seasoning well. Steam the accompanying vegetables.

When the lamb is ready, skim any visible fat from the roasting tin and deglaze the pan with the wine, stirring and boiling to reduce to 4 tablespoons. Taste and adjust the seasoning.

Presentation

Put cutlet frills on all 16 projecting bones and carve down between the chops. Serve 4 small chops on each plate accompanied by seasonal vegetables. Divide the tomato-shallot mixture between the plates and spoon 1 tablespoon of meat cooking juices beside the chops.

My wine suggestion: Merlot del Ticino: a regional wine from vineyards on the banks of the rivers of Tessin is the best accompaniment to a regional dish.

Chef's note: We serve wild asparagus with this dish in season.

FIGUE CHAUDE AU MERLOT

Hot figs in Merlot with vanilla ice cream

Serves 4

8 fresh figs
400ml/14fl oz Merlot
4 tablespoons sugar
a few redcurrants or raspberries in season, or sprigs of
mint (optional)
vanilla ice cream to serve

Cook the figs

Bring the Merlot and sugar to the boil and add the figs in a single layer. Cover the pan and cook for 5-6 minutes until just done.

Remove the figs from the pan with a slotted spoon and boil to reduce the liquid to a light syrup – about 200ml/7fl oz.

Cut the figs in half and arrange them in 4 bowls. Pour on the hot syrup. Decorate with a sprig of redcurrants and a few raspberries and pass vanilla ice cream in a separate bowl.

My wine suggestion: Merlot or champagne.

VANILLA ICE CREAM

250ml/9fl oz milk
250ml/9fl oz double cream
1 vanilla pod, split lengthways
4 egg yolks
85g/3oz sugar

Make the vanilla ice cream

Heat the milk and cream together with the vanilla pod. Beat the yolks and sugar together well, then pour on the hot milk, beating all the time. Remove the vanilla pod and return the mixture to the saucepan. On very low heat, or preferrably over boiling water, cook the custard, stirring constantly until it will coat the back of a spoon. Strain and cool, stirring occasionally. When cold, turn into an ice cream machine or alternatively freeze in the freezer, beating several times before it becomes stiff.

Figue chaude au Merlot at the Centenario

Claret jugs at the Centenario

Chez Max

Seestrasse 53, 8702 Zürich-Zollikon telephone: 1 391 88 77

Is Max Kehl a dilettante? He is certainly passionate about art. Part owner of the Galerie Belmont in Flims for twentieth century art, he is as keenly interested in the ambiance of his restaurant, where specially-commisioned murals and avant-garde sculpture blend with classical objects, as he is in wine and food. The answer is emphatically 'no', but his artistic interests have contributed breadth to his cuisine.

His parents did not share his enthusiasm for cooking and sent their thirteen-year-old to a Sunday job in a nearby restaurant to discourage him. It had the opposite effect. An apprenticeship at Baur-au-Lac, Zürich's palace hotel and hotel school in Lausanne followed, then an assistant wine waiter's job at L'Oustau de Baumanière, a spell cooking at the Dorchester in London and another as food and beverage manager in Berlin. But the exigencies of restaurant life made him swear he would embrace a more normal life style. He became a commercial traveller, which involved frequent eating out in restaurants that proved far from his liking. He consoled himself by cooking for his friends.

The job of restaurant manager at the Krone at Regensburg led to his own restaurant the Chesa – Chez Max, behind the station in Zürich. A year later the award of a Gault Millau Clé d'Or confirmed his success. In the summer of 1978 he moved to the lakeside at Zollikon with room for his art collection, but above all, space to indulge his creativity in the kitchen – acknowledged by the award of a Michelin rosette in 1984.

MENU

FILET DE SAINT-PIERRE AU BEURRE DE
COQUES
John Dory fillets with cockle butter

SUPREMES DE CAILLE AUX TRUFFES
NOIRES ET COUSCOUS DE RIZ SAUVAGE
Breasts of quail with truffles and a couscous of wild rice

SOUFFLE DE KUMQUAT AVEC SA
COMPOTE
Kumquat soufflé and compote

FILET DE SAINT-PIERRE AU BEURRE DE COQUES

John Dory fillets with cockle butter

Serves 4

4 John Dory fillets, 85g/3oz each
500g/18oz cockles
150ml/¼pt Noilly Prat, or dry white wine
1 good sized tomato
20g/⅔oz flat parsley for the garnish
135g/4½oz butter, diced
1 teaspoon grated lemon zest
pinch of paprika
1 pinch of saffron strands
salt

Prepare the cockles and garnish
Thoroughly wash the cockles. Heat a large empty saucepan with its lid until it is really hot, then tip in the cockles and cover immediately. Wait for precisely 1 minute, then pour on the Noilly Prat and remove from the heat.
Leave to cool slightly, then shell the cockles, reserving the cooking liquid. Put the cockles and their liquid into a blender and purée, then strain through a muslin-lined sieve (to remove any sand) into a small saucepan. Put the pan over a high heat and reduce until you are left with roughly 2 tablespoons of a syrupy liquid. Reserve this in the pan.
Place the tomato in boiling water for 10 seconds, transfer to cold water then peel and halve it. Remove the seeds and finely dice the flesh.
Separate the parsley leaves from the stalks and keep them cool in a small airtight container.
Make the butter and steam the fish
Reheat the cockle mixture over high heat. Whisk in 120g/4oz butter, in small pieces, adding a small batch, then whisking in the next just before the first has melted, so the texture remains velvety. Season with lemon zest, paprika and saffron, but taste the butter before adding any salt, as the cockles themselves are quite salty.
Heat the diced tomato quickly in 15g/½oz butter and season.
Season the John Dory fillets and steam them in a covered container. The cooking time will depend on the thickness of the fish, but should be about 3 minutes.

Presentation
Arrange the John Dory fillets in the centre of 4 warmed plates, pour on a little cockle butter, place a small spoonful of diced tomato in the centre and sprinkle the parsley leaves around the edge.

My wine suggestion: Meursault, Chablis or Château Y; pronouced *Ygrec,* the latter is a dry white from the same Château as Yquem, with some of the same concentration and alcoholic content, but only a trace of sweetness.

SUPREMES DE CAILLE AUX TRUFFES NOIRES ET COUSCOUS DE RIZ SAUVAGE

Breasts of quail with truffles and a couscous of wild rice

Serves 4

4 large French quails, or 8 smaller ones
120g/4oz wild rice
salt and freshly ground black pepper
60g/2oz fresh truffles
85g/3oz butter
100ml/3½fl oz white wine
60ml/2fl oz double cream
pinch of paprika

Prepare the quails by first removing the legs. These can be served, fried, with an aperitif. Cut down the breast bone and remove the breast complete with the wing (if there is one).
Prepare the wild rice for the couscous
Thoroughly wash the wild rice and boil in about 600-750ml/1-1¼pt salted water for about 35 minutes until all the water has been absorbed and the rice has puffed up. Drain and leave until cold. Then very finely chop the rice (to give it the texture of couscous).
Cut 4 good slices of truffle to garnish and keep in reserve, wrapped tightly in cling film. Chop the remaining truffle then heat for 2 minutes in 20g/⅔oz hot butter. Add the white wine, stirring to deglaze the pan, and bring it to the boil. Add 40ml/1½fl oz cream and put over high heat to reduce by half. Remove from the heat and reserve.

Whip the remaining cream until stiff and reserve in the refrigerator.

Cook the quails and finish the cream sauce

Season the quail breasts with salt, pepper and a little paprika and fry in 40g/1½oz butter, putting them in the pan skin side down to cook for 3 minutes. Turn them over and cook for 1-2 minutes on the cut side. Meanwhile reheat the wild rice in the remaining butter and check and adjust the seasoning.

Reheat the sauce then stir in the whipped cream.

Presentation

Arrange the rice 'couscous' as a nest on 4 warmed plates. Divide the quail suprêmes between them, placing them in the centre of each nest. Pour the sauce over the quails and top with a slice of truffle.

My wine suggestion: Château Beychevelle, Château Palmer or Château Cheval Blanc.

SOUFFLE DE KUMQUAT AVEC SA COMPOTE

Kumquat soufflé and compote

Serves 4

500g/18oz nice ripe kumquats
150ml/¼pt Grand Marnier Centenaire
butter and icing sugar for the moulds
6 egg yolks
1 tablespoon icing sugar
4 egg whites
100g/3½oz caster sugar

For the light sugar syrup
85g/3oz sugar
300ml/½pt water

Prepare the kumquats

Cut the kumquats horizontally in half and remove all the pips. Make the sugar syrup by dissolving the sugar in the water slowly, then boil one minute without stirring. Cook the kumquats in the syrup for 8-10 minutes.

Divide the kumquats and syrup, putting two-thirds aside for the compote. Stir 60ml/2fl oz Grand Marnier into the larger portion.

Purée the remaining kumquats and syrup in a blender then pass through a sieve into a small pan and boil to drive off as much liquid as possible; you need a thick fruit purée.

Make and serve the soufflés

Grease 6 soufflé dishes of 150ml/¼pt capacity, then dust with icing sugar, shaking out the excess. Whisk the egg yolks with the icing sugar until light. Whisk the egg whites to soft peaks, sift in the sugar and whisk to firm meringue.

Add the kumquat purée and the remaining Grand Marnier to the egg yolks and mix well. Gently fold in the meringue, using a spatula. Pour the mixture into the prepared moulds and bake in the oven at its highest setting for 3-4 minutes until nicely puffed and coloured on top; the soufflé should still be moist in the middle. Serve hot with bowls of cold compote.

My wine suggestion: Château d'Yquem. In the restaurant we also serve Champagne Deutz 'Chez Max' or Grand Marnier Centenaire, with 2 ice cubes in each glass.

Bernard Ravet

RESTAURANT DE L'HÔTEL-DE-VILLE

1040 Echallens telephone: 21 881 11 41

Bernard Ravet always wanted to be a chef. He recalls his first gourmet experience, a crawfish, newly boiled, sampled in a restaurant kitchen on an errand for his parents, and 'long gourmand moments, looking and questioning and sniffing at the stockpots' in neighbouring restaurant kitchens. His parents ran a quality grocery in Burgundy, patronised by all the decent restaurants. This gave him his chance to meet the owners, so apprenticeships were no problem. He spent several years in his native region, followed by six months, in 1964, at the Pavillon Henri IV in St-Germain-en-Laye. He then went to Vallorbe, where he married and he has remained attached to Switzerland.

He has three passions – cookery, family and friends – and they are linked in a single theme by dining and good eating. In 1980, aged thirty-four, he became proprietor of l'Hôtel-de-Ville at Echallens. It was singled out for the Clé d'Or by Gault Millau in 1980, and awarded three toques in 1984; in 1988, the restaurant gained 18 out of 20 points. In 1989 he moves to Vufflens Le Château, a restaurant and hotel in a mansion of the Louis Philippe era, surrounded by a garden, just outside Morges.

His theme is to reveal the flavours of the countryside. His cooking is subtly balanced, the products he uses absolutely fresh, each planned for and purchased at its seasonal best, so that it makes its maximum contribution in the hands of this craftsman.

MENU

CREME DE FEVETTES, GIGOTINS
ET SOT L'Y LAISSE DE POULARDE
Broad bean cream with chicken wings and 'oysters'

CHEVREUIL A GENEVRIER
ET SAUTE DE BOLETS
ET CHANTERELLES
*Saddle of venison with juniper wine lees,
fried boletus and chanterelles*

TARTE VAUDOISE A LA CREME ET
CANNELLE
Vaud cinnamon cream tart

CREME DE FEVETTES, GIGOTINS ET SOT L'Y LAISSE DE POULARDE

Broad bean cream with chicken wings and 'oysters'

I must explain the intriguing coloquial title of this recipe. *Gigotins* are chicken wings – not just the pointed tip (which is often removed), nor just the tip and middle joint (which is what freezer centres sell under this name), but all 3 joints, detached from the body at the breast.

Sot l'y laisse literally means 'the fool leaves it behind'. These are the almond-shaped pieces of flesh found on the bony side of the chicken where the thigh joins the spine above the rump, called 'oysters' in English because of their shape.

Serves 6

12 chicken wings, all 3 joints
3kg/6¾lb broad beans in the pod, about 750g/1¾lb after shelling
1 leek, white part only
100g/3½oz butter
salt and freshly ground black pepper
200ml/7fl oz Pinot Gris
200ml/7fl oz double cream
100ml/3½fl oz milk
2 black truffles
12 chicken 'oysters'

For the white chicken stock
1 chicken carcass
60g/2oz butter
200g/7oz diced mixed vegetables, onion, carrots and celery

Prepare the chicken wings

Fiddly, but not difficult, you can ask your butcher to do this. Working from the joint at the breast end, scrape the flesh back from the bone until it is exposed and draw this out, working upwards over the joint to the second bone higher up. Cut off the end bone.

The flesh will retract as it cooks, leaving the end of the second bone exposed, so that it looks like a miniature *gigot* – leg of lamb – hence *gigotin*.

Make the chicken stock

Crush the carcass and any chicken trimmings. Sweat in the butter with the diced vegetables without letting them brown. Add water to cover and simmer gently for 1 hour, skimming frequently, then strain and reserve; you should have about 400ml/14fl oz.

Prepare the broad bean cream

Pod the beans then blanch them in boiling water for a few seconds. Drain and then nick each one at one end with a fingernail. Pinch at the other end so they pop out. You need 500g/18oz podded beans.

Chop the white of leek finely and sweat without browning in 30g/1oz butter. Add two-thirds of the beans, the chicken stock, salt and pepper and the Pinot Gris, then cover and cook gently for 10 minutes.

Purée in a blender then sieve, pressing well to give a fine texture. Add the cream and the milk, warmed together, to form a thick soup. Slice one of the truffles into 2cm/¾in matchsticks and stir in. Taste and season, cover and keep warm.

Fry the gigotins and heat the garnish

Salt and pepper the *gigotins* and toss in 60g/2oz hot butter in a frying pan for 5 minutes. Add the chicken 'oysters' and cook for a further 1 minute. Everything should be crisp and golden. Drain on absorbent paper.

Finely chop the second truffle and warm it with the reserved broad beans in the remaining butter. Salt lightly.

Presentation

Serve the broad bean and truffle cream in soup plates or silver bowls. Portion out the gigotins and chicken 'oysters,' placing these on top of the bean cream, and garnish each plate or bowl with beans and chopped truffle.

My wine suggestion: Pinot Gris 1987 reserved for Bernard Ravet, from Chaudet Rivaz. Grown on the terraces above Lake Geneva, it has a very floral bouquet, with a hint of lemon and pepper.

CHEVREUIL A GENEVRIER ET SAUTE DE BOLETS ET CHANTERELLES

Saddle of venison with juniper wine lees, fried boletus and chanterelles

Serves 6

1.8kg/4¹/₂lb saddle of venison
12 juniper berries, crushed
1 sprig of rosemary
100ml/3¹/₂fl oz wine lees (see note)
salt and freshly ground black pepper
5 tablespoons oil
400g/14oz boletus mushrooms
200g/7oz chanterelles
20g/²/₃oz garlic
60g/2oz shallots
1 pinch of thyme flowers
100g/3¹/₂oz parsley
150g/5oz butter

For the venison stock
300g/11oz venison bones and trimmings
2 tablespoons oil
30g/1oz butter
300g/11oz diced vegetables, onion, carrot and celery
1 tablespoon tomato purée
500ml/18fl oz good red wine
2 sprigs of thyme
6 stalks from the parsley bunch, bruised

Marinate the venison ahead
Two days in advance, infuse the juniper berries with the rosemary in the wine lees.
The day before, remove the nerves and tendons from the saddle and peel off the papery skin to get right down to the meat. Pepper it, lay it on a tray and massage with half the infused lees. Rub it with 2 tablespoons oil, to exclude the air. Cover and leave in the refrigerator.

Make the venison stock ahead
Fry the bones and trimmings in oil in a large saucepan until they take on colour. Remove the fat pieces and add 30g/1oz butter, the diced vegetables and the tomato purée. Fry these stirring together. Thin with the red wine, add water to cover and the thyme and 6 of the parsley stalks. Simmer for 2 hours, skimming frequently then sieve: you should have 200ml/7fl oz stock. This can be done the day before.

Prepare the mushroom sauté
Clean the mushrooms, scraping rather than washing·them. Slice the boletus finely and cut the chanterelles into 3 or 4, according to size.
Chop the garlic and shallots together and add the thyme flowers. Remove the parsley stalks and roughly chop the sprigs.

Roast the venison
Salt the saddle well. Heat 2 tablespoons oil until very hot and brown on all sides. Roast it in an oven at maximum heat for 15 minutes, turning the meat over twice.
Remove from the oven and transfer to a new pan with 60g/2oz butter. Add the juniper berries and rosemary, strained from the wine lees. Lower the oven heat to 180°C/350°F/gas 4 and roast for a further 10 minutes, basting frequently. Turn off the oven, open the door, and leave the joint to rest.

Heat the sauce and prepare the mushrooms
Heat 60g/2oz butter and 1 tablespoon oil in a large saucepan and fry the mushrooms. Add the mixture of garlic, shallot and thyme flowers and toss over a high heat for 3 minutes, or until the mushrooms have lost all their juice. Add salt, pepper and the chopped parsley, check the seasonings and spoon on to a warmed serving platter.

Carve, complete the sauce and serve
Remove the fillets from the saddle whole, cut into medallions and arrange on the mushrooms. Heat the venison stock and emulsify it by gradually whisking in the drippings from the second roasting tin. Whisk in 30g/1oz butter in dice, season and serve in a gravy boat.

My wine suggestion: Pinot Noir 'Le Cartige' 1981 from J. M. Conne, Chexbres; with flavours of vanilla, morello cherries and candied fruits, its fine tannins give it a strength to match game.

Editor's note: The end of the bottle of wine – the lees – quickly turns acid in a nearly-empty bottle. One of its few uses is to replace the vinegar in a salad dressing. The acidity is deliberately used here to tenderise the venison, while helping to infuse it with juniper.

TARTE VAUDOISE A LA CREME ET CANNELLE

Vaud cinnamon cream tart

The Swiss are admirable bakers and we make superlative versions of every patisserie known in our neighbouring countries – Austria, France, Germany and Italy. Here is a very simple country tart, based on the rich cream for which Swiss cows on the high pastures are famous.

Serves 6
250g/9oz fine white flour
150g/5oz butter, diced small, plus extra for greasing the tin
85g/3oz sugar
1 egg
pinch of salt

For the cinnamon cream
2 tablespoons sugar
1 teaspoon ground cinnamon
1 tablespoon flour
300ml/¹⁄₂pt double cream

Make the pastry case
Make a well in the flour and put the diced butter, sugar, egg and salt in the middle. Mix them first with the fingertips without touching the flour, then gradually draw in the flour until a compact ball is formed. Wrap and leave in the refrigerator for at least 1 hour.

Roll out the pastry 3mm/⅛in thick and line a greased flan tin 25cm/10in diameter, fitting it well to the sides. Roll the pin over the top of the tin to remove excess pastry and prick the base in several places.

Cover with foil, spreading it over the edges and chill in the refrigerator for 30 minutes, while the oven heats.

Fill the foil with dried beans and bake the tart case in an oven at 220°C/425°F/gas 7 for 12 minutes. Remove the foil and continue cooking until the pastry is a pale golden colour – another 2-3 minutes.

Put in the cream filling
Mix the sugar and cinnamon, then reserve a third of it. Mix the remainder with the flour and sprinkle this over the base of the warm pastry case. Pour the cream over this, without mixing it and scatter the reserved sugar and cinnamon over the top. Replace in the oven at the same temperature for about 10 minutes. The tart is cooked when the mixture bubbles all over the surface and the cinnamon sugar looks as if it has melted. Cool it for at least 2 hours, until the cream has set.

My wine suggestion: Johannisberg St-Martin Mont d'Or 1982, from Dominique Fauré. This wine of the Sauternes type from the Valais region has an aroma of honey and grape flowers and is persistently aromatic.

Sweden

Welcome to an open table!
The Swedes gave us smörgåsbord —
now traditional dishes are
prepared with added art;
good food from the North,
cooked with care and talent.

Crister Svantesson

JOHANNA

Södra Hamngatan 47, Götenburg telephone: 31 11 22 60

Crister Svantesson is enthusiastic about cooking and keen to transmit this enthusiasm and share his knowledge. He has written four cookery books.

He became an apprentice at the age of fourteen in 1960. Armed with the basic knowledge for becoming a good cook, he went to France, in 1965, to perfect his craft. Here he spent three years, serving periods in several great restaurants, notably the Restaurant Colonasse and the Tour d'Argent in Paris, the Hotel Viking in Menton and then back to Paris, to work at the Relais de Suède.

In 1968 he returned to Sweden working in various restaurants until 1974, when at the age of twenty-eight he became his own employer. He bought the Johanna, on one of the principal streets in Götenburg, Sweden's canal city. Here he serves versions of traditional recipes, based on fish – Götenburg is Sweden's second port – even reindeer from the far north, and wild berries, of which the Scandinavians are particularly fond.

He is a member of the Association des Relais Gourmands and advises the Sara Hotels chain. He has received several awards including the Prix d'Honneur from Sandahl, the Swedish foundation for the encouragement of gastronomy. This was followed by the Gold Medal of the Swedish Academy of Gastronomy in 1983 – the year between our other two Swedish chefs, Bengt Wedholm and Erik Lallerstedt.

MENU

FRICASSEE DE HOMARD AU SAUTERNES
Lobster fricassee with Sauternes

FILET DE RENNE AU POIVRE, CHOUX ET BAIES DE GENIEVRE
Peppered reindeer with cabbage and juniper

MOUSSE AUX MURES ARCTIQUES
Cloudberry mousse

FRICASSEE DE HOMARD AUX SAUTERNES

Lobster fricassee with Sauternes

Serves 4

2 live lobsters, about 600g/1¼lb each and preferably female
4 ripe tomatoes
120g/4oz butter, softened
1 carrot, finely chopped
½ onion, finely chopped
100ml/3½fl oz dry white wine
100ml/3½fl oz Saúternes
100ml/3½fl oz well-reduced fish stock (page 161)
300ml/½pt double cream
salt and milled white pepper
¼ bunch chives, finely chopped

Skin the tomatoes by plunging them into boiling water for a few seconds, skin and seed them and dice the flesh.

Cook the lobsters

Drop the lobsters into a pan of boiling water and cook them for 4 minutes. Then take them out and cool them at once under cold running water.

Remove the claws, smash them with a heavy blow and pick out the claw meat in large pieces. Split the tail up the underside and remove the flesh in one piece, then cut it into rings. Reserve the eggs, which are held by the back legs and tail fins. Then split the lobster head in half. Discard the stomach but reserve the liver and any roe in the head. Mash the liver with the eggs and half the butter to make a homogenous paste.

Make the Sauternes sauce

Crush the shells. Heat the rest of the butter and add lobster shells, turning them in the hot fat. Add the carrot and onion and fry gently. Pour in both types of white wine and two-thirds of the reduced fish stock and cook, uncovered, for 20 minutes.

Pass the liquid through a sieve into a saucepan. Boil until reduced to 300ml/½pt.

Add the cream and boil again to reduce by a third. Stir in the liver and egg butter. Season to taste with salt and white pepper.

Warm the pieces of lobster in this sauce.

Presentation

Arrange the lobster on 4 warmed plates and coat with the sauce. Garnish with diced tomato and finely chopped chives.

My wine suggestion: a dry white from Sancerre – these have a pronounced taste when mature.

Editor's note: Spiny rock lobsters of the same weight may be substituted in this and other recipes for lobsters where the claws are not needed for decorative purposes. In parts of Europe they are more popular than lobsters. Minus the heavy claws, they have the convenience of having all the flesh in the tail, where it is easily extracted.

The name of this *langouste* is more of a dilemma in English-speaking countries. In Britain it is a crawfish, in America and South Africa a crayfish. The latter name in Britain is given to the small, freshwater crayfish (page 181), called *écrevisse* in France. To add to the confusion, the Americans speak of these as crawfish – it's altogether simpler to stick to the French.

FILET DE RENNE AU POIVRE, CHOUX ET BAIES DE GENIEVRE

Peppered reindeer with red cabbage and juniper

Serves 4

600g/1¼lb reindeer fillet
salt
2 tablespoons ground white pepper
40g/1½oz butter
2 tablespoons bilberries to garnish

For the red cabbage

800g/1¾lb red cabbage, shredded and marinated for
5-6 hours in 200ml/7fl oz red wine vinegar
2 tablespoons salt
100ml/3½fl oz red wine vinegar
2 tablespoons duck or goose fat
4 tablespoons honey

For the juniper and red wine sauce

2 shallots, finely chopped
10 juniper berries, crushed
100ml/3½fl oz red wine
100ml/3½fl oz brown bone stock (page 178)

Boil 1L/1¾pt water with 2 tablespoons salt and the vinegar. Add the cabbage and bring back to the boil. Drain and spread it on a cloth.
Melt the duck or goose fat in a large frying pan, add the red cabbage and honey and leave to cook over medium heat, stirring it occasionally.

Cook the reindeer and make the sauce
Salt the fillet and rub well with pepper, then fry in 30g/1oz butter, turning it until it is coloured on all sides and cooked, but still pink in the middle – about 15 minutes. Keep it warm.
Add the shallots and juniper berries to the pan and then stir in the red wine. Add the veal stock and let it reduce for a few minutes. Season with salt and add the remaining butter.

Presentation
Taste the red cabbage to check that there is the right balance between salt, sweet and sour. Spoon it on to 4 warmed plates. Slice the meat and lay it on top. Sieve the sauce, pour it round and garnish with bilberries.

My wine suggestion: Fixin Clos de la Perríre, a bold and powerful Burgundy for game.

MOUSSE AUX MURES ARCTIQUES

Cloudberry mousse

Serves 4

300g/11oz cloudberries
120g/4oz granulated sugar, or more to taste
20g/²⁄₃oz cream of semolina (see below)
200ml/7fl oz whipping cream
3 sheets gelatine
5 tablespoons water
4 biscuits to serve
2 tablespoons bilberries

Cook the cloudberries with 2-3 tablespoons water and 120g/4oz sugar for 10 minutes then cool briefly and press through a sieve. Taste and add more sugar if needed. There should be 150ml/¼pt purée. Leave until cold.
Stir the cream of semolina into the whipping cream and whisk until light and fluffy.
Soak the gelatine in 5 tablespoons water, then dissolve over hot water. Stir in to the berry purée. Gently fold in the whipped cream. Fill 4 150ml/¼pt ramekins.
Cover with 4 biscuits and chill until set.

Presentation
Run a knife round inside the ramekins and turn out the cloudberry mousses on 4 dessert plates. Garnish with some bilberries.

My wine suggestion: Grahams Malvedos port 1965.

Editor's note: Cloudberries are a small golden fruit, related to the blackberry, which grow on low bushes over large areas of northernmost Europe; they are particularly popular in Sweden. Blackberries may be substituted.

CREAM OF SEMOLINA

250ml/9fl oz milk
1 tablespoon semolina

Bring the milk to the boil and sprinkle the semolina over the top. Stir in and transfer to a bowl that fits on top a pan of simmering water. Cook gently, stirring regularly, for 30 minutes, to make a thick cream. Leave until cold.

Bengt Wedholm

WEDHOLM'S FISK

Nybrokajen 17, 111 48 Stockholm telephone: 8 104 874

'I would like to open a restaurant where we would serve nothing but sole, but in different ways. The best raw material we have in Sweden is our fish and our shellfish' says Bengt Wedholm. It's not surprising, then, that he owns one of Stockholm's best fish restaurants.

He was born in Hallsberg, not far from Stockholm. Just seventeen in 1936, he took 'whatever job I could find,' starting as an apprentice at the Gyldene Freden. In 1943 he was lucky to get a legendary chef, Julius Carlsson, as teacher at the Cecil, a relationship that was maintained for sixteen years, except for a few years he spent in Paris.

In 1958 he launched his own restaurant in Stockholm, the Rotisserie Ostergök, to which he added the first pizzeria in Sweden and a fish restaurant. Ten years later the opportunity came to buy the restaurant where he had been apprentice, the Källaren Den Gyldene Freden, and become head chef. He only left it in 1981 to open his present restaurant, just opposite the Royal Theatre at Nybroplan in Stockholm, a restaurant of spartan elegance, in several shades of grey with wooden panelling. With fish and shellfish as its stars, it was Restaurant of the Year' in 1982, when he also won the Gold medal of the Swedish Gastronomic Academy. It was awarded a Michelin rosette in 1986.

'Just plain no-nonsense cooking: the freshest fish of the best kind, prepared simply so their inherent quality is seen to advantage in the best possible manner. It is the kind of cooking I have always wanted' says Bengt Wedholm. 'It is Swedish cooking and international as well. There have always been cooks who did not want to skimp and cheat, but have insisted on quality. And this kind of cooking is appreciated more and more nowadays.'

MENU

FAGELBO
Bird's nest

SKALDJURSGRATANG
Savoury seafood ring

LINGONPARON
Lingonberry pears

FAGELBO

Bird's nest

Serves 6

20 canned anchovy fillets, finely chopped
3 tablespoons finely chopped onion
3 tablespoons capers
4 tablespoons finely chopped beetroot, pickled in vinegar
1 head of lettuce, finely shredded
9 egg yolks

Arrange the anchovies, onion, capers, beetroot and lettuce shreds in small heaps to form a ring on a big platter. Make sure that the different colours make an attractive pattern.

Slide the egg yolks into the centre, one by one, from a small plate, being careful not to break them. Show the platter to your guests.

After you have done this, stir and mix all the ingredients together – like steak tartare – before serving.

The bird's nest can also be served on individual small plates, letting each person stir and mix the ingredients.

My wine suggestion: not a wine, but beer and aquavit, or vodka.

SKALDJURSGRATANG

Savoury seafood ring

For me this is a classic dish, since it was created by my teacher, Julius Carlsson, a famous Swedish chef. He called it *'Savorie de pêcheur'*

Serves 4

300g/11oz made weight puff pastry
butter and flour for the tin
10 mussels, well cleaned
150g/5oz unshelled prawns, to give 60g/2oz after peeling
60g/2oz smoked salmon, cut into thin strips
60g/2oz Gruyère cheese, grated
30g/1oz truffle (optional)

For the egg custard
500ml/18fl oz single cream
5 eggs
½ teaspoon salt
freshly ground pepper to taste

For the hollandaise sauce
4 egg yolks
4 tablespoons water
salt and cayenne pepper
250g/9oz clarified butter (page 23)
juice of 1 lemon

For the hot mussel butter
30g/1oz butter
1 tablespoon stock from cooking the mussels
2 tablespoons chopped parsley

Line a ring with puff pastry

Grease a 1.5L/2½ pt savarin ring tin, or a 23cm/9in push-bottom ring tin, 7cm/2½in deep – what the Americans call a 'tube pan' – with butter. Sprinkle it with flour and shake off the excess. (This simple job must be done thoroughly or the pastry will stick.) Roll out the puff pastry on a lightly floured surface, so that the circle is 10cm/4in bigger all round than the diameter of the tin. Roll the pastry up round the pin and lift over the tin, then unwrap it on top. Lift the pastry edges round the outside of the tin, so that it will subside into the ring. Ease it in to line the tin, leaving at least 1cm/½in pastry hanging over the edge, to prevent the pastry slipping in. Leave the pastry intact over the hole in the middle; this helps it to keep its shape. Chill the pastry-lined tin for 30 minutes.

Prepare and put in the filling

Heat a saucepan big enough to contain the mussels in one layer. Put them in and put on the lid. Cook for 1-2 minutes, shaking the pan. Cool, discard the shells and reserve the juice.

Layer the mussels, prawns and smoked salmon into the chilled raw pastry case, sprinkling grated cheese between the layers.

Bring the cream to simmering – do not boil. Cool slightly. Whisk the eggs together, season and pour in the hot cream. Pour over the fish.

Bake the tart

Heat the oven to maximum; this must be done well in advance so the oven is very hot when you start baking. Place the tin in the bottom of the oven and bake for 20 minutes, or until the colour has turned a fine golden-brown. Cover with foil and bake for an additional 15 minutes. Lower the temperature to 200°C/400°F/gas 6 and continue baking for 20 minutes.

Let the tart rest for 5 minutes, then turn it out (or push it upwards out of the tin) and place on a plate, right side up. Trim away the pastry covering the hole, and sides if necessary.

Prepare the sauces

Make these during the last stage of baking, so they are ready when needed. Have the clarified butter ready at blood heat. Whisk the egg yolks, water, salt and cayenne together in a bowl that fits over a pan of simmering water. Whisk constantly until the mixture is thick and creamy. Remove from the heat and beat in the warm butter, a little at the time until the sauce starts to thicken, then faster. When it has been incorporated, add the lemon juice and season to taste. Melt 30g/1oz butter with 1 tablespoon of reserved mussel liquor. Beat in the parsley.

Presentation

Pour the hollandaise into the hole in the centre of the tart. Sprinkle with chopped truffle. Pour the mussel and parsley butter round the outside. Serve immediately.

My wine suggestion: Tokay d'Alsace Pinot Gris 1983 from Trimbach.

LINGONPARON

Lingonberry pears

Serves 4

8 slightly under-ripe cooking pears
½ lemon
600g/1¼lb lingonberries (see note)
400g/14oz sugar
300ml/½pt water
chilled whipped cream to serve

Peel the pears, leaving the stems on. Scrape the stems clean with a knife. Scoop out the core of the pears with an apple corer, then immerse them in cold water. Squeeze the lemon juice into the water to prevent the pears from browning.

Clean and rinse the berries then cook them with the sugar and water for 10 minutes. When cooked, they start to pop, like cranberries. Skim off any froth that rises.

Add the pears to the juice and cook for 15-30 minutes; the timing depends on the size of the pears and how ripe they are. Turn them now and then during cooking and be sure not to let them overcook and start to turn mushy: they should retain their texture. Take the pan off the heat just before you judge them to be ready, for they are then allowed to cool in the juice, and during this time they will soften a little more. Serve cold with slightly whipped cream.

My wine suggestion: not wine but mineral water would go best with these faintly tart flavours.

Editor's note: Lingonberries, also called crowberries, are a small vibrant red berry of the blueberry family. They are native to Scandinavia and Russia and less often are found in Scotland. They are a tradition in Sweden.

Erik Lallerstedt

ERIK'S

Osterlänggatan 17, Stockholm telephone: 8 23 85 00

Erik Lallerstedt is well known in Sweden for his Saturday night Food Journal *on television and a Friday radio spot. He believes 'you should love life, people and food'. 'My very biggest cooking thrill was at Frédy Girardet's. It was so fantastic that I could hardly sleep all night. I was scared: what had I dared to get into? This was almost too great a challenge. I had had other gastronomic adventures – but nothing like this.'*

The son of a Drottningholm architect, his father thought cooking was fun, often being the one to cook Sunday dinner. His own first attempts at cooking were in an up-country hotel.

He then spent four years training at the Hasselbacken school in Stockholm.

His first commercial enterprise was a shop selling fish and shellfish in Ostermalmshallen, a well-known indoor market selling the best and freshest delicacies. With the shop went a restaurant specialising in seafood. In 1980 he launched – literally – Erik's restaurant och Ostronbar, on a rebuilt barge moored alongside Strandvägen, a popular promenade. It won a Michelin rosette in 1984, and the gold medal of the Swedish Gastronomic Academy.

In 1986 he started a new Erik's, where the big dining room on the second floor has a view of the bronze of St George and the Dragon outside. 1988 brought him a Michelin rosette.

'My style of cooking is rather traditional,' he says 'but this does not mean that I don't try out new dishes or ideas. Swedes are rather conservative in their eating habits and you ought to give your guests' tastes priority – but it is always nice to surprise them.'

MENU

MATJESILL SOUFLE MED KAVIARSAS
Pickled herring soufflé with cold caviar sauce

UGNSBAKAD LAX MED APPLE OCH
CURRYSAS, GURKA OCH OSTRONSVAMP
*Baked salmon with curried apple sauce, cucumber
'noodles' and oyster mushrooms*

VARM BJORNBARSSOPPA MED
VANILJGLASS OCH MANDELFLAN
Hot blackberry soup with ice cream and almond wafers

Matjesill soufle med kaviarsas

Ugnsbakad lax med apple och currysas, gurka och ostronsvamp

Varm Björnbärssoppa med vaniljglass och mandelflan

MATJESILL SOUFLE MED KAVIARSAS

Pickled herring soufflé with cold caviar sauce

Serves 4

3 medium-to-large fillets of matje herring, salted and seasoned, often sold canned

For the soufflé
60g/2oz butter
40g/1 ½oz flour
250ml/9fl oz milk
4 egg yolks
3 egg whites
salt and freshly ground black pepper

For the cream and caviar sauce
300ml/½pt crème fraîche (page 250)
2 tablespoons salted smoked cod roe paste (Kalles Kaviar) or puréed smoked cod's roe

Make the soufflé mixture
Melt the butter and work in the flour with a wooden spoon; cook for a minute. Add the warm milk and bring to the boil, stirring all the time. Simmer for another 2 minutes. Stir a little hot sauce into the yolks, then pour this back into the pan off the heat.
Cut the herring into pieces and chop in the food processor. Add to the soufflé and season.
Bake and serve the soufflés
Butter 4 ovenproof ramekins, 150ml/¼pt capacity. Whisk the egg whites until stiff with a pinch of salt. Stir a little into the herring mixture to lighten it, if it seems stiff, then fold the herring mixture into the whites with a spatula, cutting it in lightly. Turn the mixture into the ramekins, smoothing the top and wiping away any spills.
Bake in an oven heated to · 200-240°C/400-475°F/gas 9-10 for 10-12 minutes until nicely risen, but not dry in the middle.
While the soufflés are in the oven, make the sauce by stirring together the crème fraîche and cod's roe paste.
Serve the hot soufflés immediately, accompanied by the cold sauce.

My wine suggestion: not a wine, but beer and ice-cold aquavit.

UGNSBAKAD LAX MED APPLE OCH CURRYSAS, GURKAS OCH OSTRONSVAMP

Baked salmon with curried apple sauce, cucumber 'noodles' and oyster mushrooms

Serves 4

4 pieces of salmon fillet, each 200g/7oz
½ cucumber
salt and freshly ground black pepper
300g/11oz oyster mushrooms
2 tablespoons olive oil
4 pastry fish (see note)
4 sprigs of marjoram

For the curried wine sauce
40g/1 ½oz butter
1 shallot
30g/1oz flour
100ml/3 ½fl oz white wine
100ml/3 ½fl oz fish stock (page 161) or milk or cream
salt and freshly ground black pepper
1 teaspoon curry powder
2 tablespoons apple juice

Make the curried apple sauce
Melt 30g/1oz butter and fry the shallot until transparent. Sprinkle with the flour and work this in, then add the white wine and fish stock milk or cream. Bring gently to the boil, stirring and season to taste.
In another small pan heat the remaining butter and work in the curry powder. Let it cool a little then scrape into the wine sauce, stirring until smooth. Add the apple juice and bring gently to simmering. Keep the sauce hot.
Prepare the vegetables and bake the fish.
Peel the cucumber, halve it and remove the seeds with a teaspoon. Cut it into fine strips on the mandolin. Blanch these green vegetable 'noodles' for 1-2 minutes in boiling, lightly salted water; they should retain some crispness. Keep the cucumber hot.
Cut the oyster mushrooms into strips. Heat the oil and add them. Let them sizzle over a high heat so that they do not cook in their own plentiful juices – which give them the French name of *pleurottes* or 'weepers'. Season with salt and pepper and keep them hot.

Season the salmon fillets on both sides. Bake them on a greased ovenproof ceramic platter at 120°C/250°F/gas ½ for 5-7 minutes.

Presentation

Pour a pool of curried wine sauce on to 4 warmed plates and place a fillet of salmon and pastry fish on each one. Arrange the cucumber 'noodles' on one side and the fried oyster mushrooms topped with a herb sprig on the other and serve at once.

My wine suggestion: Pouilly-Vinzelles.

Editor's note: Make the pastry fish like the *fleurons* on page 168, cutting out the fish with the point of a knife.

VARM BJORNBARSSOPPA MED VANILJGLASS OCH MANDELFLAN

Hot blackberry soup with ice cream and almond wafers

Serves 4

200g/7oz fresh or defrosted blackberries
150g/5oz icing sugar
1L/1¾pt water
½-1 tablespoon arrowroot

For the vanilla ice cream
1 vanilla pod
100g/3½oz icing sugar
600ml/1pt double cream
4 egg yolks

For the almond wafers
30g/1oz butter
2 tablespoons sugar
2 tablespoons heavy sugar syrup (page 252)
3 tablespoons flaked almonds
1 tablespoon flour

Make the vanilla ice cream

Split the vanilla pod and scrape out the vanilla seeds. Mix them with a little of the measured sugar as they are so tiny. Heat the cream with the vanilla pod and the seedy sugar and bring to boiling point.

Whisk the egg yolks with the remaining sugar until light and fluffy. Remove the vanilla pod and pour the hot cream down on the eggs, stirring all the time. Return the cream to the pan and cook over very low heat, preferably over just-simmering water, stirring with a wooden spoon, until the custard will just coat its back. Strain and cool the custard, stirring occasionally, then chill.

Freeze in an ice cream maker, or in the freezer, beating several times before the mixture is stiff.

Make the almond wafers

Melt the butter with the sugar and sugar syrup. With a wooden spoon work in the flaked almonds and then the flour. Grease 2 baking trays and dot the almond mixture on to the trays, a spoonful at a time, and spacing them well out, as they will spread.

Bake 1 tray at a time at 180°C/350°F/gas 4 until they are a light brown round the edges, about 7-8 minutes. Let them rest ½ minute then quickly remove from the tray with a palette knife, draping them over a rolling pin, to give a curved shape. When crisp, cool on a wire rack and store in an airtight tin if made ahead.

Cook the hot blackberry soup

Put the blackberries in a saucepan and add the sugar and water, stir and bring to the boil. Simmer for 10 minutes, the fruit should be just disintegrating into the liquid as it reduces. Strain the soup through a sieve, pressing the fruit down well with a wooden spoon, but not forcing it through – there should be about 600ml/1pt liquid.

Check the consistency; if it does not seem thick enough, make a paste with the arrowroot and very little water. Reheat the blackberry liquid, stir a little into the arrowroot and return to the pan. Do not let the soup wait, simmering, if it has been thickened – arrowroot can separate again on long boiling.

Presentation

Serve the hot soup in bowls, topped with a scoop of vanilla ice cream and pass the almond wafers.

My wine suggestion: try the rich flavours of a medium Madeira, or red port or Sauternes.

Benelux

A land won from the sea, it is famous for plain things well done —

like mussels and mayonnaise and good, sweet Flemish beer.

For simple things are very well done in the Low Countries,

and nowadays the cooking is far from plain.

Pierre Romeyer

PIERRE ROMEYER

Chaussée de Groenendaal 109, 1990 Hoeilaart, Brussels, Belgium telephone: 2 657 0581

'If there had not been a war,' this virtuoso cook and sauce-maker says 'and my mother had not taken so much trouble to make sure I never went hungry, I am almost certain I would not have become a chef.' An interest born of need bred the gourmand. His first mentor was Georges Michel, a giant of a man with a personality to match, who ran the Auberge Alsacienne in Brussels, and taught him the disciplines of the kitchen.

From there to the bottom rung at the Savoy in Brussels, during the reign of Julien Vermeersch, where he stayed until 1948. After military service he returned to the Savoy, now under another master, Maixent Coudroy, but followed Vermeersch to the Carlton. Aged twenty-five, he won the Prosper Montagné Prize in 1955. It would have been logical for the Carlton to feature the dish that made him Belgium's top chef, but unfortunately it was a sauce dish and house rules kept his name off the menu. He gave notice.

He cooked for the world's luminaries at the 1958 Brussels Exhibition, then decided to open his own restaurant, first the Val Vert at Groenendaal in Hoeilaart, where he gained first one then two Michelin rosettes. Then, in 1967, he moved to the Maison de Bouche in the same area: a handsome house, surrounded by lawns and pools with swans, it is now named after him. It gained three rosettes in its opening year — surely a record. He is proud of these only 'because they reflect my love of doing things well.'

Honours followed, both personal ones like the Chevalier de l'Ordre de Leopold II and, in 1979, the coverted Gault Millau Clé d'Or, a nouvelle cuisine award rarely won in Belgium. His dishes are 'inspired by a classic technique, but bear my own very light touch.'

MENU

HOMARD AUX FINES AROMATES
Lobster in aromatic cream

RABLE DE LIEVRE AUX CANON HALL
D'OVERYSE-HOEILAART
Saddle of hare with Canon Hall grapes

ARLEQUIN A LA MANDARINE NAPOLEON
Orange liqueur and chocolate cake

HOMARD AUX FINES AROMATES

Lobster in aromatic cream

Serves 2

*2 female lobsters, preferrably Norwegian, each 600g/
1¼lb
1L/1¾pt unsalted fish stock (page 161)
500ml/18fl oz Riesling
salt and freshly ground black pepper
500ml/18fl oz double cream
100g/3½oz butter, in dice
lambs' lettuce or celery leaves to garnish*

For the mirepoix

*100g/3½oz each chopped carrots, celery, shallots and
white of leek
1 sprig of thyme
2 bay leaves
cloves from ½ garlic bulb*

For the cooked garnish

*clarified butter (page 23) for deep frying
50g/1¾oz carrots, sliced
50g/1¾oz celery stalks, cut across in crescents
50g/1¾oz white of leek, sliced diagonally
50g/1¾oz pickling onions, sliced in rounds
50g/1¾oz French beans, halved lengthways*

Cook and prepare the lobsters

Put the fish stock, Riesling and the mirepoix
into a large pan and add a pinch of pepper but
no salt. When the·liquid boils, plunge in the
lobsters, cover and boil for 10 minutes. Take the
lobsters from the pan and remove the tails and
claws. Return the claws to the pan for 5 minutes
to finish cooking.

Turn the lobster tails on to their backs and
remove the coral, which is held between the tail
fins and the back legs. Press this through a fine
sieve and reserve the purée.

Twist all the legs off the body and add them to
the boiling liquid.

Cut the lobster tail up the underside and remove
the shell. Cut the tail meat into discs and
reserve.

When the claws are ready, remove them and
boil the liquid, without a cover, to reduce to
120ml/4fl oz. Remove and reserve the legs. Add
the cream and boil to reduce again to 120ml/

4fl oz. Press the sauce through a fine sieve and
thicken it by stirring in the puréed coral and
then the diced butter. Season to taste.

Meanwhile smash the claws with a hammer and
extract the meat, in as large pieces as possible.

Prepare the garnish

Heat clarified butter in a wide pan to a depth of
1.5cm/½in and fry all the vegetables except the
beans. Boil the beans briefly. Drain on absorbent
paper and season lightly.

Presentation

Arrange the lobster head at the edge of each
warmed plate, facing outward. Behind it arrange
four legs, making a ring round the plate and
make a splayed tail with.the beans opposite the
head.

Spoon sauce into the middle and on it arrange
the claw meat and the tail, sliced lengthways,
with the red skin uppermost. Arrange the
vegetables decoratively inside the ring made by
the legs. Flash in a very hot oven to warm
through again, then garnish the head on either
side with lambs' lettuce or celery leaves and
serve.

My wine suggestions: a fine white burgundy from
Puligny Montrachet, which combines finesse
with plenty of body.

Homard aux fines aromates

Râble de lièvre aux Canon Hall d'Overyse-Hoeilaart

The carving table at Pierre Romeyer

RABLE DE LIEVRE AUX CANON HALL D'OVERYSE-HOEILAART

Saddle of hare with Canon Hall grapes

Serves 4

saddles from 2 hares
40 Canon Hall grapes
100ml/3½fl oz champagne cognac
salt and freshly ground black pepper
30g/1oz butter
new potatoes, boiled in their skins, to serve

For the poivrade cream
120g/4oz cold butter, diced
85g/3oz mirepoix, made up of chopped carrot, celery,
onion and garlic
1 sprig of thyme
1 bay leaf
1 tablespoon redcurrant jelly
250ml/9fl oz sauce poivrade (see right)
1 tablespoon Belgian mustard
250ml/9fl oz double cream

Prepare the grapes and cook the hare saddles
Peel the grapes, removing all the pips. Soak them in the cognac. Put them on the edge of the stove in a pan, to be warmed later, but don't let them cook.

Melt 30g/1oz butter in a heavy flameproof dish. Season the saddles and cook them on top of the stove, turning regularly, until done but still pink in the middle – about 15 minutes. Remove to a warm serving platter.

Make the poivrade cream
Add the mirepoix to the juices in the pan and sweat over low heat. Add the redcurrant jelly, thyme and bay leaf. Moisten with the basic sauce poivrade and bring to the boil. Leave to cook for 15 minutes. Pass through a fine sieve into a pan. Drain the juices from the grapes and add to the pan. Stir in the mustard and the cream and boil to reduce again until you have about 175ml/6fl oz sauce. Season to taste.

Whisk in the diced butter over a very low heat, adding a few lumps at a time, then adding more just before the previous lumps melt, so that the sauce has a velvety texture.

Presentation
Remove the fillets whole from either side of the saddles. Carve thinly and arrange the slices in a flower shape on 4 warmed plates. Spoon grapes into the centre of each one and pour the poivrade cream round the outside of the meat. Serve small new potatoes, boiled in their skins with the dish.

My wine suggestion: a red burgundy: Bonnes-Mares would harmonise particularly well.

SAUCE POIVRADE

Peppercorn sauce

250g/9oz bones and trimmings from the hare
30g/1oz onions, roughly chopped
30g/1oz carrots, roughly chopped
30g/1oz celery stalk, roughly chopped
2½ cloves garlic
2 bay leaves
10 thyme sprigs
6 juniper berries, crushed
2 tablespoons black peppercorns, crushed
500ml/18fl oz red wine (burgundy or claret)
1 tablespoon oil
30g/1oz flour
500ml/18fl oz brown bone stock (page 178)
120ml/4fl oz sieved tomato (passata)

Marinate all the hare trimmings, vegetables, herbs and spices in red wine for 12 hours. Drain the hare trimmings and vegetables, saving the red wine. Sort out the hare from the vegetables. Colour the hare bones and trimmings in hot oil in a casserole over a high heat. When they are browned, add the chopped vegetables, herbs and spices from the marinade and sprinkle with the flour. Stir this in, then cover the casserole, turn the heat to very low and leave the vegetables to sweat for 10-15 minutes.

Remove the cover, turn up the heat and add the red wine marinade. Boil to reduce by half. Add the brown bone stock and sieved tomato and leave to simmer for 2 hours, then strain through a fine sieve – you will have about 700ml/1¼pt.

ARLEQUIN A LA MANDARINE NAPOLEON

Orange liqueur and chocolate cake

Serves 6

For the chocolate sponge
3 eggs
120g/4oz caster sugar
100g/3½oz flour
30g/1oz potato flour (fécule), sifted
1 teaspoon cocoa
butter and flour for the tin

For the chocolate cream and sponge
100g/3½oz dark chocolate, broken
1 egg yolk
200g/7oz crème fraîche (page 251)
2 tablespoons sugar
½ teaspoon kirsch

For the Mandarine Napoléon layer
4 leaves gelatine, broken up
60g/2oz caster sugar
grated zest and juice of ½ orange
1 tablespoon Mandarine Napoléon liqueur
2 egg yolks
100ml/3½fl oz crème fraîche (page 251)
2 egg whites

For the cake decoration
4 big oranges
4-5 strawberries
30ml/1fl oz white wine
juice of ½ orange
20g/⅔ oz caster sugar
¼ teaspoon powdered gelatine
60ml/2fl oz whipping cream
1 tablespoon caster sugar
1 tablespoon cocoa, sifted

Start by making the sponge base
Grease a cake tin 20cm/8in diameter. Line the base and grease again. Dust with flour.
Beat the eggs and sugar in a mixer-bowl. Move the bowl from the mixer to sit over a pan of simmering water and hand-whisk until light and much increased in volume, then whisk in the mixer until cold. Sift the dry ingredients together, sift over the egg mix and gently fold in. Pour in the cake mixture and bake in an oven at 180°C/350°F/gas 4 for 20 minutes, or until done. Cool for 2 minutes in the tin, then turn out, peel off the lining paper, cool and chill.

Make the chocolate layer
Melt the chocolate over hot water and stir in the egg yolk and a little crème fraîche until smooth. Whisk the remaining crème, fold in the chocolate and chill.
Dissolve the sugar in 2 tablespoons water, boil for 1 minute, stir in the kirsch and leave to cool.
Pin a folded paper strip round the sponge to stand 7.5cm/3in above the surface. Brush the sponge top with the syrup. Spoon in the chocolate cream and chill for 1 hour.

Make the Mandarine Napoleon layer
Soak the gelatine in 3 tablespoons water, then dissolve over hot water.
Whisk together 30g/1oz sugar, the orange zest and juice, liqueur and yolks. Stand the bowl over simmering water and whisk until light and thick – like zabaione. Whisk in the gelatine. Stand the bowl in a larger one containing water and ice cubes and cool.
Whip the crème fraîche in a large bowl then whisk in the orange mousse.
Put the egg whites and remaining sugar in the mixer-bowl. Stand this, off the heat, on the pan of simmering water (the warmth will increase the volume). Return to the mixer and whisk at high speed to make meringue.
Fold together the orange mousse and the meringue, then spoon on top of the cake. Leave to set for 4 hours. Remove the paper border.

Make the cake decoration and glaze
Peel the oranges, removing the outside membrane with the peel. Then cut down between the membranes, removing each orange segment. Lay them round the top of the cake, with more in the middle. Centre the strawberries.
Put the wine, orange juice, sugar and gelatine for the glaze in a small pan and bring to the boil, stirring. Cool until partially setting. Brush over the fruit several times. Coat the outside of the cake with cocoa.
Whip the cream and sugar then pipe tiny rosettes round the top of the cake.

My wine suggestion: Muscat Beaumes de Venise.

Arlequin à la mandarine Napoléon at the Pierre Romeyer

Christian Ulweling

AUBERGE DU MOULIN HIDEUX

Route de Dohan 1, 6831 Noirefontaine, Belgium telephone: 61 46 70 15

Far from being hideous, Le Moulin Hideux, nestling at the water's edge in the bottom of a little valley, in the forest of Ardennes, is surrounded by beautiful lakes and waterfalls. A twisting back road will take you to this former mill, once one of a pair, from which the name comes: 'y deux moulins.' Le Moulin Hideux was the first restaurant outside France to be on the Relais and Châteaux list of agreeable lodgings with good food.

The Moulin's owners, Charles and Martine Lahire, both come from families of great restaurateurs. His uncle, Henrion Raymond, was a well-known Belgian chef who owned the Val-de-Paix and the Moulin Hideux had been in his family since 1945. Henrion Raymond trained his nephew, who worked beside him for twenty years – and he also trained the Moulin's present head chef.

Christian Ulweling did not start out to cook; he began by studying electricity but realised he preferred cooking. His aunt ran the Val-de-Paix, and he started working there in 1966. In 1970, when Henrion Raymond moved to the Moulin, he took over the kitchen at the Val-de-Paix, holding on to its existing Michelin rosette. When the Val-de-Paix was sold, he moved on to the Moulin Hideux, becoming head chef in 1981, ten years later. He is now a Maître Cuisinier of Belgium.

It is a traditional house that has not followed the trend of nouvelle cuisine, though it is still inventive in its recipes. In autumn a great variety of game, mushrooms and wild berries from the woods are served, and its use of local ingredients is highly original in an area rather better known for the simplicity and basic quality of the dishes.

MENU

GOUJONNETTES DE TURBOT AU BASILIC
Fingers of turbot with basil

CHEVREUIL A LA SAUCE POIVRADE
Venison in peppercorn sauce

MILLE-FEUILLES AUX FRUITS ROUGES
Puff pastry slice with red fruit

GOUJONNETTES DE TURBOT AU BASILIC

Fingers of turbot with basil

Serves 4

600g/1¼lb turbot fillets, skinned
salt and freshly ground black pepper
a few basil leaves, chopped
butter for greasing
100ml/3½fl oz white wine
100ml/3½fl oz fish stock (page 161)
cherry tomatoes, green beans or mange tout, steamed,
to serve

For the vegetable stock

1 carrot, chopped finely
1 leek, white part sliced in a fine julienne
1 pickling onion, sliced in a fine julienne
½ red pepper, seeded and sliced in a fine julienne
1 celery stalk, sliced in a fine julienne

For the butter and basil sauce

½ lemon
1 teaspoon cream
100g/3½oz cold butter, diced

Put all the vegetables for the vegetable stock in a pan and cover with about 120ml/4fl oz water. Bring to the boil and simmer for 5 minutes, then strain out the vegetables.

Cook the turbot fingers

Cut the turbot fillets into finger-sized pieces. Season them with salt, pepper and a little chopped basil and place them in a buttered ovenproof dish.

Heat the white wine and fish stock together and pour over the fish. Cook in the oven at 200°C/400°F/gas 6 for 3 minutes. Remove the fish from the cooking liquid and keep it warm.

Make the butter and basil sauce

Pour the cooking liquid into a small pan and boil to reduce to 2 tablespoons. Add the lemon juice and reduce slightly. Whisk in the cream and then start adding the butter, a few dice at a time, whisking over low heat, adding more as each batch is incorporated. Whisk in the warm vegetable stock, check the seasonings and add more chopped basil to taste.

Presentation

Pour the butter sauce on 4 hot plates and arrange the fingers of turbot. Garnish with cherry tomatoes, green beans or mange tout.

My wine suggestion: a Pouilly Fumé from the Loire, from M.O.Bailly; it has a flinty aroma, a slightly smoky flavour and a greenness which comes from the Sauvignon grape.

CHEVREUIL A LA SAUCE POIVRADE

Venison in peppercorn sauce

Serves 4

600g/1¼lb loin of venison
salt and freshly ground black pepper
chestnut purée to serve
cranberry compote to serve

For the venison stock

1kg/2lb venison neck and shoulder bones, and
venison trimmings
1 carrot, chopped
1 onion, chopped
a bouquet garni
6 black peppercorns, roughly crushed
60ml/2fl oz olive oil
1L/1¾pt dry white wine, plus 2 tablespoons
2 tablespoons wine vinegar

For the peppercorn sauce

1L/1¾pt brown chicken stock (page 250)
1L/1¾pt game stock (page 109)
12 black peppercorns, roughly crushed
30g/1oz butter, in dice
salt and freshly ground black pepper
1 teaspoon redcurrant jelly (optional)

Make the stock ahead

Put the venison bones and trimmings in an earthenware dish with the chopped vegetables and peppercorns and add the olive oil and white wine. Leave to marinate overnight.

Next day, drain off the liquid. Skim off the olive oil into a roasting pan and put over medium heat. Add the bones and vegetables, turning them until they are coloured on all sides. Add the wine vinegar and 2 tablespoons white wine and let reduce until almost disappeared. Transfer everything to a stock pot. Add the marinade juices and the chicken and game stocks. Let the stock simmer for about 3 hours; it will reduce from 3L/5½pt to about 500ml/18fl oz. Strain out the bones, meat trimmings and vegetables and leave until cold. Skim off all fat.

Roast the venison and complete the sauce
Add 12 broken peppercorns to the stock and simmer for a further 40 minutes; the liquid should reduce to about 200ml/7fl oz.

Season the venison and roast in a small buttered tin at 200°C/400°F/gas 6 for 10 minutes. Then remove from the tin and keep warm while the meat rests for 10 minutes before carving.

Strain the pepper sauce into the venison drippings in the meat tin. Whisk in the diced butter to give the sauce a gloss. Season to taste with salt and pepper; if the sauce is slightly too acidic, correct it with a little redcurrant jelly.

Presentation
Carve the meat into 8 slices, arranging 2 on each warmed plate. Serve chestnut purée and cranberry compote with each one and pour a little pepper sauce round the meat.

My wine suggestion: Château Figeac 1975, an outgoing St-Emilion with a lively aroma; from the Merlot and Cabernet Franc grapes, it has a hint of Cabernet Sauvignon.

MILLE-FEUILLES AUX FRUITS ROUGES

Puff pastry slice with red fruit

Serves 4

200g/7oz made weight puff pastry
flour for rolling
about 120g/4oz granulated sugar
250ml/9fl oz whipping cream
200g/7oz strawberries, hulled
200g/7oz raspberries
200g/7oz redcurrants, off the stalks
a few mint leaves
60g/2oz icing sugar, sifted

For the rum pastry cream
175ml/6fl oz milk
3 egg yolks
60g/2oz sugar
20g/²⁄₃oz flour, sifted
15g/½oz butter, in tiny pieces
2 tablespoons dark rum

Make the rum pastry cream
Heat the milk. Cream the yolks and sugar together and gently work in the flour, beating to make a smooth paste. Whisking rapidly, add the hot milk, a little at first, then faster.

Return to the pan and cook over low heat, whisking constantly so that thicker patches are dispersed. Turn into a bowl and dot with butter, to prevent a skin forming.

When cold, beat in the butter and add the rum.

Bake the mille-feuilles
Roll out the puff pastry on a lightly floured surface to a long narrow rectangle, then cut from it a strip 30 x 10 cm/12 x 4in. Place it on a dampened baking sheet and sprinkle with most of the sugar. Bake in an oven heated to 220°C/425°F/gas 7 for 15 minutes, or until it is nicely puffed up and golden. Remove from the tray to a wire rack and leave until cold.

Assemble and decorate the dessert
Whip the cream with 30g/1oz sugar until soft peaks form, to make crème chantilly. Fold this lightly into the cold rum custard.

With a sharp knife split the pastry rectangle horizontally. Use a piping bag fitted with a wide nozzle and spoon in about two-thirds of the rum cream. Pipe custard on to the bottom rectangle, close to the edge – this makes a neat join when the pastry is reassembled. Fill the centre of the pastry with custard. Reserve a few of the best fruit for the top, then arrange the rest on the custard, in such a way that every slice will contain every fruit. Top with the remaining pastry slice.

Decorate the top, piping it with the remaining custard. Arrange the reserved fruit and mint leaves on top and sift a little icing sugar over.

My wine suggestion: champagne

Pierre Wynants

COMME CHEZ SOI

Place Rouppe 23, Brussels, Belgium telephone: 2 512 29 21

Pierre Wynants has always been 'comme chez soi' in the pretty cream-coloured house with green woodwork on a Brussels square, for he was son of the restaurant owner, and it had been in the family since 1926. Aged sixteen he began training at the Savoy in Brussels. He learned English in Cleethorpes and continued his apprenticeship at Le Moulin Hideux, then moved to Paris to Le Grand Véfour under Raymond Oliver, and on to La Tour d'Argent. Back in Belgium in 1961, he spent a month running the kitchens of Prince Albert, the King's brother. He then returned to Comme chez Soi, progressively taking over the cooking. The restaurant gained its second Michelin rosette in 1966.

On the death of his father in 1973, Pierre and his wife Marie-Thérèse, who runs the dining room, took over. The restaurant 'has always had the relaxed style of a bistro' says the owner, and is now prettily refurbished in the art nouveau style of Victor Horta. He has published a history of the restaurant and also, in 1985, a collection of his own recipes. Influenced by the easy and flexible bourgeois cooking of his father, Pierre Wynants' own cooking could be described as a more hearty, Belgian offshoot of French nouvelle cuisine. He thinks of it as 'the most natural possible, employing the minimum of foundation sauces from the classic kitchen and using the maximum of local products.' Not a front-of-the-house convivialist, he enjoys 'putting the touch of personal originality' – acknowledged by three Michelin rosettes since 1979 and four Gault Millau toques in 1988.

MENU

ROUGETS BARBETS AU COULIS DE
TOMATES ET DE FEVES DE MARAIS
Red mullet served with tomato sauce and broad beans

JARDINIERE D'AILES DE CAILLES, FINE
CREME DES BOIS
*Garden bouquet of quails with a cream from
the wild woods*

L'EMINCE DE POIRE CARAMELISEE EN
FEUILLETE, SAUCE AUX PISTACHES
Puff pastry with caramel pears and pistachio sauce

ROUGETS BARBETS AU COULIS DE TOMATES ET DE FEVES DE MARAIS

Red mullet served with tomato sauce and broad beans

Serves 4

500g/18oz red mullet fillets, you will need 3-4 fillets per person; ask your fishmonger to scrape the skin well but not remove it
2 small, bright red, fresh tomatoes
4 asparagus spears, preferrably Mechlin and not too large, stalks scraped
salt and freshly ground black pepper
85g/3oz shelled young broad beans
pinch of dried savory
100ml/3½fl oz white chicken stock, well-seasoned (page 96)
4 small spring onions
12 chive leaves
30g/1oz butter
2-3 teaspoons double cream
a few sprays of chervil, or another garden herb, to garnish

For the tomato sauce

400g/14oz large, bright red, fresh tomatoes (add 1 teaspoon tomato purée if the tomatoes are inadequately red)
30g/1oz red pepper, coarsely chopped
40g/1½oz onion, coarsely chopped
60g/2oz leek, white part only
175ml/6fl oz white chicken stock (page 96)
2 small garlic cloves, finely chopped
1 sprig of thyme
1 bay leaf
1 teaspoon coriander seeds, crushed

Prepare the vegetables

Blanch the small tomatoes for 10 seconds, peel them, halve and remove the seeds. Reserve them in a small ovenproof dish.

Cook the asparagus spears in salted water for 10 minutes: they should be slightly crisp. Cut them into 5mm/¼in dice. Cook the broad beans in salted water with savory for 8-10 minutes then strain. Heat 100ml/3½fl oz chicken stock and add the beans. Purée together in a food processor then sieve and season.

Make the sauce

Blanch and peel the large tomatoes, cut into 4 and put in a saucepan with the chopped pepper, onion and the leek and pour in the chicken stock. Add the garlic, thyme and bay leaf and bring to the boil. Simmer over a very low heat for 20 minutes. Remove the thyme sprig and bay leaf, purée in a food processor and return to the saucepan. Add the coriander seeds, put over low heat and leave to infuse for 5 minutes (add tomato purée if the colour is poor), then press through a fine sieve. Season with salt and pepper; if the coulis is too thick, thin it with a little water.

Assemble the garnishes

Cut the spring onions to a uniform length – 7.5cm/3in measured from the white base. Make as many small lengthways cuts as possible along the green part of the onions. Place in cold water ½ hour before serving, so these open up to a tassel.

Cut the chives into 7.5cm/3in lengths and put them in the same water.

Cook the fish and get everything ready

Heat the tomato sauce and the bean purée. Blot the fish fillets well and heat the butter in a non-stick pan (2 if necessary) until a light brown. Fry the fish quickly for 1 minute on each side; the skin should colour slightly. Season and keep warm. In an oven at 200°C/400°F/gas 6 heat the small tomato halves for 1 minute. This is to take the chill off them: they must remain raw.

Presentation

Heat the asparagus dice in the bean purée and pile into the tomatoes, dribbling with ½ teaspoon double cream. Drain and blot the spring onion tassels and plant them, base down, in the bean purée. Add the blotted chives. Arrange on one side of the plate.

Fan out the fish fillets with their tails on the tomato. Pour a little bean purée round the tomato, and tomato sauce between the fish, at the head end. Garnish each head end with a sprig of chervil. Serve piping hot with the remaining tomato sauce in a sauceboat.

My wine suggestion: Sancerre 'Clos du Chêne Marchand' from B. Bailly-Reverdy; choose a young vintage – its delicate fruitiness will go well with the freshness of this dish.

JARDINIERE D'AILES DE CAILLES, FINE CREME DES BOIS

*Garden bouquet of quails with a cream
from the wild woods*

Serves 4

*6 large quails
30g/1oz butter
salt and freshly ground black pepper
your choice from: broccoli or cauliflower florets, green
beans, asparagus spears, courgette slices, baby carrots,
new potatoes, mange tout and petits pois*

*For the morel cream
100g/3½oz fresh morels
10g/⅓oz butter
200ml/7fl oz brown chicken stock (page 250)
150ml/¼pt double cream
100ml/3½fl oz truffle juice
60ml/2fl oz brown bone stock (page 178)*

Prepare the quails

Pull the legs of the quails outward (the opposite of trussing) and use a sharp knife to cut them off, through the joint. Reach into the necks to remove the wishbones, then take each breast off the birds, working with a knife down the breast bone. This will give you 12 portions of each type.

Prepare the vegetable bouquet

Make small bouquets of broccoli or cauliflower heads. Trim green beans or asparagus spears to a uniform length. If young vegetables are not available, trim older ones to a standard shape and size (called turning them), choosing them with an eye to colour as well as taste.

Make the morel and truffle cream

Cut off any earthy stem ends from fresh morels and wash them. Cut them in half and drain on a cloth. Then cut them up, the stems into long strips, the heads into large pieces.

Melt the butter over medium heat and add the morels. Cook for 2 minutes, stirring constantly. Add the chicken stock, bring to the boil and simmer gently for 5 minutes. Strain through a fine sieve, reserving the morels, and return the juices to the heat. Boil to reduce by two-thirds. Add the cream and boil again to reduce to 100ml/3½fl oz. Return the morels to the pan, add the truffle juice and 30ml/1fl oz brown bone stock, season to taste and keep warm.

Cook the quails and complete the sauce

Place a wide shallow pan over fairly high heat and heat the butter to a light brown. Put in the quail pieces, skin side down. Brown them, seasoning with a little salt and pepper. Turn them over and season again. Turn down the heat slightly and fry them for 4-5 minutes. The thigh pieces will be ready a minute before the breast pieces. Remove and reserve in a warm place.

Add the remaining brown bone stock to the pan and swirl it round to heat and deglaze. Add this to the morels and cream.

Meanwhile, steam the vegetables, each for the appropriate length of time – they should remain crisp.

Presentation

Pour the morel cream in the centre. In the restaurant we serve the breasts only on the vegetables, in order not to crowd the plates, and serve the thighs as part of a second service.

My wine suggestion: Crozes-Hermitage, Domaine de Thalabert from Paul Jaboulet Aîné, a great mature wine: durable, spicy and velvety.

Editor's note: The size of quails varies quite considerably. In France you will find much larger ones than the 100g/3½oz cleaned quails of Italy or Britain. You could increase the number of smaller quails to 8; however, serving the thighs as part of the main course – arrange them in a catherine wheel between the breasts – will make large enough portions in this menu.

L'EMINCE DE POIRE CARAMELISEE EN FEUILLETE, SAUCE AUX PISTACHES

Puff pastry with caramel pears and pistachio sauce

Serves 4

2 ripe pears, preferably Comice
60g/2oz shelled pistachios
about 120g/4oz sugar
½ lemon
175g/6oz made weight puff pastry
4 mint leaves (pungent if possible)

For the custard
250ml/9fl oz milk
2 large egg yolks
40g/1½oz sugar
few drops of bitter almond essence

Prepare the pistachios

Bring about 300ml/½pt water to the boil in a small pan and add the shelled pistachios. Blanch for 2 minutes then drain and cool in cold water. Drain again, dry in a cloth then remove the skins. Place them on a baking sheet in an oven at 200°C/400°F/gas 6 (or higher) and bake for about 2 minutes: they must be completely dry and very slightly toasted.

Make the custard

Bring the milk just to the boil. Put the yolks into a mixer bowl, add the sugar and beat until the mixture turns white and thick. Pour on the hot milk, beating all the time.

Return the milk to the saucepan and put over low heat, stirring all the time with a wooden spoon. Cook until the custard coats the back of the spoon, but do not let it boil. Pass through a fine sieve and leave to cool, stirring occasionally. Then add a few drops of almond essence: the effect should be subtle, rather than strong.

Make a syrup to coat the pears

In a very tiny pan heat 2 tablespoons water and 10g/⅓oz sugar until the sugar dissolves, then leave to cool and add the lemon juice.

Make the pastry squares

Roll out the puff pastry on a lightly floured surface to a square 3mm/⅛in thick and cut into four 6-7cm/2½-2¾in squares. Rinse a baking sheet and place the squares on it. Bake at 200°C/400°F/gas 6 for 15 minutes or until risen and golden.

Caramelise the pears

Heat a caramelising iron (see note). Peel the pears, cut in half and remove the stalks. Scoop out the cores with a teaspoon and cut across into 5 or 6 slices. Put them on a baking sheet and gently push them out, so the slices overlap slightly. Brush them with the prepared syrup (this will make them shiny and also stop them going brown). Sprinkle 1 tablespoon sugar over each pear half, making sure it is evenly distributed.

Press the carmelising iron, which should be almost red-hot, gently but quickly on to the sugar to caramelise it. Repeat the process a second time if the pears are not fully caramelised. You need to do this under a powerful extractor or by an open window, as a lot of smoke is generated.

Completing the slices

Remove the pastry squares from the oven and slice them in two horizontally. Use a fork to remove any uncooked pastry from the inside, then put them back in the oven, inside upwards, for 2-3 minutes until crisp and a good brown colour.

Presentation

Place the pastry squares in the middle of hot dessert plates. Use a palette knife to place the pear halves across them diagonally. Half cover with the pastry lid. Pour about 1½ tablespoons almond custard round them in the plate and sprinkle the custard with pistachios. Decorate with a mint leaf and serve immediately.

My wine suggestion: Clos Labère Sauternes, Société du Château Rieussec, a beautiful young vintage, which will end this meal on a supple note.

Editor's note: Some shops selling patisserie equipment sell electric caramelising irons, while a few kitchen stores sell a small round iron on a long handle (called a salamander) which can be heated until glowing and red on a gas, solid electric plate or solid fuel cooker. Few domestic grills are hot enough to perform the restaurant trick of turning granulated sugar to caramel, though sometimes demerara sugar is successful.

Pierre Fonteyne

LE BRUEGEL
Damse Vaart Zuid 26, 8350 Oostkerke Damme, Belgium telephone: 5050 03 46

'I believe I inherited my culinary skill from my mother. Watching her cook made me want to be a chef. I was equally influenced by my father, who for two generations defended tradition from the dining room.' Pierre Fonteyne's apprenticeship was served in Belgium — he feels particularly indebted to Emile Isabeau and Georges Nollet for their help. He and his wife Cécite, who is a welcoming hostess, have owned the Bruegel since 1963.

It is a small restaurant, seating thirty-five at the most, in the pure Flemish style, near enough to Damme to hear the bells from the square tower. The flat countryside is distinctive, a scene of interlacing canals with rows of poplars. At the Bruegel the cooking is distinctive, too. A neat white house with trim hedges and garden, it nestles in a corner, beside a bridge and a lock, on the canal that joins Bruges to the coast.

'Every chef is essentially an individualist,' says Pierre Fonteyne, 'it's the real reason for choosing the profession. Each day I have the possibility of creating something new or changing something that exists. It's the magic side of this profession that permits one always to surpass oneself.' The first Michelin rosette, 'a moment of pure pride', was awarded in 1973 and the second followed in 1978. He defines his own style as 'a creative cuisine which nevertheless respects scrupulously the classic foundation which my masters taught me. I have the greatest respect for the produce of my country and accordingly give a privileged place to the products of local farms.'

MENU

FILET DE BARBUE BRAISE AUX WITLOOF
Braised fillet of brill with chicory

BECASSINE ROTIE AUX CHOU VERT, COULIS DE TRUFFES ET POMME LIARD
Roast snipe with green cabbage, truffle sauce and potato crisps

MARQUISE AU CHOCOLAT AVEC CREME AU CAFE ET CARAMEL
Chocolate mousse with coffee and caramel cream

Filet de barbue braisé aux witloof

FILET DE BARBUE BRAISE AUX WITLOOF

Braised fillet of brill with chicory

Serves 4

4 brill fillets, 150-175g/5-6 oz each
8 firm heads of chicory
60g/2oz butter
freshly grated nutmeg
salt and freshly ground black pepper
4 tomatoes
120ml/4fl oz white wine, Coteaux Champenois or the Ladoix served with it
2 tablespoons fish stock (page 161)
250ml/9fl oz whipping cream
1 egg yolk

Finely slice the chicory heads across into rings. Melt 30g/1oz butter and lightly fry them, without allowing them to brown. Season with a little nutmeg, salt and pepper. Put the tomatoes in turn into boiling water for 10 seconds. Peel and quarter them, removing the seeds and juice. Put the white wine and fish stock in a small pan and boil to reduce to 60ml/2fl oz. Add half the cream and let the sauce thicken slightly. Taste once more and season. Add the remaining cream, mixed together with the egg yolk, and warm through. Do not let the mixture boil from this point.

Meanwhile season the brill fillets on both sides and fry in the remaining butter, without letting them brown.

To serve, spoon the chicory into 4 plates. Place a brill fillet on top of each one and coat with the sauce. Arrange the tomato quarters round the fish. Put in the oven at 220°C/425°F/gas 7 for 30 seconds to glaze.

My wine suggestion: Ladoix 'Les Grechons,' Domaine Michel Mallard; one of the great white burgundies, it is well matched with the slight bitterness of the chicory.

BECASSINE ROTIE AUX CHOU VERT, COULIS DE TRUFFES ET POMME LIARD

Roast snipe with green cabbage, truffle sauce and potato crisps

Serves 4

8 snipe
1 small green cabbage, about 400g/14oz after trimming
salt and freshly ground black pepper
250g/9oz farm butter
freshly grated nutmeg
120ml/4fl oz white chicken stock (page 96)

For the truffle sauce
120ml/4fl oz ruby port
1 tablespoon truffle juice
75ml/2½fl oz well-reduced brown bone stock (page 178)
30g/1oz truffle, finely chopped

For the potato crisps
2 potatoes, each 200g/7oz, preferably Binch
2 tablespoons goose fat

Prepare the vegetables
Shred the cabbage finely and blanch it in plenty of boiling salted water for 5 minutes. Melt 100g/3½oz butter in a large pan, put in the cabbage, seasoning with salt, pepper and nutmeg and moistening with the stock. Cover the pan and leave to simmer slowly for 30-45 minutes.

Trim the potatoes to the shape of large, extra-long corks and slice the thickness of a coin. Heat the goose fat on top of the stove and add the potato slices. Stir well so that they are coated with fat. Put into the oven at 180°C/350°F/ gas 4 with the snipe and cook for the same length of time.

Roast the snipe and make the sauce
Smear the snipe, using 60g/2oz butter, and season them well. Roast in the oven for 10 minutes – 12 at the most – basting frequently.

Pour the port into a small pan and boil to reduce to 60ml/2fl oz. Add the truffle juice then the clear meat stock and season with a little salt and pepper. Cook for 5 minutes.

Thicken the sauce by whisking in the remaining

butter, a few dice at a time, adding more before the last batch has melted, so that the sauce is creamy. Add the finely chopped truffle.

Presentation

Arrange the drained cabbage on warmed plates in a half moon at the bottom, with a small pile opposite. Place 2 snipe on each one, their heads resting on the cabbage pile, and lightly coat them with the truffle sauce. Garnish with potato crisps.

My wine suggestion: a claret from the Pomerol region – wine in which it is often possible to detect a hint of truffles, for example Château La Conseillante, Château L'Evangile or Château Trotanoy.

MARQUISE AU CHOCOLAT AVEC CREME AU CAFE ET CARAMEL

Chocolate mousse with coffee and caramel cream

Serves 6

250g/9oz butter
250g/9oz icing sugar, sifted
120g/4oz cooking chocolate (callebaut)
3 egg yolks
60ml/2fl oz kirsch
1 tablespoon grated fresh coconut
1 vanilla pod
3 egg whites
24 chocolate coffee beans, to decorate

For the coffee and caramel sauce
250ml/9fl oz milk
200ml/7fl oz very strong, freshly made coffee
3 egg yolks
1 tablespoon caramel sauce (see right)

Chop the butter, which should be at room temperature, then beat in a mixer-bowl with the icing sugar. Melt the broken chocolate in a bowl over simmering water. Stir well, making sure it is not too hot, and mix into the butter and sugar. Add the egg yolks, kirsch and coconut and beat in.

Slit the vanilla pod lengthways and scrape out enough tiny seeds to cover the tip of a round-bladed knife. Add to the mixture.

Whisk the egg whites until stiff peaks form. If the chocolate mousse seems stiff, stir in a little white, then fold in the rest lightly.

Grease an 850ml/1½pt rectangular tin – a long thin terrine shape is needed – and spoon in the mousse. Chill for 3-4 hours.

Make the coffee and caramel cream

Put the milk and coffee in a saucepan and bring to the boil. Whisk the yolks well and pour on the boiling liquid, whisking all the time. Pour back into the pan (or the top of a double boiler) and cook over low heat, stirring continously until slightly thickened, when the custard will coat the back of a spoon. Remove from the heat and add a large spoonful of caramel sauce. Leave until cold.

Presentation

Run a knife round inside the tin, then turn out the chocolate mousse. Cut into slices – 12 if you used a thin tin. Pour a pool of coffee cream on to each plate and arrange a slice of marquise.

Decorate with a chocolate coffee bean on 4 corners. Since this is a composition in browns, in the restaurant we add touches of colour and vary the texture – mint leaves of course, coarsely-ground commercial sugared rose petals, little piles of orange zest ground with sugar, flaked toasted almonds and some more of the coconut that went into the marquise.

My wine suggestion: a pink champagne will freshen your overstressed palate and also add colour to the table; I suggest Dom Ruinart.

CARAMEL SAUCE

250g/9oz caster sugar
2-3 tablespoons water

Cook the sugar and water together in a small heavy-bottomed pan until the colour turns to caramel. Immediately take off the heat and pour in 120ml/4fl oz water to arrest cooking. Bring back to the boil, stirring to dissolve the caramel then cool.

Bécassine rôtie aux chou vert, coulis de truffes et pomme liard at Le Bruegel

Marquise au chocolat avec crème au café et caramel at Le Bruegel

Cas Spijkers

DE SWAEN

De Lind 47, 5061 HT Oisterwijk, The Netherlands telephone: 4242 19006

'Put your soul into your cooking, be at one with the products you are using. Be a master of your technique. But remember, too, that there is no one, definitive moment when a chef's career reaches its apogee. There is always another day tomorrow.' These are the principles behind a culinary renaissance in the south of Holland wrought by Cas Spijkers.

Dutch by birth, his father was a master tailor and going to good restaurants was the family hobby. His father helped choose the best kitchens in which to learn: the Chalet Royal, the Prinses Juliana Hotel, and the Hotel Negresco in Nice. In 1976 Cas Spijkers rocketed to fame, when he won the Netherlands highest award, the Chef's Silver Cap.

In 1978 he joined the new team at De Swaen as chef and within three years gained it a Michelin rosette. A book followed, Cas Spijkers and his Swan. A white building with nine windows, joined by a long loggia, the Swan has its own bakery and smokes its own fish, meat and game. A very big man, with monumental hands, Cas Spijkers' cooking is known for its light, subtle flavours. In 1983 he was awarded a second Michelin rosette.

'Cooking is the ultimate form of self-mastery, starting with the art of coming home every day with the best the market has to offer' he says. 'When you look at your product properly you perceive something: that's your inspiration!' His hero is Alain Chapel 'for the intelligence in the food — cuisine so thought-through, so beautifully sober.' Restraint is a virtue. 'Leave the items to be what they are: natural. Most chefs do too much or too little.'

MENU

TURBOT FARCI D'HUITRES AU MARCHAND DU VIN ROUGE
Oyster-stuffed turbot with red wine sauce

PALETTE DE CANARD A LA SAUGE
Medley of duck with sage

PECHE BLANCHE POCHEE DE SAUTERNES, MOUSSE D'AMANDE ET COMPOTE DE FRAMBOISE
White peaches poached in Sauternes, with almond mousse and strawberry compote

TURBOT FARCI D'HUITRES AU MARCHAND DU VIN ROUGE

Oyster-stuffed turbot with red wine sauce

Serves 4

4 turbot fillets, 500g/18oz together, from a fish of about 1kg/2lb
1 egg white
4 oysters, preferrably from Zeeland
30g/1oz butter
salt and freshly ground white pepper
150ml/5fl oz double cream

For the red wine sauce
500g/18oz turbot head and bones
500g/18oz chicken carcass, broken up
75ml bottle Mas de Gourgonnier
1 onion, roughly chopped
1 leek, white part only, roughly chopped
1 carrot, roughly chopped
a sprig of thyme
2 bay leaves
1 teaspoon arrowroot

For the garnishing vegetables
your choice of asparagus tips, freshly podded peas and some cubed tomato flesh for colour

Stuff the turbot

Skin the turbot fillets: put them skin-side down, hold the tail with salted fingers and work the flesh off with a knife. Trim to four 100g/3½oz portions. Cut each of these lengthways to give two thin slices.

Make the stuffing from the turbot trimmings by beating the egg white into the fish, then 60ml/2fl oz cream. Force the mixture through a sieve.

Using a piping bag to put a row of stuffing down 4 slices of turbot.

Open the oysters by inserting a knife into the hinge and remove from the shell. Place them on top of the stuffing and top each one with 7g/¼oz of butter. Cover with a second slice of turbot, pressing down gently to make a neat sandwich.

Place the turbot fillets on a buttered plate, which will fit into your steamer, and season with salt and pepper.

Make the red wine sauce

Wash the fish bones and head under running water. Drain and put in a saucepan with the chicken carcass and cover with the red wine. Bring to the boil very slowly, so that the fish soaks up the wine, skimming the surface of impurities that rise. Add the flavouring vegetables and herbs and cover the pan. Simmer slowly for 1½ hours, then strain out the bones and vegetables and pass the liquid through a muslin-lined sieve into a clean pan. Bring to the boil: there should be about 175ml/6fl oz.

Make a paste with the arrowroot and stir into the liquid; bring gently back to the boil, stirring until smoothly thickened. Season to taste. Reheat as needed but do not let this sauce simmer continuously, as arrowroot can separate again on continual cooking.

Steam the fish and prepare the garnish

Steam your chosen selection of vegetables, timing them carefully to be ready when the fish is. Asparagus tips may be steamed on a rack, but the peas will need a shallow container; allow 20-25 minutes. Add the chopped tomato flesh on a small plate 1-2 minute before the end, to heat through without losing texture.

Meanwhile, steam the fish in a covered container for about 5 minutes.

Presentation

Arrange a stuffed turbot fillet on each of 4 warmed plates and pour the red wine sauce round it. Arrange the vegetables in colourful groups and add a spoonful of whipped cream to each plate to give a colour contrast to the main sauce.

My wine suggestion: Chinon 'Clos de l'Echo,' Couly-Dutheil 1983: a fine, fresh fruity Loire wine to go with fish in a red wine sauce, or alternatively, a white Hermitage.

PALETTE DE CANARD A LA SAUGE

Medley of duck with sage

Serves 4

4 Barbery (grey) ducks, innards reserved
60g/2oz duck's liver
75g/2½oz butter
salt and freshly ground black pepper
4 good Savoy cabbage leaves
2 shallots, finely chopped
2 cloves garlic, crushed
200ml/7fl oz truffle juice
1 teaspoon Armagnac
4 thin strips, cut from a long leek
400g/14oz small boiled turnips, heated in
100ml/3½fl oz double cream
200g/7oz chanterelles, fried in 40g/1½oz butter
20g/⅔oz truffle, sliced

For the red wine sauce
1 onion, 1 leek and 1 carrot, finely chopped
2 beefsteak tomatoes, chopped
75cl bottle Mas de Gourgonnier
200g/7oz mushrooms
100ml/3½fl oz brown chicken stock (page 250)
2 sage leaves
¼ celeriac (100g/3½oz), finely chopped
1 thyme sprig
1 bay leaf

For the beer pancakes
120g/4oz flour
5 eggs
120ml/4fl oz Pilsner lager
300ml/½pt milk
60g/2oz melted butter for frying

Prepare and roast the ducks
Reserve the stomach, hearts and livers. Salt the ducks inside and cook at your lowest oven setting for 10 hours. Cool the ducks on their sides on a tray in the refrigerator. Save the juices, cut off the legs (not used in this recipe), and remove the breast fillets.

Make the red wine sauce
Brown the chopped carcasses in a tin in the oven at 180°C/350°F/gas 4 with the vegetables. Add the tomatoes. Transfer to a stock pot, deglazing with the red wine. Add the mushrooms with the sage leaves, celeriac, thyme, bay leaf and pepper. Simmer, covered, for 4 hours.

Prepare the cabbage parcels
Slit open the stomachs, clean then peel them. Open and wash the hearts. Simmer in stock until tender – about 1 hour. Meanwhile clean all 5 livers and cut into small pieces. Fry in butter, seasoning well, until tender.
Blanch the cabbage leaves for 1 minute, drain on a cloth and cut out the hard stem base.
Drain the hearts and stomachs and chop like the liver. Mix together, distribute between the cabbage leaves and roll into parcels.

Make the duck wing ragout
Fry the wings in 40g/1½oz butter in a casserole, until brown. Add the shallots, garlic, truffle juice and Armagnac. Strain in red wine sauce to cover (reserving a little for serving); press the sieve contents well. Cover and cook in the oven at 180°C/350°F/gas 4 for 20 minutes until tender.
Remove the duck wings and strip off all the meat; chop finely. Skim all fat from the sauce and boil until thick, then add the reserved duck juices and return the wing meat.

Make the beer pancakes and little purses
Mix the batter and fry in the butter, making 4 thin pancakes – using about 1½ tablespoons batter each – in a small crêpe pan.
Divide the ragout between them. Pull up the edges and tie round the neck with leek strip.
Cook the turnips and chanterelles.

Heat the meats
Arrange the cabbage parcels and pancake purses on a buttered tray. Strip off the skin, cutting the breasts into strips and add. Heat through thoroughly in the oven at 190°C/375°F/gas 5 for 6 minutes. Cut the skin into thin strips and crisp in 30g/1oz butter.

Presentation
Arrange a cabbage parcel, garnished with sliced truffle, a 'purse' and the breast strips garnished with crisp skin on each plate. Pour round them a little warmed red wine sauce and add the turnips and chanterelles.

My wine suggestion: La Romanée-St-Vivant, Marey Monge 1971, a fine intense wine.

PECHE BLANCHE, POCHEE DE SAUTERNES, MOUSSE D'AMANDE ET COMPOTE DE FRAMBOISE

White peaches poached in Sauternes with almond mousse and strawberry compote

Serves 4

4 white peaches
75cl bottle of Sauternes
200g/7oz sugar
1 vanilla pod
½ cinnamon stick
segments of 1 orange
segments of 1 lemon

For the almond mousse
60g/2oz ratafia biscuits
30g/1oz marzipan
40ml/1½fl oz milk, hot
5g/⅙ oz powdered gelatine
2 tablespoons water
325ml/11fl oz whipping cream
4 teaspoons Cointreau

For the strawberry compote
20g/⅔oz raisins
1 tablespoon Cointreau
150g/5oz strawberries

For the pastry leaf decoration
60g/2oz butter, diced, plus extra for greasing
85g/3oz sugar
75g/2½oz white of egg (from 2 large eggs)
60g/2oz flour, plus extra for dusting
seeds scraped from ¼ vanilla pod

Poach the peaches
Blanch the peaches very briefly in boiling water, then peel them. Cut them in half and remove the stone.

Put the Sauternes, sugar, vanilla pod and cinnamon stick in a saucepan with the fruit segments. Bring to the boil and add the peaches. Simmer, covered, until tender, about 5-6 minutes, then leave in the liquid until cold.

Make the almond mousse
Crumble the ratafia biscuits and marzipan into the hot milk and stir until smooth. Sprinkle the gelatine over the hot water in a cup, let it soak briefly, then dissolve over hot water. Stir into the mixture. Place the bowl in another larger one containing ice cubes and stir until it seems thick and cold.

Whip the cream to soft peaks and use a spatula to gently fold it in. Flavour with Cointreau. Line 4 ramekins or small moulds, at least 120ml/4fl oz in capacity, or a single mould 500ml/18fl oz in capacity, with cling film and then fill with the mousse. Chill until needed.

Make the strawberry compote
Soak the raisins in Cointreau. Use a slotted spoon to remove the peaches from their Sauternes syrup, and bring it to the boil. Boil until it has reduced to one-quarter. Add the strawberries and simmer for 2 minutes. Leave the syrup until cold, then add the raisins.

Make the pastry leaves
First take a piece of cardboard, about 1mm/⅛in thick (or the plastic lid of a freezer box), draw a leaf shape about 10cm/4in long, and cut out the interior with a sharp knife, leaving the surrounding intact, to make a stencil.

Make the pastry by mixing all the ingredients in a large bowl; do not do this too vigorously – a food processor can be used. Butter a large baking sheet and sprinkle lightly with flour. Place the stencil on it and use a palette knife to fill the leaf shape. Repeat 4 times.

Bake the biscuits in an oven at 200°C/400°F/gas 6 for 7-8 minutes, or until light brown.

Remove one by one from the baking sheet with a fish slice or palette knife and immediately arrange them over a rolling pin, so they set to an attractive curved leaf shape. Cool on a wire rack when set and store in an airtight tin.

Presentation
Unmould the almond mousse(s), slice if necessary, and arrange on 4 plates with a drained peach. Spoon strawberry and raisin compote on one side of the plate and arrange a leaf biscuit on each one.

My wine suggestion: Château Raymond Lafon 1975: the nuances of peaches and strawberries are complete wedded to a very fine Sauternes.

Tony Tintinger

CLAIREFONTAINE

9 rue de Clairefontaine, L-1341 Luxembourg telephone: 46 22 11

Writing about food, rather than cooking it, was Tony Tintinger's first professional contact with the world of cuisine. Born at Pétange, a small town on the coalfield of southern Luxembourg, he studied in Belgium and Germany before basing himself in Frankfurt. Here his gift for languages – he speaks six – led him to take up a career as a journalist specialising in travel and tourism. This gave him experience of many hotels and a view of cuisine round the world. His interest in the latter was strengthened by the many contacts he cultivated with chefs.

With his wife Margot he opened his first small business in Esch-sur-Alzette, when he was twenty-five. At first they served only beers and wine, but he quickly introduced light dishes, lovingly prepared, to accompany them. By now he was committed to the idea of being a chef and an extra-mural course at hotel school and working short periods with a number of celebrated chefs added to his experience. Full of optimism, in 1975 he transformed his small bistro into a restaurant. The following year he progressed again, spending for weeks with the master Roger Vergé. Back in Luxembourg, his own restaurant was acknowledged the best in his home town.

In 1984 an ambition was realised and he moved to a new restaurant, luxuriously appointed, at the heart of the capital, where he has a faithful clientele of bankers, ministers and businessmen. As many come regularly, the menu changes frequently with daily dishes, and he specialises in light, creative lunches for lovers of good food.

MENU

DUO DE TURBOT ET DE SAUMON EN ROBE VERTE AU BEURRE DE CIBOULETTE
Green-coated duo of turbot and salmon with chive butter

TOURNEDOS D'AGNEAU A L'ARDENNAISE
Tournedos of lamb, Ardennes style

GRATIN DE MANGUES ET DE PAPAYES
Mango and papaya gratin

DUO DE TURBOT ET DE SAUMON EN ROBE VERTE AU BEURRE DE CIBOULETTE

Green-coated duo of turbot and salmon with chive butter

Serves 4

400g/14oz turbot fillets
400g/14oz wild salmon, the same thickness as the turbot
2 large undamaged spinach leaves
1 tomato, blanched, skinned and deseeded
a little melted butter
1 courgette for the optional garnish

For the chive butter
85ml/3fl oz champagne
1 shallot
60ml/2fl oz double cream
120g/4oz cold butter, diced
60ml/2fl oz whipping cream
salt and freshly ground black pepper
1 bunch chives, finely chopped

Prepare the fish

Cut the fish fillets to make 4 long triangles of turbot and the same number of salmon. A triangle of each fish will fit together to make a larger elongated triangle. Blanch the spinach leaves by pouring water on them and draining. Plunge immediately into cold water, then pat dry on a tea towel.

Place a triangle of each fish on half a spinach leaf and fold it round two-thirds of the fish, so the pointed end is enclosed, but pink and white fish project at the wide end.

Prepare a big steamer, wide enough to take all four parcels. Cut the tomato flesh into diamonds, ready to garnish the plate.

Start making the chive butter

Put the champagne and chopped shallot in a small saucepan and boil until the liquid has virtually evaporated. Add the double cream to the pan and boil again, to reduce by half.

Steam the fish; complete the butter sauce

Place the fish parcels in the upper part of the steamer, cover and steam for 6-7 minutes. Remove and drain the parcels on absorbent paper, patting the tops dry.

Over very low heat, whisk the diced butter, a little at a time, into the sauce, adding each new batch before the last has melted, so that the sauce acquires a creamy consistency. Then add the whipping cream which will make the sauce lighter. Do not allow it to boil from this point. Season and add the chives.

Presentation

Transfer the green parcels to 4 heated plates, where they will look like green horns, with the coloured fish just peeping out. Brush with melted butter to give them a good sheen.

Pour a pool of sauce near the wider end of the fish triangle and arrange 3 diamonds of red tomato on the other side of the fish, pointing towards it.

In the restaurant we use courgette slices to make a 'fish tail' for the narrow end of each triangle, though this is optional. To do this, use a medium-sized courgette, halved lengthways and trimmed so it is about 1.5cm/½in thick. Cut a lozenge shape from each one. Slit each one lengthways, to two-thirds of the way up, to form eight thin strips, still joined at one end. Fold every other strip back, splaying the others out like a fish tail. Flash in the oven to warm.

My wine suggestion: Cos Koeppchen, a Luxembourgeois Moselle Riesling from Domaines Mathes, 1983 Commune de Wormeldange, one of the greatest wines of Luxembourg: golden in colour with an almost glycerine softness.

TOURNEDOS D'AGNEAU A L'ARDENNAISE

Tournedos of lamb, Ardennes style

Serves 4

1 saddle of lamb, weighing 1.4kg/3lb, boned to give 2 loins of lamb, trimmed of all fat, making 500g/18oz meat
200g/7oz caul,
soaked in water (page 165)
salt and freshly ground black pepper
10 good rashers smoked bacon, trimmed
15g/½oz butter
1 tablespoon oil

For the stuffing
2 tablespoons parsley
1 garlic clove, finely chopped
2 tablespoons 1-day-old breadcrumbs
1 tablespoon olive oil
1 tablespoon Dijon mustard

For the peppercorn wine sauce
1 shallot, chopped
30g/1oz butter
1 tablespoon redcurrant vinegar
75ml/2½fl oz full-bodied red wine
250ml/9fl oz lamb stock (page 164)
1 teaspoon pink peppercorns (baies roses – page 250)
1 teaspoon green peppercorns

For the garnish
150g/5oz tagliatelle
pinch of powdered saffron (optional)
1 teaspoon chopped truffle
4 broccoli florets
8 flower shapes, cut from carrot slices
butter

Make the stuffing and stuff the loins
Slit each loin lengthways and three-quarters of the way through. Combine the parsley, garlic, breadcrumbs and oil. Season the inside of the loins with pepper and spread with mustard then the filling. Drain and dry the caul well, then spread it out flat. Spread out the bacon rashers, slightly overlapping, on the caul making a rectangle the length of the lamb loins. Shut the loins on the filling and place, side by side on the bacon (cut upward), so that the rashers will wrap across them. Pepper the lamb and roll up in the bacon and then the caul. Tie with string.
Cook the lamb
Brown the loins on all sides in butter and oil in an ovenproof dish. Cover the roll with foil and cook in the oven at 240°C/475°F/gas 9 for 5 minutes. Baste with the juices, then rest (covered) for 10 minutes.
Prepare the garnish
Cook the tagliatelle in boiling salted water with the saffron, drain and toss in butter with a little chopped truffle. Boil the broccoli and carrot flowers briefly. Toss in butter.
Make the peppercorn wine sauce
Fry the shallot in half the butter. Deglaze the

pan with redcurrant vinegar and red wine, boiling until the liquid has almost evaporated. Add the lamb stock and boil to reduce by a third. Strain, then whisk it in a blender with 15g/½oz butter to thicken it. Add both colours of peppercorns and allow to infuse for a few minutes. Season lightly.
Presentation
Slice the loin into 4 and arrange on a pool of sauce with a coil of tagliatelle on one side and the vegetables on the other.

My wine suggestion: Château Latour 1976, a year noted for its dryness.

GRATIN DE MANGUES ET DE PAPAYES
Mango and papaya gratin

Serves 4
2 ripe mangoes, peeled and sliced
2 ripe papayas, peeled, seeded and sliced
175ml/6fl oz whipping cream

For the confectioner's custard
250ml/9fl oz milk
1 vanilla pod, split lengthways
3 egg yolks
85g/3oz caster sugar
20g/⅔oz cornflour
30g/1oz butter

Make the confectioner's custard
Bring the milk to the boil with the vanilla pod. Whisk the egg yolks and sugar until pale and whisk in the cornflour.
Remove the vanilla pod from the milk and pour this down on the yolks, whisking all the time. Return to the pan and bring to the boil. Cook for 1 minute, stirring. Whisk in the diced butter and leave until cold, stirring occasionally.
Grill and serve the gratin
Arrange the fruit in 4 ovenproof dishes. Fold the cream into the custard, pour over the fruit and brown at maximum oven heat.

My wine suggestion: Gewürztraminer, séléction grains nobles Domaine Hugel.

GLOSSARY

Technical jargon has been avoided in this book. However, here are some helpful notes about ingredients, some basic recipes, and some tips and guidance about cooking.

Amuse-Gueule
A tit-bit before dinner – often free with the aperitifs. The French means 'mouth tickler'.

Aspic
A stock made with bones will jelly if sufficiently reduced. Very slow simmering and scrupulous skimming may produce a clear jelly – Raymond Blanc prefers this method. Most stocks, however, are cloudy and need clarifying for aspic – described on page 105. For a terrine check that the aspic is firm enough to support the ingredients, by chilling a little on a plate. If it fails the test, gelatine can be added, or the stock reduced further and retested. Consistency is important too – aspic must not be rubbery. Rinse out the terrine with cold water first, to ease unmoulding.

Baies Roses
Pink peppercorns were once the darling of the nouvelle cuisine, both for their colourful appearance and their spicy taste. Black peppercorns go through a pink phase, but baies roses are unrelated and come from the Madagascar pepper, grown on Reunion Island, or the Florida holly. They are less often used now – and are banned in the US – because both types can cause allergic reactions.

Bain-Marie
Delicate egg mixtures require a heat below boiling – or never exceeding it. The dish or container stands in a roasting tin surrounded by hot water. In an oven this will rise to boiling, on a stove, it will simmer quietly. A water-bath of cold water plus ice is used for cooling custards quickly.

Brown Bone Stock
Also called veal stock or *fond de viande* in French, recipes are given on page 178.

Brunoise
The smallest of all chopped vegetables, these tiny dice – peppercorn-sized – are used for decoration. If you control the pulsing carefully this can be done in a food processor, but tomato must be chopped by hand.

Butter Sauces
There are two main types: in the first a small amount of butter is added for gloss then boiled to emulsify it.
The second is 'mounted butter' which replaced the butter-and-flour roux as a quicker, lighter way of thickening sauces. It is a spontaneous sauce, combining well with reductions. Cold butter dice are whisked into a flavourful liquid on low heat, or with the pan on, then off, the heat. The idea is to keep the butter in suspension, without letting it melt; it gives the sauce a rich, cream-like texture.

Chicken Stock
There are two main types. The recipe for white stock is on page 96.
For a brown stock, the chicken bones and carcass are seared in a very little oil in a hot oven for 30 minutes. Vegetables including onions, garlic, peppercorns, thyme and bay leaf are added and roasted to a good brown colour. Add water, simmer and skim for 30 minutes.
Raymond Blanc thickens the strained stock with arrowroot; he sometimes uses this instead of the less-accessible brown bone stock.
Both types will jelly when reduced and both can be clarified for aspic (if the colour is suitable for the dish); see Aspic.

Court Bouillon
Literally a short-cooked broth, this is usually a fish stock cooked for under 30 minutes, because long cooking would turn it bitter. It may also be of vegetables – page 13.

Crème Fraîche

On the Continent 'fresh cream' is slightly acidic in taste, and will not pipe well, so recipes call for this, or for *crème fouettée* when a whipping cream is needed. To make *crème fraîche*, stir 150ml/¼pt buttermilk (or failing this, 1 tablespoon soured cream) into 250ml/9fl oz double cream. Bring to blood heat then leave in a warm place for 6-8 hours. It will keep in the refrigerator for 10 days, and can be boiled in a sauce without separating..

Deglaze

A way of securing any meat juices that have escaped during cooking. Skim off all cooking fat and add wine or water to the pan. Boil to reduce and concentrate. To avoid burning in a large or flat pan, chefs will often take it off the heat as the liquid bubbles up and return it several times, until almost boiled away.

Degrease

Add a tablespoon of cold water to raise the fat on a hot liquid, before skimming with a spoon. Remove the final fat by drawing strips of absorbent paper across the surface.

Double-Boiler

Not the same as a bain-marie, though used for a similar purpose. A pan (or bowl) on top of another containing simmering water is used to ensure that cooking takes place below boiling. Water in the bottom pan should not boil and should not touch the upper vessel.

Fish Fumet

Well-reduced fish stock is used for sauces. The stock is reduced after straining, or it might turn bitter. It will gel when cold.

Fish Stock and Shellfish Stock

A recipe is given on page 161. Chefs differ in approach: some like Eckart Witzigmann and John Burton-Race like to fry the bones in butter, others omit the mushrooms. Sole and turbot bones are a firm favourite. Opinions differ, too, about fish offal: Raymond Blanc removes the gills with scissors from a fish head when including it. Lobster stomachs are generally not used.

Galantine

A poultry breast, or a whole bird, stuffed and then served hot or cold.

Gelatine

Leaf gelatine is preferred because there is little danger of lumps. Soak the sheets then add them directly to a hot liquid, or melt over hot water in 3-4 tablespoons water and add to a cold liquid. 1 tablespoon powder is the equivalent of 2 sheets.

Julienne

Short vegetable strips of matching size and length, usually about 5cm/2in long. For citrus julienne, pare the zest finely, then pile and slice as thinly as possible. To make the zest edible, boil it in plenty of water to get rid of the bitterness. It is then refreshed in cold water. Repeat this at least twice.

Mandolin

A kitchen cutter named for its resemblance to the musical instrument. Used for cutting long and extremely thin vegetable strips.

Meat Glaze

In French *glace de viande*, not the jellied juice from a roast, but made by boiling brown bone stock to reduce by half until it jellies. A meat stock with bones, page 68, can also be used.

Mirepoix

Roughly chopped or diced vegetables, often with bacon, used as braising base for meat.

Nage

The cooking liquid for shellfish, the name is in origin poetic – the liquid in which it swam. Nowadays it is a fashionable term which includes vegetable stock as well as fish, and may be the sauce of a dish, or even soup.

Oven Temperatures

Fan ovens give a consistent, steady heat. Conventional ovens are hotter at the top and moreover vary as they go off and on. With the short oven times used by professional chefs, the difference between the two may be marked. If you are not using a fan oven, use your eyes as well as a kitchen timer!

Parsley
Sprigs are not used in white stocks for they discolour them. In any case, broken stalks have more flavour – and the root even more.

Peppercorns, Green
Unlike black peppercorns, the green, half-ripe corns are edible – usually sold in brine.

Pomme Maxime
Raymond Blanc's useful and elegant potato cakes: peel 4 potatoes to make cylinders 4cm/1½in diameter, then slice them 2mm/⅛in thick. Brush 4 tartlet rings with clarified butter, stand on a baking tray, arrange the potatoes slices inside, seasoning and brushing with butter. Colour in a hot oven (220°C/425°F/gas 7) for 3-4 minutes, then flip them over with a palette knife. Sprinkle with more clarified butter and cook for a further 4 minutes.

Potato Flour
Also known as *fécule*, it has an advantage over arrowroot, for it will thicken without being brought back to the boil – avoids curdling.

Quenelles
An egg shape – more elegant than a ball – it can be achieved in ice cream by a long shallow scoop that is then rolled. Mousses are usually shaped with a spoon beneath and on top. The shape is excellent for light poaching.

Reduction
This concentrates the flavour of a stock for sauce – don't salt ahead. It's part of the nouvelle cuisine heritage that the juices of the dish are reduced to emphasise them, rather than introducing new or masking tastes.

Refresh
After swift boiling, vegetables are plunged in iced water (or more commonly at home, under a cold running tap) to arrest cooking and fix the colour. Citrus zest is treated this way.

Sieve, Conical
Called a *chinoise* in French, this fine-mesh sieve will transfer a liquid to narrow jug. A tamis or drum sieve is used for pressing through meat mixtures – a wide surface is easier to work on with a fibrous mixture.

Sweat
Technically to cook vegetables without browning until softened. They give up water, hence the name, become pliable and lose bulk.

Sweetbreads, Calf
The oval ones from near the heart are a much better buy than the long dangly ones from the throat, though they are often sold as a pair. They should be a firm white, with no bruising or scent. A good size is 200g/7oz, though restaurants tend to snap them all up; big ones weigh twice this. They need advance soaking and blanching, described on page 178.

Syrups
Sugar content is measured by a floating gauge called a saccarometer; for example 30° is heavy syrup, made from 250g/½lb sugar dissolved in 250ml/½pt water. Stock syrup (the heaviest) uses 500g/1lb sugar with 250ml/½pt water.

Tomato Flesh
Neat cubes of tomato flesh, without skin, juice or seed, are called concassé tomato. Literally *concassé* means crushed – for other vegetables it means roughly chopped.

Toque
The chef's tall white hat is used a a badge mark by restaurant guide Gault Millau.

Turned Vegetables
Trimmed with a small paring knife to an identical shape and size, vegetables look better on the plate, but this also makes for more precise cooking times.

Vegetable Garnish, Hot
Vegetables are blanched until barely cooked, then refreshed under cold water. At the last moment they are swiftly reheated in butter with 2 tablespoons water – highly convenient!

Vegetable Stock
A simple one is given on page 232, a very sophisticated one on page 13.

INDEX